Five Black Preachers in Army Blue
1884-1901
The Buffalo Soldier Chaplains

FIVE BLACK PREACHERS IN ARMY BLUE
1884-1901
The Buffalo Soldier Chaplains

Alan K. Lamm

The Edwin Mellen Press
Lewiston•Queenston•Lampeter

Library of Congress Cataloging-in-Publication Data

Lamm, Alan K.
    Five Black preachers in Army blue, 1884-1901 : the Buffalo soldier chaplains / Alan K. Lamm.
       p.   cm.
    Includes bibliographical references and index.
    ISBN 0-7734-2249-8 (hard)
    1. United States. Army--Chaplains--History. 2. United States.
Army--Afro-Americans--History. 3. United States. Army--Chaplains-
-Biography. 4. United States. Army--Afro-Americans--Biography.
5. Chaplains, Military--United States--Biography. 6. Afro-American
clergy--United States--Biography.   I. Title.
UH23.L36   1998
355.3'47''092273--dc21   98-44211
[B]   CIP

A CIP catalog record for this book is available from the British Library.

The Edwin Mellen Press   The Edwin Mellen Press
Box 450   Box 67
Lewiston, New York   Queenston, Ontario
USA 14092-0450   CANADA L0S 1L0

The Edwin Mellen Press, Ltd.
Lampeter, Ceredigion, Wales
UNITED KINGDOM SA48 8LT

Printed in the United States of America

Dedicated to

Melissa and Anderson Lamm

TABLE OF CONTENTS

Preface

The unique, ground breaking role of the African-American chaplain in the United States Army, is a story that has not been told in a coherent form until Dr. Alan K. Lamm's study. In many ways the role of the Army chaplain, white or black, is one often ignored by most military historians. Until the question of that role is addressed directly, the chaplain tends to disappear from the historical equation. For example, when the 1st Volunteer Cavalry Regiment and Theodore Roosevelt charged up Kettle Hill in 1898, there was a regimental chaplain, Henry Brown, with them; and when Task Force Smith fought at Osan in 1950 during the Korean War, Chaplain Carl Hudson was a part of that operation. Lamm's work opens a door on one facet of the history of Army chaplaincy.

The story of the black chaplain began in 1863 with the formation of the initial regiments of the U.S. Colored Troops. The 1st U.S.C.T. was recruited from the Baltimore area, and its chaplain was the Reverend Henry M. Turner of the African Methodist Episcopal Church, the first black chaplain in the Regular Army. Most of the chaplains who served with the 166 U.S.C.T. regiments were white, but 13 were black. Some state regiments including the 54th and 55th Massachusetts Infantry regiments also had black chaplains.

After the Civil War, while a number of black regiments were made a part of the Regular Army, their chaplains were white. Beginning in 1884 a gradual change was instituted whereby black chaplains were reintroduced into these positions. By 1898 all four of the Army's black regiments had African-American chaplains. When Chaplain Allen Allensworth of the Twenty-Fourth Infantry Regiment retired as a Lieutenant Colonel in 1906, he was not only the highest-ranking black officer in the history of the U.S. Army, but also the second highest-ranking chaplain. This unique situation continued down until the outbreak of World War II. In 1936, for example, of the eight highest-ranking African-American in the Army, five were chaplains.

Lamm's study of the African-American Army chaplain covers a period in history often referred as a nadir of the black experience in America. The great hopes engendered by the end of slavery had been dimmed with the introduction of a rigorous system of segregation in the South in the aftermath of Reconstruction, and the legal recognition of this inferior status by the Supreme Court decision in the *Plessy vs. Ferguson* case of 1896. Violent repression against African-Americans in the South was widespread, while in the rest of the country, the role blacks was circumscribed by isolation in a societal and cultural sense. It is within the context of these times that Lamm examines the activities of these five black Army chaplains. Each one was different, and their responses to the situation they found themselves in was different. Some were more successful than others were. Yet, on the whole, they stand as a unique success story for the African-American, in a time of repression.

The careers of these black chaplains, with one exception, were successful within the context of the nexus of legal, social, and cultural barriers which faced the African-American in late nineteenth-century America. While not minimizing the difficulties that they endured, Lamm properly delineates their role within the institutional context of the U.S. Army.

William J. Hourihan, Ph.D.
U.S. Army Chaplain Branch Historian
Fort Jackson, South Carolina

I

Introduction

African America soldiers made up nearly one-fifth of the cavalry and one-tenth of the total United States Army in the West during the last quarter of the nineteenth century. Led by white officers, these black men served in four regiments: the Ninth and Tenth cavalry, and the Twenty-fourth and Twenty-fifth Infantry. Unlike the all-white units, a chaplain was assigned to each black regiment primarily to serve as teacher for the mostly illiterate new recruits. Initially the chaplains for these all-black regiments were white, but eventually five black men accepted the call to minister to the troopers of these units.

African America soldiers faced hardships, deprivations, and dangers in their quest to open up the West to settlement. Their Native American foes respected them and gave the black army men the nickname "Buffalo soldiers" as a sign of deference. The black troopers' relationship with white soldiers with whom they served, and with the white settlers they protected was tense and contradictory, for the whites needed the Buffalo soldiers and yet despised them solely because of their race.

Most history books have overlooked the contributions of the Buffalo soldiers, but lately a number of publication have appeared that have sought to rectify this oversight. William H. Leckie's 1967 book, *The Buffalo Soldiers: A Narrative of the Negro Calvary in the West*, was one of the first and remains today as a classic on the exploits of the Ninth and Tenth Cavalry. Arlen L Fowler's *The Black Infantry in the West, 1869-1891* complements Leckie by addressing the contribution of the Twenty-fourth and Twenty-fifth Infantry. Even more recently other publications have appeared such as Monroe Lee Billington's *New Mexico's Buffalo Soldiers, 1866-1900* (1991), to name but one. These books are fine additions, but they all lack attention to the role of the chaplains who served in the Buffalo soldier regiments and especially the five African America chaplains. At best they offer only a page or two on these clergymen; at worst, they ignore the chaplains altogether. The plain fact is that most military historians are simply not interested in the work of the chaplains.

On the other hand, when religious scholars have taken up the story they have committed another over sight: namely, they tended to pass over chaplains as military men. For example, Stephen Ward Angell's book, *Bishop Henry McNeal Turner and Afro-American Religion in the South*, is an excellent work, but he devotes only half of one chapter to Turner's time as the first black chaplain to serve in the federal armed forces. Ward's primary focus is on Turner as a bishop in the African Methodist Church (A.M.E.).

Therefore, the goal of this book is to fill avoid that has been left by scholars; that is, to examine the life and ministry of the five Regular Army Buffalo soldier chaplains primarily *as* Army chaplains.[1] The second original contribution to scholarship is its examination, for the first time, of all five chaplains together. The method used is the case study and the approach taken is twofold: the life and work of each chaplain is explored within the context of a brief history of the particular regiment.

The first chapter provides the background for the Buffalo soldier chaplains by examining African America Christianity. Past scholars have slighted this form of religion by dismissing it as a poor imitation of white Christianity. This chapter demonstrates that African America Christianity was not a shoddy copy, but rather something unique formed from the merger of the slave's African heritage with the slave experience and evangelical Protestantism. African America Christianity, rich

---

[1]The focus of this work is on the Regular Army chaplains and does not include chaplains who served in the militia or Volunteer units.

and unique because of its strong folk religion element, was a religion of liberation which provided strength, hope, and dignity to men and women beaten down but not broken by slavery. As Gayraud S. Wilmore has written, "transplanted Africans, denied access to other forms of self-affirmation and group power, have used religion and religious institution as the principal expression of their peoplehood and their will both to exist and to improve their situation."[2] Through their religious faith, blacks discovered "the power to get at and transform the depths of suffering and bondage and oppression toward hope and fulfillment and joy."[3] Because the Buffalo soldier chaplains were ministers, understanding their religious heritage is crucial.

The second chapter explores the forerunners of the Buffalo soldier chaplains, the fourteen African Americas who served as military clergymen in the American Civil War. That war was an important transition period for the army chaplaincy. When the conflict began, countless unqualified and even unsavory characters flocked to join the ranks of the Union army as chaplains. These scandalous rogues hurt the reputation of the military clergymen, but, inspired by numerous complaints by soldiers and the decent chaplains, Congress overhauled the entire branch in 1863. In that same year, the first of nearly 180,000 African Americas entered the Union army in 166 all-black regiments. Each regiment had its own chaplain but only fourteen of these men were African America. The earlier professionalization of the chaplaincy, however, ensured that these black ministers were the best quality. All fourteen left the army by the war's end, but they helped to establish a high standard and solid reputation upon which the later Buffalo soldier chaplains were able to build.

Nearly twenty years passed between the end of the Civil War and the donning of an army uniform by another black clergyman, because most black

---

[2]Gayraud S. Wilmore, <u>Black Religion and Black Radicalism: An Interpretation of the Religious History of Afro-American People</u> (Marynoll, N.Y.: Orbis Books, 1986), 221.

[3]Charles L. Helton, "The Tragic in Black Historical Experience," <u>Duke Divinity School Review</u>, Vol. 38, No. 2 (Spring 1973).

preachers were too busy trying to meet the needs of the freedman in the Reconstruction South to consider joining the army and moving. But by 1884, Reconstruction was over and the heroic exploits of the men in blue on the western frontier had caught the attention of the American public and of the African America community in particular. The first three case studies examine the careers of the African America chaplains assigned to the black cavalry regiments: Henry V. Plummer, the first commissioned in 1884 and detailed to the Ninth Cavalry; his replacement, George W. Prioleau, the fourth to receive a commission in 1895; and William T. Anderson of the Tenth Cavalry who was the fifth black clergyman commissioned in 1897. The final two cases studies examine the careers of the African America chaplains who served in the all-black infantry units: Allen Allensworth of the Twenty-fourth Infantry, the second African America minister to be commissioned in 1886; and Theophilus Steward of the Twenty-fifth Infantry, the third commissioned in 1891.

The third chapter focuses on Henry V. Plummer , and his successor, George W. Prioleau of the Ninth Cavalry. Plummer's historic career began with much promise but was cut short by court-martial and dismissal from the service basically because he was too assertive for a black man in the 1890s. His subsequent replacement, George W. Prioleau, faced another kind of racism as the only Regular Army chaplain to spend any length of time in the Jim Crow South.

The fourth chapter looks at the role of Williams T. Anderson of the Tenth Cavalry. Anderson was unique because he was a medical doctor as well as a clergyman, and, because he was the only black chaplain in the Regular Army who was deployed to Cuba with his unit during the Spanish-American War. He also has the distinction of being the first African American officer to command a United States Army post. Chaplain Anderson was much less confrontational than Plummer and Prioleau in his approach to combating racism which is probably why he was able to rise to the rank of major. But even he could not escape prejudice and in the end was forced into an early retirement despite his strong and vehement protests.

4

The fifth chapter explores the life and work of Allen Allensworth of the Twenty-fourth Infantry. Like Chaplain Plummer, Allensworth was Baptist minister (the rest were A.M.E. pastors). Like Plummer, Prioleau, and Anderson, he, too, was a former slave who came "up from slavery" to carve out a better life for himself. He was a gifted teacher whose educational reforms were recognized by his civilians peers and were ultimately adopted army-wide. He rose higher than any black officer of his era by reaching the rank of lieutenant colonel. After his retirement from the army he started Allensworth California, the first all-black community in that state. Allensworth was an accommodationalist whose approach to battling racism was similar to Booker T. Washington's in many respects.

The final chapter investigates the ministry of Theophilus Gould Steward, who was the only northerner, the only one who was the product of a racially mixed marriage, and the only free-born Buffalo soldier chaplain. While most chaplains were primarily men of action, Steward was also a deep thinker and prolific writer. His much more confrontational style in combating racism was similar in several respects to that W.E.B. Du Bois and makes for an interesting comparison with Allensworth.

Because these men were all different individuals with various and sundry backgrounds, common themes are not always readily apparent; nevertheless, a few emerge. A cursory examination reveals that all but Steward were born into slavery; all five lived to the "airplane age." Each was part of the struggle of African Americans to emerge from slavery and find their way in American civilization with pride, dignity, and self-worth. All five believed that the best way for their people to face the new challenges presented by freedom was through education and Christianity.

All five of these men have much to teach about the evolution of AfricaAmerican religion and culture between the late antebellum period and the beginning of the twentieth century. Their struggles suggest how African American Christianity, with its folk religion core, was formed on the Old South plantations and then evolved in order to meet the new hurdles confronting the freedmen in an age of black ecclesiastical freedom. Their efforts illustrate how the competing visions of Book T. Washington and his accommodationist view and W.E.B. Du Bois and his resistance view were implemented in an army setting. Their battles indicate how former slaves rose to success as army officers only to face that same old foe, racism, in a new and subtle form.

They also believed that the military provided young, black males with the best opportunity for acquiring the skills, discipline, and character development needed in order to compete in American society, a view that has been widely held in the black community throughout most of the twentieth century. Therefore, while the Buffalo soldier chaplains recognized that racism existed in the army, they persistently adhered to the belief that the military's positive aspects outweighed the bad.

In their quest to create a new and better life for themselves and their people, all the Buffalo soldier chaplains encountered rampant racism both from soldiers and civilians alike, and each fought back in his own unique way. Plummer, Prioleau, and Steward were quite aggressive in standing up for their rights; Anderson, and especially Allensworth, took a more politic approach.[4] But no matter what means or methods they employed, all five were men of pride and dignity, and all five faced great odds in their quest to minister to their soldiers as Regular Army chaplains.

Therefore, if there is one continuous theme or thread that can be found running consistently through the lives of these men, that theme is "double consciousness" spoken of by W.E.B. Du Bois in his classic book, *The Souls of Black Folk*. Double-consciousness was the "double life of every American Negro...as a Negro and as an American," brought on by racism and prejudice. This doubleness or dualism produced psychological and emotional confusion, tension, and competition which ultimately led to "two souls, two thoughts, two unreconciled

---

[4]It is probably no coincidence that only Anderson and Allensworth advanced past the rank of captain. Anderson retired as a major, and Allensworth as a lieutenant colonel.

striving; two warring ideals in one dark body, whose dogged strength alone keeps it from being torn asunder." The end result was a "double life, with double thoughts, and double duties, and double social classes" creating "double words and double ideals, [which] tempt the mind to pretense or to revolt, to hypocrisy or to radicalism."[5]

Du Bois resolved his double-consciousness dilemma by moving to the African nation of Ghana. The Buffalo soldier chaplains stayed in the United States and sought to reform the system within by confronting racism, educating their soldiers, serving a role models, and proclaiming the gospel.

---

[5]W.E.B. Du Bois, The Souls of Black Folk (1903; repr: New York: Bantam Books, 1989), xxi, 3.

CHAPTER I

AFRICAN AMERICAN CHRISTIANITY

The beginning and very basis of any understanding of black United States Army Chaplains, 1884-1901, must start with the religious heritage which formed them into men and leaders. These men were not only chaplains; they were also African American chaplains. As African Americans their religious heritage, complete with a strong tradition of black folk religion, made them unique and distinct from their white peers. This chapter is an examination of African American Christianity and focuses on the three elements which merged to form this unique black folk religious expression: the African heritage, the slave experience, and evangelical Protestantism.[1]

Both black and white theology share much in common and yet there are many differences as well. For example, both entail objective references such as holy things beyond and outside human beings; and a subjective side in the form of expression and experience. For both blacks and whites, religion is also a way of acknowledging and understanding an ultimate reality. But the genesis of African American Christianity is found in West Africa -- not Europe. Further, the religious expression which African Americans founded was created as a social and theological necessity,

---

[1]Most blacks were primarily influenced by the evangelical wing of Protestantism in their quest to create something new, African American Christianity. Therefore, Roman Catholicism, Islam, and other forms of religious expression will not be explored.

for, in the context of slavery, blacks were defined as "things" rather than as men and women. Therefore, blacks took the Protestant evangelical religion of this masters, merged it with their West African heritage and slave experience, and created something new and different, African American Christianity, complete with a strong black folk religion core in tact. Thus the creation of African American Christianity was a conscious effort on the part of blacks to find meaning for their lives, as well as worth and dignity as human beings despite being told that they were something less.[2]

I

The African Heritage

Most slaves brought to America came from West Africa. The culture of this region continued to make an impact on their lives and their religion even after they were rudely resettled in the New World. Therefore, it is important to understand the African heritage if one is truly to appreciate African American Christianity. Although religion different somewhat between the various West African peoples like the Akan, Ewe, Yoruba, Ibo, and others, there was a common pattern. First, these peoples believed in a Supreme Creator who was remote, usually identified with the sky, and was aloof from the activities of the lesser gods and of humanity. The High God was given various names by West African tribes such as *Olorun* among the Yoruba peoples, *Chukwu* among the Ibo, *Nyame* among the Ashante people, and so forth. *Olurun* gave people their fates at creation. Over time, though, these fates have

---

[2]Gayraud S. Wilmore, Black Religion and Black Radicalism: An Interpretation of Afro-American People (Maryknoll, N.Y.:Orbis Books, 1986), 2-4. See also Milton C. Sernett, Black Religion and American Evangelicalism: White Protestants, Plantation Missions, and the Flower of Negro Christianity, 1787-1865 (Metuchen, N.J.: The Scarecrow Press, 1975), 17-19. Albert J. Raboteau, Slave Religion: The "Invisible Institution" in the Antebellum South (New York: Oxford University Press, 1978), 4-6. Gayle Felton, Class lectures from "The Black Church in America," Duke University, 1987.

been forgotten and now can only be retrieved by divination. *Esu* stands in opposition to *Olorun* and serves as the trickster and sometimes mediator between humans and *Olorun*. Because of the remoteness of the Supreme Creator from his creation, few prayed to him. Instead, most concentrated their attention on the lesser gods and on the spirits of their dead ancestors, both thought to be close to this world.[3]

The lesser deities included the gods of lighting, thunder, rivers, lakes, and so forth. Many felt these lesser gods served as mediators between themselves and the High God. These lesser divinities also had names. The Ashanti called them *abosom*; the Ibo, *arose*; the Yoruba, *orisha*. These were the gods who caused daily events to occur in the lives of everyday people, both good and bad. Therefore, people had to appease them through praise, sacrifice, and obedience.[4]

Much of this worship took place at local altars, shrines, and temples dedicated to the various divinities. The priests who headed these shrines offered worship and praise, as well as serving as diviner and herbalist. After being trained and initiated, which included 'dying' and being resurrected, the new priest was given the ability to serve as a medium between the gods and humanity. This was carried out through ecstatic trances or 'spirit possession' accompanied by shouting and dance which revealed which god was trying to communicate. Most people became affiliated with the god of their parents.[5]

Charms, amulets, and witchcraft also played a role in West African religion and had strong ties with medicine as well. West Africans believed that illnesses were caused by "spiritual" as well as "natural" causes. Therefore, their priests doubled as

---

[3]Raboteau, 8-9. See also C. Eric Lincoln, ed., The Black Experience in Religion (New York: Anchor books, 1974), 313. Noel Q. King, African Cosmos: An Introduction to Religion in Africa (Belmont, CA: Wadsworth Publishing Company, 1986), 8-9. Warren Matthews, World Religions, 2nd ed. (Minneapolis: West Publishing Company, 1995), 75.

[4]Raboteau, 9-1. King, 9-10.

[5]Raboteau, 10-11. Lincoln, 288-291. See also Arna Bontempts, ed., Great Slave Narratives (Boston: Beacon Press, 1969).

"root doctors." Charms and amulets were employed to heal sicknesses, ward off diseases, or cause people to fall in love. West Africans also feared witches who used these same devices to inflict harm on innocent people.[6]

In addition, West Africans believe that spirits were present in the world, too. They thought that spirits could be found in certain trees, etc., and that these spirits had to be taken into account through taboos, sacred medicine, and so forth less they cause a person harm. Second, they believe that the spirits of their ancestors were very near at hand. These they divided into two types: the spirits of their founding fathers and mothers; and those of their recently deceased ancestors. The second type of spirits acted as intercessors in the spirit realm for their living relatives. They also taught right living which encouraged people to conduct themselves in a way which would be approved of by their ancestors. Finally, most West Africans believed in an overreaching life-force that surrounded and permeated the world sometimes called a sacred cosmos by scholars. West Africans called this life-force *Da* or *Nyam*, a word which is linguistically akin to the word yam, an important African food and sustainer of life. This life force was very important, indeed, the key to all that was.[7]

West Africans were very anthropocentric in regards to their views on humanity. They held no great distinction between humans and spirits, no concept of original sin, and certainly no devaluation of humanity in light of the spirit world. They were positive, optimistic, and believed that each person was endowed with a soul or spirit which he or she must care for. The ultimate goal was to reunite one's soul with the High God at death. This was the reason funerals and grave sites became very important among African Americans. Breaking up personal possessions

---

[6]Raboteau, 14-15.

[7]Raboteau, 11. King, 15-16. Felton.

12

and half-burying them in the top of the grave aided the deceased in their return to the Supreme Creator. The worse thing to happen was to die and fall from memory.[8]

Many of these specific features such as emphasizing the spirit world, breaking up personal possessions for burial, shouting, dancing, the closeness of the sacred and secular worlds, the positive view of nature, etc., persisted among slaves even after they were brought to the New World. Most scholars in this camp now insist that these links between Africa and America consisted of subtle rather than clear-cut African carry-overs which is described as the "soft impact" theory.

The thesis that West African influences continued to impact slaves in America is relatively new. Robert E. Park, writing in a 1919 article for *The Journal of Negro History*, laid out a different view which soon became the traditional position. In a much quoted statement he wrote:

> My own impression is that the African Tradition which the Negro brought to the United States was very small. In fact, there is every reason to believe, it seems to me, that the Negro when he landed in the United States, left behind almost everything but his dark complexion and his tropical temperament. It is very difficult to find in the South today anything that can be traced back to Africa.[9]

Not only were all traces of their African heritage erased, but he also implied that blacks were intellectually inferior and unable to create a culture of their own. Instead, they merely developed a poor copy of white culture including a shoddy copy of the Christian faith.

Writing in the 1950s when the major goal of civil rights advocates was integration, E. Franklin Frazier saw religion as both a "refuge" which protected blacks, and as a hindrance which prevented them from being fully integrated into American society. His analysis of African American religion led him to draw on

---

[8]Bontempts, 14. Charles Ball, Fifty Years in Chains (1837; repr., New York: Dover Publications, 1970), 265. Felton.

[9]Robert E. Park, "The Conflict and Fusion of Cultures with Special Reference to the Negro," Journal of Negro History 4 (1919): 116.

Park's thesis that slavery caused a total break with the African heritage of blacks. He believed that the Christianity slaves developed was used to fill a void left by their forgotten African heritage.[10]

While Park and Frazier maintained that the African heritage was lost to blacks imported as slaves to this country, a few other scholars challenged this traditional opinion: for example, W.E.B. Du Bois in *The Souls of Black Folk;* and later, Carter G. Woodson in his book *History of the Negro Church.* Both men's pioneering studies led them to the conclusion that definite African antecedents remained in Africa-American religion. Their works soon inspired others like Newbell N. Puckett to write books such as *Folk Beliefs of the Southern Negro*, and articles like "Religious Folk Beliefs of Whites and Negroes" published in the *Journal of Negro History.* Puckett countered that black Christianity was not a poor copy of white Christianity, but instead was an attempt by blacks to create something select. In particular, he argued that African cultural elements survived and provided a strong basis for black religion.[11]

But one of the best criticisms of the traditional point of view came from Melville J. Herskovits, an anthropologist and Director of African studies programs at schools like Columbia University, Howard University, and Northwestern University. Herskovits brought to the examination of African America culture and religion a much broader background than most observers of this day. In a well-researched book entitled *The Myth of the Negro Past,* he made a strong case for the influence of the African heritage on slave religion in a chapter entitled "Africanisms

---

[10]E. Franklin Frazier, The Negro Church in America (New York: Schocken Books, 1963), 1-4, 71-73, 86.

[11]Newbell N. Puckett, Folk Beliefs of the Southern Negro (Chapel Hill, 1926). Journal of Negro History, 16: 9-35, 1931. See also W.E.B. Du Bois, The Souls of Black Folk (1903; repr.: New York: Bantam Books, 1989) and Carter G. Woodson, The History of the Negro Church (Washington, D.C.: Associated Publishers, 1945).

14

in Religious Life." Specially, he cited language structure, folk art, dance, spirituals, and so forth as direct links between the old world and the new.[12]

Herskovits demonstrated that the focus of study must include a broad spectrum of African culture in order to understand fully the interrelationship of African culture and religion, and the impact this made on African American Christianity. This was necessary for, as G.J.A. Ojo has written, "African life in general is thoroughly permeated by religion. It is no overstatement to say that religion is not just one complex of African culture but the catalyst of the other complexes."[13] For instance, dance, music and poetry were very important in West African life, employed to express joy, grief, love, hate, religion and to celebrate great events in the life of the people like battles, festivals, religious activities, and so forth. African musicians were more than just entertainers, then, they served the tribe by recounting its saga through music, dance, stories, magic and mime which meant that they were "living encyclopedias" who were highly trained experts in history, law, and liturgy.[14]

Rhythmic music and action by the observers like patting their feet, clapping, swaying to the beat, and so on, accompanied these songs, driven by the beat of African drums. These drums were usually made of hollowed logs up to fourteen inches in diameter, and were played with sticks or the palms of one's hands. Other instruments included the marimba, banjo, flute, and harp. Later when Africans were imported to the new world as slaves, they carried their music, body rhythm, voice,

---

[12]Melville, J. Herskovits, The Myth of the Negro Past (Boston: Beacon Press, 1958), 207ff.

[13]Quoted in Eugene Genovese, Roll, Jordan, Roll: The World the Slaves Made (New York: Vintage Books, 1976), 210.

[14]Chaplain (Major) Allen K. Lowe, "Black Traditions in Christian Worship" Military Chaplains' Review (Summer 1992), 49-50.

and instrumentation with them which would prove crucial in the formation of the African American Christianity.[15]

Much effort has been made by scholars to find and then trace African vestiges back to Africa. Some of their efforts have been successful; others have not. It is important to realize that Africans imported to North America came from different regions and had various languages and traditions. Nevertheless, they did have a common "style of life" which bound them together and which was preserved even after they arrived in North America. This common style of life consisted of subtle rather than clear-cut carry-overs and, as noted, has been called "the soft impact" theory. As one scholar has written:

> Though they varied widely in language, institutions, gods, and familial patterns, they shared a fundamental outlook toward the past, present, and future and common means of culture; expression which could have well constituted the basis of a sense of common identity and world view capable of withstanding the impact of slavery.[16]

The main point is that African vestiges did survive and helped to shape black culture and black religion even after the Africans were rudely introduced to the New World via slave experience.

II

The Slave Experience

The American system of slavery differed from that of ancient times because it was permanent, based on race, and dehumanizing. Because this New World

---

[15]Lowe, 50.

[16]Lawrence W. Levine, Black Culture and Black Consciousness: Afro-American Folk Thought from Slavery to Freedom (New York: Oxford University Press, 1977), 4.

slavery was so devastating, the traditional African understanding of life and religion was severely damaged, though never lost. This section traces the history of the slave experience, demonstrates the impact it made on both blacks and whites in the American South, and shows how the slave experience formed a critical component in the formation of African American Christianity.

The Muslims were some of the first to become involved in slave trading in the Middle Ages. Soon tales of African wealth in slaves and other desirable items reached the Portuguese who moved to enter the lucrative market. By 1444 the Portuguese were the leaders in the slave trade followed by the Spanish. Because the African states were still quite powerful, Europeans welcomed them as equal partners in this venture. Indeed, this was an era in which black and white kings greeted one another in friendly, respectful terms. Many Africans had no problems with the slave trade for they has been enslaving captured black prisoners of war for centuries. Further, black slaves brought to Portugal were few in number, quickly intermarried with the local population, and were viewed as fellow human beings by the Portuguese.[17]

It was the Spanish who created the major turning point in the African slave trade. First, the New World's demand for labor for the new sugar plantations began to outstrip the supply of Native American workers. Second, Bartolome de Las Casas, a Dominican priest, wrote a book entitled *In the Defense of Indians* which documented the awful abuses inflected on Indian slaves by the Spanish. Therefore, the Spanish turned to Africa to find replacements for their Indian slaves. The Spanish found that Africans were more resistant to European sicknesses like venereal diseases, and that imported blacks could not escape and blend back into the forests as easily as local Native Americans. Therefore, by the early 1500s large

---

[17]Lerone Bennett, Jr., <u>Before the Mayflower: A History of Black America</u> (1962; repr., New York: Penguin Books, 1986), 31-33,47.

numbers of Africans were being imported to the Caribbean and Central and South America.[18]

The first blacks brought to what would become the United States occurred in Jamestown, Virginia in 1619. That August, Dutch traders delivered twenty Africans apparently as indentured servants, not as slaves, though historians are not entirely clear on this issue. Like white indentured servants, they were bound to the land for five to seven years; after that, they were set free and could become landholders or artisans. An example of the ease in which they successfully entered English New World life can be found in the story of a black man named Anthony Johnson, who came from England to America as an indentured servant in 1621. After working off his servitude, he started purchasing land. By 1651, Johnson owned 250 acres and had five servants, including white ones. He and his son, John, were instrumental in establishing one of America's first black communities along the Pungoteague River in Virginia. Many other African Americas joined Johnson; some, however, chose to live in integrated communities in which they held public office and intermarried with whites, not just in Virginia, but also in Massachusetts, New York, and other colonies as well.[19]

By 1660, a major change began to occur in the way in which blacks were treated in the English colonies. Before, blacks and whites apparently socialized with one another quite freely. In large part this was because most shared the same lot as servants, and because blacks brought to America had already learned English via their period of "seasoning" in the West Indies. Then, too, blacks were few in number, making up only five percent of the population of the Chesapeake region.

---

[18]Bennett, 34-35.

[19]Lawrence H. Leder, America-1603-1789: Prelude to a Nation (Minneapolis: Burgess Publishing Company, 1978), 48-49. Felton. See also Marshall Smelser, American Colonial and Revolutionary History (New York: Barnes and Noble, 1962), 48. Bennett, 34-38, 40, 41. Eric Foner and John A. Garraty, eds., The Reader's Companion to American History (Boston: Houghton Mifflin Company, 1991), 991-995.

After 1660, however, planters began to acquire more slaves than servants because declining death rates now made slaves more cost effective, since a one-time cash outlay resulted in a lifetime worker. Longer life spans also meant that slave families could be formed thus producing even more slave children. This is an important factor, because rumors of harsh conditions in the Chesapeake led to reduction in the numbers of indentured servants.[20]

Now that larger numbers of blacks were being imported to work the highly profitable tobacco fields, it was necessary to import them directly so that forthwith more than eighty percent were brought straight from Africa. Without having been "seasoned" first, these Africans knew no English and had not been exposed to Christianity. Because they had much less in common with whites, owners found it fairly easy to develop a rationale for permanent bondage for these "heathen like creatures."

This rationalization process took place gradually. In 1661 the Virginia House of Burgesses made a legal distinction between black and white servants for the first time, when it referred to blacks as "servants indentured for life," and laid out a different set of punishments for them should they disobey their masters. In 1662 a law was established that made children born to blacks, servants for life, too. Finally in 1670, slavery was clearly established when the Burgesses declared that "all servants not Christians imported into this colony by shipping [i.e., blacks] shall be slaves for their lives; but what shall come by land [i.e., Indians] shall serve until thirty years of age."[21] Native American captives could easily run away back to their homes, while white indentured servants often slipped away to North Carolina and merged with the free population; but the African stood out. With the increasing

---

[20]James W. Davidson and others, Nation of Nations: A Narrative History of the American Republic (New York: W.W. Norton and Company, 1994), 59-61. Allen Weinstein and Frank Otto Gatell, eds., American Negro Slavery (New York: Oxford University Press, 1973), 27-29.

[21]Leder, 49. Weinstein and Gatell, 29-36.

demand for tobacco, constant shortage of labor, and strange ways of blacks imported directly from Africa, justifying permanent slavery became readily acceptable.

Europeans, who had initially led the slave raiding parties, now turned to African allies to help them meet the insatiable demand for more slaves. These African allies received iron, cloth, rum, and glass beads in the exchange. Soon the machinery of the slave trade was refined to a science with "factories" being set up all along the West African coast, and a "Triangular Trade" taking place across the Atlantic between the New World, the West Indies, and Africa.[22]

The last leg of the Triangular Trade which brought the Africans over was called the "Middle Passage." One to two hundred black men and women were stuffed into spaces so tight that they could not sit upright. As one "lucky" survivor later wrote, conditions were so bad that "with the loathsomeness of the stench, and [the sounds of people] crying together, I became so sick and low that I was not able to eat." Perhaps one out of every six died before they completed the 5,000 mile, twelve to fifteen week journey. Dysentery was the most common cause of death; others simply committed suicide through starvation or strangulation. [23]

For those who survived, another one-quarter were likely to perish in the first year if their final destination was the Chesapeake Bay area, with death rates in Carolina running even higher. Adding to their misery was the fact that unlike earlier black imports, these new slaves coming directly from Africa were totally unfamiliar with English language and customs, thus making their first impressions even more bewildering.[24]

---

[22]Foner and Garraty, 994-995. Davidson, 61. John W. Blassingame, The Slave Community: Plantation Life in the Antebellum South (New York: Oxford University Press, 1972), 6-8.

[23]Ball, 184-186. Davidson, 61. W.D. Weatherford, The Negro from Africa to America (New York: George H. Doran Company, 1924), 82-85. Bontempts, 22,30,77.

[24]Davidson, 61. Peter Wood, Black Majority: Negroes in Colonial South Carolina from 1670 through the Stono Rebellion (New York: W.W. Norton and Company, 1974), 79-80. Bontempts, 27, 34.

The slave trade was quite profitable and continued in the United States until a compromise in the Constitutional ratification process ended it in 1808. Slavery had existed for centuries, but this New World slavery was different for three reasons: first, it was permanent; second, it was based on race; and third, it was dehumanizing.[25]

In 1919 Ulrich Bonnell Phillips published a landmark book entitled *American Negro Slavery*, in which he asserted three arguments that have framed the discussion of slavery to the very present. First, he maintained that slavery was a dying economic institution that was unprofitable to both the individual slave owner and the South in general. Second, he contended that slave life was not all that horrid despite tales of woe woven by abolitionists. Finally he wrote that slaves were such easygoing and slow-witted -- "Sambos" -- that they did not really mind slave life.[26]

Since than scholars have found many deficiencies in Phillips' reasoning. Most economic historians, for instance, now argue that slavery, and especially the plantation, was highly profitable and efficient and most likely would not have died out anytime soon. Indeed, a recent study has shown that by the 1830s, masters were using imported watches to keep up with the work pace of their slaves so that they were able to transform slavery into a modern, highly efficient factory-style system.[27] Still others have challenged Phillips' benign view of slavery. Stanley Elkins' book

---

[25]W.E.B. Du Bois, The Suppression of the African Slave Trade to the United States, 1638-1870 (1898; repr., New York: Russell and Russell, 1965), 60-61. Thomas F. Gossett, Race: The History of an Idea in America (New York: Schocken Books, 1965), 28-31, 40-43. Felton. See also Bontempts, 10, 25, to compare African slavery to its American counterpart.

[26]Thomas A. Bailey and Davis M. Kennedy, The American Pageant: A History of the Republic (Boston: D.C. Heath, 1991), 360-361. U.B. Phillips, American Negro Slavery (1918; repr. Baton Rouge: Louisiana State University Press, 1966), 514.

[27]Mark M. Smith, Mastered by the Clock: Time, Slavery, and Freedom in the American South (Chapel Hill: University of North Carolina Press, 1997).

Slavery, for example, compared slave life to that in a Nazi concentration camp. He asserted that both were "total institutions" which "infantilized" their victims.[28]

Others, like Kenneth Stampp have taken a position somewhere between the two extremes presented by Phillips and Elkins. In *The Peculiar Institution,* Stampp argued that, although nearly three-fourths of all southerners owned no slaves, the slave system dominated southern life through the economic and political power of the planters. He also demonstrated the complexity of slaveholding with its variations from region to region. Slaveholding families in the Upper South (Virginia, North Carolina, Tennessee, and Arkansas) tended to own fewer blacks, for instance, due to cost and greater crop diversity. It was the Deep South (South Carolina, Georgia, Alabama, Mississippi, and Louisiana) where most slaves lived, concentrated on large plantations.[29]

No matter what state, though, the status of a child in slave society always depended on the status of its mother, for in many cases, some slaves looked white. A mulatto child was generally considered black if he or she was one-eighth percent black. Some states, however, went even farther and designated a person a negro if he or she were one-thirty-third percent black. Such strict regulations were deemed necessary because of the frequent sexual assaults committed against slave women by their white masters and overseers either through bribes or force if trinkets failed to elicit a favorable response. Black abolitionist Frederick Douglass accurately summed up the plight of black females when he wrote that the "slave woman is at the mercy of the fathers, sons or brothers of her master."[30]

---

[28]Stanley M. Elkins, Slavery: A Problem in American Institutional and Intellectual Life (Chicago: University of Chicago Press, 1959), 104-106. Bailey and Kennedy, 360-361.

[29]Phillips, 514. Kenneth M. Stampp, The Peculiar Institution: Slavery in the Antebellum South (1956; repr., New York: Alfred A. Knopf, 1972.), 6, 29, 31-33. Bailey and Kennedy, 360-361.

[30]Frederick Douglass, My Bondage and My Freedom (1855; repr., New York), 60. Blassingame, 82-85. Bontempts, 271-272.

These sexual assaults not only posed a constant threat to the black female, but they also served to hinder the development of strong family ties among the slaves. Black men tried to protect their mates but could do little if their masters were persistent in their advances. Often times black couples were separated by the sale of one partner for legal marriage between slaves was not permitted. As John Blassingame has noted, the "most brutal aspect of slavery was the separation of families."[31] In this environment, multiple sexual relationships developed among the slaves as a sheer necessity. Nevertheless, blacks did have a great deal of respect for monogamous relationships as noted by ex-slaves like Lunsford Lane who noted of his 1828 marriage that he was:

> bound as fast in wedlock as a slave can be. God may at any time sunder that band in a freeman; either master may do the same at pleasure in a slave. The [marriage] bond is not recognized in law. But in my case it has never been broken; and now it cannot be, except by a higher power.[32]

Most slave families lived in barracks or crude cabins if they were owned by planters, or perhaps in the same house if they were the property of less well-to-do slave owners. The majority served as field hands, while a small minority worked as servants, artisans, and so forth. Life as a house crew member was generally better than that of a field hand, especially for those field hands who were controlled by sadistic overseers who routinely beat them. But the house crew had the disadvantage of being under the constant supervision of whites.[33] Whether slaves worked in the "big house" or in the fields, their lives were under the total control of the master, for

---

[31]Blassingame, 87-89.

[32]William Loren Katz, ed., Five Slave Narratives: A Compendium (New York: Arno Press, 1968), 10-12. Theodore Rosengarten, Tombee: Portrait of a Cotton Planter with The Journal of Thomas B. Chaplin 91822-1890) (New York: William Morrow and Company, 1986), 109-110.

[33]Harvey Wish, ed., Slavery in the South: First-Hand Accounts of the Antebellum American Southland from Northern and Southern Writers, Negroes, and Foreign Observers (New York: Farrar, Strass and Giroux, 1964), 77-81. Ball, 112, 139, 146-147.

as Stampp has pointed out, the entire slave system was based on fear, intimidation, and a sense of helplessness, coupled with poor food, long hours, and inferior medical care.

Eugene D. Genovese's book, *Roll, Jordan, Roll: The World the Slaves Made*, has added another crucial element to our understanding of the slave experience, and that is the concept of paternalism. Genovese wrote:

> A paternalism accepted by both masters and slaves -- but with radically different interpretations -- afforded a fragile bridge across the intolerable contradictions inherent in a society based on racism, slavery, and class exploitation...For the slaveholders paternalism represented an attempt to overcome the fundamental contradiction in slavery: the impossibility of the slaves ever becoming the things they were supposed to be.[34]

Paternalism permitted slaveholders to rationalize holding another human being against their will. Paternalism stifled black revolt because it tied blacks to a master rather than to one another. The plantation owner lived like a medieval lord in his castle and all those who lived there under him -- wife, children, and especially slaves -- were his to rule. Finally, paternalism forced the slaves to direct their creative energy inward which eventually resulted in the formation of African American Christianity,

The American system of slavery was quite dehumanizing. Any illusions to the contrary are quickly dismissed by the words of the planters themselves. Perhaps the best example is the 4 March 1858 "Mud-sills Speech" made by James Henry Hammond, U.S. Senator from South Carolina, in response to an address the previous day by Senator William Seward of New York. In addition to declaring that "Cotton is king," Hammond defended slavery with these words:

> in all social systems there must be a class to do the menial duties, to perform the drudgery of life. That is, a class requiring but a low order of intellect and but little skill. Its requisites are vigor, docility,

---

[34]Eugene Genovese, Roll, Jordan, Roll: The World the Slaves Made (New York: Vintage Books, 1972), 5.

fidelity. Such a class you must have, or you would not have the other class which leads progress, civilization, and refinement. It constitutes the very mud-sills of society and of political government; and you might as well attempt to build a house in the air, as to build either one without the other, except on this mud-sill. Fortunately for the South, she found a race adapted to that purpose to her hand...We use them for our purpose, and call them slaves.[35]

Hammond's arrogant views were not atypical. But ironically the diaries of men like Hammond and other antebellum planters suggest that, despite their lordly proclamations, they, too, were entrapped by the very same slave system. For instance, planter journals are full of cases of slave intransigence which required constant attention diverting overseers and planters from other pursuits. Examples of this obstinance ran the course from passive resistance like feinting illness, work slowdowns, and pretending not to understand orders, to more contentious acts, like theft and escape attempts.[36]

Planter women were especially susceptible to this sense of reverse bondage for they were caught between domineering husbands and the demands of managing the slaves during periods of frequent absences by their spouses. Elizabeth Fox-Genovese has captured this ironic twist successfully in her book, *Within the Plantation Household: Black and White Women of the Old South;* so too does *A Northern Woman in the Plantation South: Letters of Tryphena Blanche Holder Fox, 1856-1876,* edited by Wilma King. A planter women named Sarah Gayle expressed this feeling well when she noted: "I despise myself for suffering my temper to rise at the provocations offered by my servants. I would be willing to spend the rest of my life at the north, where I never should see the face of another negro."[37]

---

[35]Carol Bleser, ed., Secret and Sacred: The Diaries of James Henry Hammond, a Southern Slaveholder (New York: Oxford University Press, 1988), 272-273.

[36]Rosengarten, 157-159, 635ff.

[37]Elizabeth Fox-Genovese, Within the Plantation Household: Black and White Women of the Old South (Chapel Hill: University of North Carolina Press, 1988), 22. See also Wilma King, A

Two things stand out as a result of the slave experience. First, because of the devastating and ruthless effects of New World slavery, the traditional African understanding of life and religion were severely damaged, though never lost. What blacks needed was to assimilate elements from their new home with vestiges from the past to form a new coherent world-view to help them adjust. As Eugene Genovese wrote: "The slaves' efforts, therefore, aimed at ordering this [new] world, at rendering it rational, and at explaining those things which their oppressors could not or would not explain to them."[38] Second, by the 1830s black-white frustrations intensified making life even less bearable for blacks. This was because southerners became fearful of losing control of their slaves because of Nat Turner's bloody revolt, and the increasing belligerent tone taken by northern abolitionist groups. In this environment, merely subsisting from day to day was a major accomplishment for the typical bondsman. But with the advent of the Second Great Awakening, the slave would acquire a new coherent world-view and means of resistance that would prove amazingly affective, and that was through the adoption and modification of evangelical Protestant Christianity.

III

Evangelical Protestantism

The religion that would prove to make the greatest influence on the life of American slaves, and later, black Army chaplains was evangelical Protestantism.

Northern Woman in the Plantation South: Letters of Tryphena Blanche Holder Fox, 1856-1876 (Columbia: University of South Carolina Press, 1993), 31,36,47,86,106-107,131,152.

[38]Genovese, 231.

26

Beginning in the seventeenth-century Europe, evangelical Protestantism made its initial impact on African Americans in the Great Awakening of the 1730s and 1740s. But its biggest impact on the black community came, however, in the Second Great Awakening which occurred during the first part of the nineteenth century.

Evangelicalism is a term that is often used but its history and even meaning are somewhat elusive. Evangel is the root for evangelical and it comes from a Greek transliteration of the word *euaggelion*. The original Biblical denotation refers to the "good news" ("gospel" in the Anglo-Saxon tongue) Jesus preached concerning the coming kingdom of God.[39]

The word evangelical came into usage during the time of the Reformation to identify Protestants, and particularly those who believed salvation came by grace through faith based on their reading of the Bible. In time the meaning narrowed so that evangelicals were Protestant Christians who had undergone an intense personal conversion -- the "born again" experience mentioned in John 3:1-13. They also adhered to a strict moral life, saw the Bible alone as their source of authority, and shared these experiences with the goal of converting others.[40]   As one church historian has described it, evangelicalism is:

> much more a mood and an emphasis than a theological system [with a] stress upon the importance of personal religious experience [and is a] revolt against the notion that the Christian life involved little more than observing the outward formalities of religion.[41]

---

[39] Alan Richardson and John Bowden, eds., The Westminster Dictionary of Christian Theology (Philadelphia: Westminster Press, 1983), 192-193. See also Mark 1:14-15.

[40] Richardson and Bowden, 192-193,

[41] Winthrop S. Hudson, Religion in America 4th ed., (New York: MacMillan Publishing Company, 1987), 77.

Evangelical Protestantism emerged in the seventeenth-century Europe, after the religious fervor that had flowed freely during the heady days of Martin Luther and John Calvin subsided. History has shown a predictable pattern emerge time and again: namely, that the new ideas and creative impulses that cascaded so effortlessly from the first generation of imaginative spirits tends to become hardened, rigid, and dogmatic as time passes on. That was precisely what happened to much of Protestant Christianity in the German states by the end of the Thirty Years' War. In the aftermath, intellectual acquiescence and orthodoxy became the key criteria for proper adherence to the faith, with faith itself becoming less of a personal relationship with God than a proper understanding of church tenets.

Evangelicalism sprang up as a revolt against this rigid, overly cerebral form of Christianity. The direction of evangelical Protestantism was ultimately shaped by the efforts of the seventeenth century Continental Pietists and English Puritans who inspired them. This story is a complex and interconnected one, for it sprang forth simultaneously in several locations with writers in one country influencing those in another. A few illustrations will make the emergence of evangelical Christianity more lucid.

The Continental Pietists were led by Philip Jacob Spener who lived in Germany from 1635 to 1705. He become convinced of the need for spiritual revitalization of the Lutheran faith, in part after reading books by Continental writers like Johann Arndt and English Puritan authors like Richard Baxter. These publications emphasized that true Christian living required a critical self-examination of one's religious faith, a quest for holiness, and high standards of personal morality, as opposed to mere intellectual assent to correct doctrine.[42] To risk oversimplification, Spener and his Pietist followers emphasized a religion of the heart rather than the head. As he noted in his most famous book, *Pia Desideria*: "whoever grows in learning and declines in morals is on the decrease rather than the

---

[42]Philip Jacob Spener, Pia Desideria (1675, repr., Philadelphia: Fortress Press, 1982), 8-9.

increase."[43] Spener's ideas spread which resulted in an infusion of new life into the Protestant faith, not only in Germany, but in the rest of Europe and eventually North America.

The Moravians were instrumental in bringing Pietism to America when the first of many emigrated from Germany to Georgia in 1735, just at a time when much of the old religious enthusiasm of the original colonial settlers had waned.[44] On that same voyage with the Moravians were two brothers, John and Charles Wesley, both young Oxford educated Anglican missionaries. Legends abound as to what transpired between the Wesley brothers and the Moravians. What is known for certain is that the Wesleys were deeply moved by the sincerity of the Moravians' humble but sturdy Christianity. Both in Georgia and later back in England, John kept in touch with the Moravians. Already a pious soul, Wesley at last found answers he had been seeking all his life on his Christian pilgrimage under the mentoring of one of them, Peter Boehler, who led him to conversion on 24 May 1738.[45]

Wesley finally broke relations with the Moravians two years later, but the debt both he and evangelical Protestantism owed them was immeasurable. A translucent example of this influence can be seen in a typical Wesley sermon such as "The Scripture Way of Salvation." This sermon, published in 1765, was in response to the Scottish Glasites or Sandemanians who claimed that faith was merely intellectual assent to the gospel, a view which Wesley and all evangelicals denied. In a passage which sums up evangelical thought quite eloquently, Wesley wrote that:

---

[43]Spener, 105.

[44]Sydney E. Ahlstrom, A Religious History of the American People (New Haven: Yale University Press, 1972),237-239. Moravians are known officially as the Unitas Fratum. They are descended from the followers of John Hus. After being nearly annihilated during the Counter-Reformation, the Moravians went underground until conditions permitted them to reemerge in the eighteenth century under the protection of Count Nicholas Zinzendorf. Jon Sensbach's 1991 Ph.D. dissertation, "A Separate Canaan: The Making of an Afro-Moravians World in North Carolina, 1763-1856," describes the efforts by Moravians to convert the few slaves they owned.

[45]Jerald C. Bauer, ed., The Westminster Dictionary of Church History (Philadelphia: Westminster Press, 1981), 860.

at the same time that we are justified, yea, in that very moment, sanctification begins. In that instant we are born again, born from above, born of the Spirit: We are inwardly renewed by the power of God. We feel the love of God shed abroad in our heart by the Holy Ghost which is given unto us; producing love to all mankind, and more especially to the children of God; expelling love of the world, the love of pleasure, of ease, of honor, of money, the love of pride, anger, self-will, and every other evil temper; in a word, changing the earthly sensual, devilish mind, into the mind which was in Christ Jesus.[46]

Through Wesley's influence evangelical Protestantism spread both in Anglican Britain and in religiously diverse North America. This is crucial for it was evangelical Protestantism that made the biggest impact on the lives of the slaves because it was this form of Christianity that most appealed to them. Second, it is important because the revivals connected with evangelical Protestantism persuaded some religious groups like the Quakers to see slaves as human beings with eternals souls leading them to condemn slavery.

Wesley's friend and fellow Oxford "Holy Club" member, George Whitefield, proved to be the key player in the Great Awakening. This was the religious revival that swept the colonies in the 1730s and 1740s, introduced blacks to evangelicalism, and resulted in the establishment of evangelical Protestantism as the most potent religious force in America. Through this revival evangelical Protestantism came into its own complete with the features that would soon become standard fare: lay testimonials, dramatic conversions, and dynamic, extemporaneous preaching designed to appeal to one's heart via the emotions. All of these feature were new religious innovations and they would prove to be highly compatible with the African heritage of the slaves.[47]

---

[46] Albert C. Outler, ed., John Wesley (New York: Oxford University Press, 1964), 271,274.

[47] Hudson, 62-69. James D. Essig, The Bonds of Wickedness: American Evangelicals Against Slavery, 1770-1808 (Philadelphia: Temple University Press, 1982), 10-14.

If the Great Awakening of the 1730s and 1740s won America to the evangelical cause, it was the Second Awakening during the early nineteenth century which won over American blacks. Indeed, while the Great Awakening established evangelical Protestantism as the most potent religious force in America impacting all denominations and parts of the country, the number of slaves converted during this time was relatively small. The Presbyterian minister Charles Colcock Jones wrote that before the Second Awakening "On the whole...but a minority of the Negroes, and that a small one, attended regularly the house of God, and taking them as a class, their religious instruction was extensively and most seriously neglected."[48] The Second Awakening reversed this trend dramatically as the numbers show. For example, from 1846 to 1861 the Methodist Episcopal Church, South, increased its black membership from 200,000 in 1845, to 400,000 by 1860. In Mississippi, black members outnumbered whites by five-to-one thanks to the revivals so that the largest Baptist church in the state, the Natchez Baptist Church, had 422 members: 62 white and 380 black.[49] Figures like these demonstrate that impact of the Second Great Awakening on the African American community was quite dramatic.

The story of the Second Great Awakening is more difficult to trace than the earlier colonial revival, however, for it, too, like the entire evangelical movement, developed simultaneously in several locations. Some of the first stirring began in the 1790s at Yale College led by its president, Timothy Dwight. Other instances occurred at Hampden-Sydney and Washington colleges. But the most dramatic out-pouring came west of the Appalachians.

A catalyst in this story was the Presbyterian minister James McGready who pastored three small churches in rugged Logan County, Kentucky. He was a dynamic preacher who got results immediately upon his arrival. In 1800, McGready and three other Presbyterian ministers, accompanied by a Methodist preacher, John

---

[48]Raboteau, 149.

[49]Raboteau, 175-176, 200.

McGee, joined forces. After four days of subdued services, the Methodist McGee, who reportedly could no longer restrain himself, rose, and called on the people "to let the Lord Omnipotent reign in your hearts." When a women in the crowd "shouted" for mercy, McGee began shouting and, in his words, "exhorting with all possible ecstasy and energy." Soon a score of others were screaming for heavenly mercy as well.[50]

In August 1801 at nearby Cane Ridge, McGready and Barton W. Stone organized another large camp meeting, as it was called. That revival lasted a full week, drew between ten and twenty-five thousand people, and proved to be the most dramatic outbreak of revival to date. The crowds that gathered that summer were as a rule rough and hardy frontier types not given to refined manners or cosmopolitan tastes. Lacking a certain amount of self-discipline and decorum, the effects of the revival on them were less restrained. Stone described some of the manifestations of those converted noting how they were affected by "bodily agitations or exercises" such as "a piercing scream" which led to them falling "like a log on the floor, earth, or mud" as if "dead." At the same time, others developed the jerks, began dancing, barking, or running uncontrollably.[51]

The Presbyterians were bothered by the emotional outbursts, but the Methodists delighted in them. Within a few years these camp meetings became a regular feature in Methodist life. And more importantly, the revival soon spread east engulfing thousands in its path.

If George Whitefield served as a culminating force in the Great Awakening, Charles G. Finney did the same in the Second Awakening. Trained as a lawyer, Finney went on to become a minister, theology professor, and president of Oberlin College in Ohio. Oberlin, in turn, later became a major stopping point along the

---

[50]Hudson, 132.

[51]Mark A. Noll and others, Eerdmans' Handbook to Christianity in America (Grand Rapids, Michigan: William B. Eerdmans Publishing, 1983), 173. Ahlstrom, 433, 434.

Underground Railroad. But it was his work as an evangelist that won him the most fame, especially with the introduction of his "new measures." Finney's radical new approach involved simple, direct preaching utilizing colloquial language, prepared and argued like an attorney's brief, and designed to appeal to people's free will. Bringing the camp meeting to the more settled east, he transformed it into the "protracted meeting" which lasted for several days and even weeks. At these meetings he prayed for people by name and called on the uncommitted to sit in the front at the "anxious bench." And perhaps the thing that shocked his conservative opponents even more than his softening of Calvinist theology, was his encouragement to women to pray and speak out at his meetings.[52]

Finney's greatest success came in New York's Erie Canal region -- Utica, Rochester, Rome -- during the winter of 1830-1831. The revival fires were so "hot" that the area was henceforth dubbed the "burned-over district." Finney was especially successful in recruiting the nascent business and professional classes that were forming in this era of the emerging market. With the boom-and-bust economic times, evangelical Protestantism offered support and comfort in an uncertain world. Further, the values that the revivalists such as Finney stressed, self-discipline and restraint, honesty and hard work, fit well with the needs of business and industry.[53]

The Second Great Awakening assured evangelicalism's role as the dominant type of Christianity in the first half of nineteenth century America. Membership roles soared in the three predominant evangelical denominations: Methodist, Baptist, and Presbyterian. The Methodists, for example, went from 58,000 members in 1790 to over a million in 1844. By 1840 an estimated half of Americans were connected to some type of church. For whites, evangelicalism fit with the Jacksonian age

---

[52]Donald W. Dayton, Discovering an Evangelical Heritage (New York: Harper and Row, 1976), 16. Edwin S. Gaustad, ed., A Documentary History of Religion in America to the Civil War (Grand Rapids, Michigan: William B. Eerdmans' Publishing Company, 1983), 337, 338.

[53]Davidson, 417, 418.

because of its emphasis on democracy, optimism, and the common people.[54] For blacks, evangelicalism Protestantism would prove to be the most appealing religious force to date.

The Second Awakening also had another impact and that was the unleashing of the spirit of reform. As hopes of the coming millennial heightened, Finney converts fanned out to transform America by making improvements in prisons, asylums, promoting temperance, and most importantly the abolition of slavery which would prove to have a profound impact on African American Christianity.

IV

The Emergence of a Unique Black Religion

Stripped of much of their African heritage, treated like animals rather than human beings by the slave experience, and indoctrinated with a white version of evangelical Protestantism to believe that their plight was the will of God, African Americans were beaten down but not broken. Instead, they were forced to direct their imagination and energy inward to create a coherent world-view to help them cope. They were successful through the merger of their African heritage, slave experience, and evangelical Protestantism. What they created was something new and unique: African American Christianity.

Although some Africans imported to North American were Muslims, the vast majority practiced traditional African religion. Upon coming to this country, a few converted to the Christian faith. The best example of this is Anthony and Isabella who were baptized in Jamestown, Virginia shortly after their arrival in 1619. Later their son, William, was baptized an Anglican as well. But when large numbers

---

[54]Davidson, 417, 418.

arrived in the 1660s and the attitudes toward them changed, some whites began to argue against trying to convert the slaves altogether. People in this camp maintained that preaching and teaching the gospel to slaves would interfere with their work. Others feared that the revolutionary potential of the gospel message might lead to insurrections. Some complained that Africans had no souls, thus making all attempts at evangelism useless. Still others wondered if a fellow Christian could be held in bondage. Virginia's House of Burgesses helped to clear up some of these questions when it ruled in 1667 that baptism did not mean emancipation. Yet efforts to convert slaves in the early Colonial period were few, with Moravians and Quakers proving to be the only exceptions.[55]

Another reason blacks did not join Christian churches in the early Colonial period involved a lack of interest by the slaves themselves. The Anglican missionary wing, the Society for the Propagation of the Gospel, made some attempts to reach them, but most blacks felt that the Anglican faith was too stiff and formal to meet their needs. The Reverend Francis Le Jau's reports to his superiors from Goose Creek, South Carolina, between 1706-1717, provide excellent insights into these struggles.[56] Other slaves complained that all they ever heard from white ministers were sermons exhorting them to be obedient to their masters. As one slave later wrote, "The Gospel was so mixed with slavery, that the people could see no beauty in it, and feel no reverence for it."[57] And this situation remained until the advent of the Second Awakening which witnessed the biggest change in church-black relations.

By the 1830s when the Second Awakening was at its peak, evangelicals launched a full scale effort to convert blacks -- but for different reasons. Many

---

[55]Raboteau, 97-105, 115-116. Noll, 215-218. Felton. Susan Markey Fickling, Slave-Conversion in South Carolina, 1830-1860 (Columbia: University of South Carolina Press, 1924), 9-10. Ball, 162, 164.

[56]See: Frank W. Klingberg, ed., The Carolina Chronicle of Dr. Francis Le Jau, 1706-1717 (Berkeley: University of California Press, 1956).

[57]Sernett, 64.

northern evangelicals like Benjamin Lundy linked evangelism and the emancipation of the slaves. Lundy was a supporter of the American Colonization Society which had been founded in 1816 to promote gradual, voluntary liberation and the resettlement of former slaves in Africa. Lundy represented the moderate, gradualist approach to emancipation which attracted some evangelicals, Quakers, and many southern planters.[58] Other northerners like Theodore Dwight Weld, a Finney convert, were more radical and became abolitionists.[59] Frustrated by the limited achievements of the gradualists, and the implicit racism of the American Colonization Society, Weld turned Lane Seminary and later Oberlin College into hotbeds for abolitionist agitation. Oberlin was instrumental in training a whole generation of future anti-slavery leaders, as well as becoming one of the nation's first integrated college.

The connection between evangelicalism and abolitionism is so strong that it cannot be overemphasized. Abolitionists viewed their cause as a sacred calling and conducted their meetings like revival services. Harriet Beecher Stowe claimed that her highly influential book, *Uncle Tom's Cabin*, was written by God. The following plea by the Anti-Slavery Society of Boston is typical of the passion and religious tone of so many abolitionists. They wrote:

> This [abolitionism] is the greatest missionary enterprise of the day. Three millions of *Christian*, law-manufactured heathen are longing for the glad tidings of the gospel of freedom. Are you a friend of the Bible? Come, then, and help us restore to these millions, whose eyes have been bored out by slavery, their sight, that they may see to read the Bible. Do you love God whom you have not seen? Then manifest that love, by restoring to your brother whom you have seen his

---

[58] Mary Beth Norton and others, A People and a Nation: A History of the United States, 4th edition (Boston: Houghton Mifflin Company, 1994), 375-376.

[59] Weld, a Presbyterian, later married Angelina Grimke' who, along with her sister Sarah, were also strong abolitionists during this period. Initially, the Grimke' sisters were Episcopalians but later became Quakers partly because of the early Quaker stand against slavery. See Gerda Lerner, The Grimke' Sisters from South Carolina.

rightful inheritance, of which he has been so long and so cruelly deprived.[60]

While the cause of abolitionism was not popular one, it was an extremely important manifestation of the evangelical spirit. Indeed, members of the American Anti-Slavery Society were considered fanatics by most Americans -- northerners as well as southerners. Ministers who preached abolitionist sermons often had their churches and parsonages burned. Lewis Tappan, a prominent abolitionist supporter and financier of Oberlin College, suffered a mob attack on his home. And sadly, all but one or two city newspapers came out in full support of the mob against Tappan! Others were like the Reverend Elijah Lovejoy who paid the ultimate price by sacrificing his life for the cause. Nevertheless, by 1838, the American Anti-Slavery Society claimed 1,350 auxiliaries and 250,000 members.[61]

Whites were not the only ones engaged in abolitionism, however. Paula Giddings' book, *When and Where I Enter,* describes the role of black women in the abolitionist movement.[62] But one of the most powerful black abolitionist voices was Frederick Douglass who was especially effective in criticizing the hypocrisy of Christians owning slaves. In his autobiography, he wrote:

> I love the pure, peaceable, and impartial Christianity of Christ: I therefore hate the corrupt, slave holding, woman-whipping, cradle-plundering, partial and hypocritical Christianity of this land. Indeed, I can see no reason for calling the religion of this land Christianity.

---

[60]William L. Andrews, ed., From Fugitive Slave to Free Man: The Autobiographies of William Wells Brown (1848 and 1880, repr., New York: Mentor Books, 1993), 25.

[61]H. Shelton Smith, Robert T. Handy, and Lefferts A. Loetscher, American Christianity: An Historical Interpretation with Representative Documents, Volume II (New York: Charles Scribner's Sons, 1963), 173. Noll et al, 261.

[62]Two key black female abolitionists were Sojourner Truth and Harriet Tubman. Truth escaped slavery and worked as a street corner preacher. Later she joined William Lloyd Garrison's abolitionist group, and after the Civil War helped the Freedman. Tubman was a key figure in the Underground Railroad which helped hundreds of slaves to escape to freedom in the North.

I look upon it as the climax of all misnomers, the boldest of all frauds, and the grossest of all libels.[63]

Douglass was absolutely relentless in his reprimands, citing the counterfeit nature of those who sold men "to build churches, women to support the gospel, and babes to purchase Bibles for the *poor heathen! all for the glory of God and the good of their souls!"*[64]

Other black abolitionists like the fiery David Walker were even more radical. Born free in Wilmington, North Carolina to a free mother and slave father, he eventually settled in Boston where he ran a used clothing store and became involved in the black Baptist church and Underground Railroad. In his 1829 work, *Appeal,* he called on blacks to rise up in revolt against their white oppressors. Veiled in millennialist language, he told slave holders that their day of judgement was near stating, "I call God -- I call angels -- I call men, to witness, that your DESTRUCTION *is at hand,* and will be speedily consummated unless you REPENT."[65] Walker's subtle but obvious call of an armed insurrection frightened many like William Lloyd Garrison within the white abolitionist camp, as well as many blacks. The South reacted by putting a price on his head.[66] But what seemed so radical and impossible in 1829, would soon come to fruition within the following decades with the black preacher Nat Turner's bloody revolt in 1831, John Brown's Kansas and Virginia raids in the late 1850s, an ultimately the American Civil War which claimed the lives of over 600,000 soldiers.

Today historians debate the impact of abolitionists on American national life, but most agree that they were extremely influential in pressuring the South, and in

---

[63]Frederick Douglas, <u>Narrative of Frederick Douglass, An American Slave</u> (Boston: Anti-Slavery Office, 1845), 77-82, 118-125.

[64]Douglas, 118-125.

[65]Quoted in Sernett, 195.

[66]Sernett, 188.

eventually transforming the North to their cause. They did this by raising difficult questions and pointing out the obvious contradiction of slave holding *and* Christianity. They helped to force slave holders into giving more attention to the religious needs of their bondsmen which was crucial in the formation of African American Christianity. And their constant prodding, plantations missions, tracts and articles served as a constant reminder to southerners that the eyes of the larger world were upon them.

White abolitionist speakers like Wendell Phillips and Lucy Stone were influential, but so too were the powerful black voices of Harriet Tubman and Sojourner Truth. Likewise white writers like William Lloyd Garrison and Harriet Beecher Stowe advanced the cause tremendously, but so did the fiery black writer David Walker and eloquent speaker Frederick Douglass. Thus abolitionism gave blacks an opportunity to express themselves and serve as living proof that the notion of black inferiority was absurd.

Southern evangelicals caught up in the Second Awakening committed themselves to slave conversions, too, but for radically different reasons. Slave problems like the Gabriel Prosser and Denmark Vessy conspiracies, and Nat Turner's revolt convinced even the most reluctant masters that bondsmen needed to Christianized; the hope was that such a transformation would lessen their rebelliousness.[67] Many planters felt that Christianity would also serve as a means of social control.[68] Southerners saw slave conversions as having another benefit as well: they helped to ease the conscience of slave holders by winning blacks to the cause of Christ. The hope among planters was that by bringing slaves into the church the entire slave system might be softened somewhat from within and reformed.

---

[67]The Bible speaks of humility (Matthew 5:1-12; 18:1-5, etc.), forgiveness (Matt. 18:21-35, etc.), obedience to the state (Romans 13:1-7,etc.), love (I Corinthians 13), and the acceptance of slavery (Philemon, etc.).

[68]Genovese, 186

Many planters also believed that Christianizing the slaves would diminish the growing arguments of northern abolitionists like Theodore Weld and others against the "peculiar institution." By the 1830s, the work of people like Weld, the Grimke' sisters, and others was starting to have an impact on southerners. Southern church leaders were forced to take a stand: they could either adopt the high ground against slavery as John Wesley has advocated, and as the Quakers had actually done; or they could accept the status quo, focus primarily on the souls of the slaves, and render unto "Caesar the things which are Caesar's."[69]

The powerful influence of the slave holders eventually carried the day and through a gradual process several churches were won over to the proslavery argument. Soon men like Methodist leader William Capers and Presbyterian minister Charles Colcock Jones pushed hard for mission work among the slaves. Thus, the camp meetings of the Second Awakening were interracial from the start with blacks sometimes outnumbering whites. Black participation in the camp meetings and revivals delighted southerners to no end and helped bolster their evolving slave ideology.

The first generation of slave holders believed slavery to be simply a temporary expedient employed for the short run because of the severe labor shortage. They recognized that slavery was not an ideal system but thought that it would be phased out over time. Then a second phase of slave ideology emerged with the advent of Eli Whitney's cotton gin and subsequent revolution in the textile industry. Now the increased profits from cotton production made slave holders feel more dependent on forced labor thus leading them to think of slavery as a permanent but necessary evil.

Finally by the 1830s, a third phase in thinking occurred brought on by southern fears of slave revolts, pressure from northern abolitionists, and the growing realization that the South was losing ground to the North in Congress due to the

---

[69]Genovese, 186.

North's growing population. Now southern writers began to justify slavery as a positive good noting how blacks had been removed from primitive Africa, civilized, Christianized, and were certainly better off than northern factory workers.[70]

Southern ministers, many of whom were slave holders themselves, eagerly joined this chorus offering Biblical references to support slavery such as the now infamous declaration that blacks were the cursed descendants of Ham.[71] Robert Lewis Dabney, a Presbyterian theologian, wrote the following: "Here is our policy then, to push the Bible argument continually, to drive Abolitionism to the wall, to compel it to assume an anti-Christian position." The Reverend James Henley Thornwell of South Carolina took much the same approach noting that the:

> Scriptures not only fail to condemn Slavery, they as distinctly sanction it as any other social condition of man. The Church was formally organized in the family of a slave holder; the relation was divinely regulated among the chosen people of God; and the peculiar duties of the parties are inculcated under the Christian economy. Opposition to slavery has never been the offspring of the Bible...[72]

Thornwell's relentless logic was inescapable: either one agreed with this view, or else one stood in direct opposition to the Bible. Ironically, however, northern Abolitionists eluded Thornwell's well-laid trap altogether in two ways. First, many northern evangelicals were beginning to embrace progressive revelation which led them to give more weight to the New Testament rather than the Old, which was a much different approach than that taken by southerners. Second, rather than

---

[70]Genovese, 185, 186. Matthews, 137-138.

[71]Genesis 9:18ff.

[72]The Collected Writings of James Henley Thornwell, D.D., LL.D., quoted in Smith, Handy, Loetscher, 176. See also James O. Farmer, The Metaphysical Confederacy: James Henley Thornwell and the Synthesis of Southern Values (Macon, Georgia: Mercer University Press, 1986).

41

appealing to the Old Testament style "letter of the law," they made their case based on the "spirit of the law," particularly the Golden Rule and Jesus' Law of Love.[73]

Nevertheless, southerners pressed their attack and insisted that a divinely ordained social order existed in which God was on top, followed by angels, white men, white women, and finally blacks (a few even claimed that blacks were not human, but rather a different species altogether). Armed with such proof, southerners convinced themselves that since slavery was their God-given responsibility, emancipation would not only be neglectful of one's sacred duty, it would also disrupt the heavenly inspired social order. It is not surprising, then, that such diametrically opposed positions so dogmatically held would eventually lead to schism between northern and southern evangelicals which is precisely what happened to Methodists in 1844, Baptists in 1845, New School Presbyterians in 1857, and Old School Presbyterians in 1861.[74]

Once they headed down this slippery slope, southern clergy found themselves forced to join with secular folk in making the proslavery argument. They did this by moving beyond just a scriptural defense of slavery to a political and social defense as well. Specifically, they challenged the Jeffersonian doctrine of equality and argued for "social inequality, class stratification, male dominance, and subordination of the laboring classes to personal authority."[75] For southern clergy, the root of the growing infidelity and secularism, liberal theologies and popular democracy that they saw threatening western civilization was the system of free labor that created wage slaves, and which bred "egotism and extols personal license at the expense of God-

---

[73]Smith, Handy, and Loetscher, 177-178.

[74]Smith, Handy, and Loetscher, 178. Ball, 288-289. See also Charles Reagan Wilson, Baptized in Blood: The Religion of the Lost Cause, 1865-1920 (Athens: University of Georgia Press, 1980), 3-7. Winfred B. Moore and Joseph F. Tripp, Looking South: Chapters in the Story of an American Region (New York: Greenwood Press, 1989), 39.

[75]Moore and Tripp, 31-32, 37. See also Eugene D. Genovese, The Slave holders' Dilemma: Freedom and Progress in Southern Conservative Thought, 1820-1869 (Columbia: University of South Carolina Press, 1991), 15-18.

ordained authority." Southerners saw themselves, then, as the last bulwark against social and political anarchy, the last "bastion of Christian social order" because their labor system alone rested "upon a Christian social system."[76]

Meanwhile, as white northerners and southerners were busy debating religion, blacks were taking matters into their own hands. The first indications of this occurred at the camp meetings. As stated earlier, key features here included shouting and ecstatic behavior in which both white and black participants engaged. But observers noted that blacks seemed especially enthusiastic in their response to the point that their religious frenzy frightened some whites. Scholars like Melville Herskovits and Albert J. Raboteau have maintained that such religious frenzy was a direct folk religion carry-over from Africa. Herskovits wrote, "the tradition of violent possession associated with these meetings is far more African than European, and hence there is reason to hold that, in part at least, it was inspired in the whites by this contact with Negroes."[77] Raboteau concurred adding:

> In the camp meeting the slaves met with encouragement. The proclivity of the slaves for "bodily exercises" was not due to any innate emotionalism; nor was it totally due to the need of an oppressed class to release pen-up tension. Rather the slaves tended to express religious emotion in certain patterned types of bodily movement influenced by the African heritage of dance.[78]

God Struck Me Dead: Voices of Ex-Slaves is an excellent primary source in the study of the emergence of African American Christianity from the African heritage, slave experience, and evangelical Protestantism. Here, former slaves talk about "shouting," for instance, in which participants yelled and sometimes leapt

---

[76]Genovese, The Slave holders' Dilemma, 37,38. Wilson, 3-7. See also Farmer, 390-393; and E. Brooks Holifield, The Gentlemen Theologians: American Theology in Southern Culture, 1795-1860 (Durham, 1978).

[77]Herskovits, The Myth of the Negro Past, quoted in Raboteau, 60-61. See Ball, 165, who wrote his book in 1837 for the continuing influence of African traditions.

[78]Raboteau, 61.

from pew to pew in a religious frenzy. When asked why, one responded that: "I shout because there is a fire on the inside. When I witness the truth, the fire moves on the main altar of my heart, and I can't keep still." Another testified that "we children of God shout because of that love that wells up in our bosom. It is a love which runs from heart to heart and from breast to breast. We have to cry out."[79]

Long suppressed by plantation masters, other African folk religion features that had been discouraged by the slavery experience also manifested themselves at this time and merged with evangelical practices. One striking example, and one of most important, was the use of spirituals. Former slave Robert Anderson described this folk religion element as follows:

> Their music is largely, or was..a sort of rhythmical chant. It had to do largely with religion and the words adopted to their quaint melodies were largely of a religious nature. The stories of the Bible were placed into words that would fit the music already used by the colored people. While singing these songs, the singers and the entire congregation kept time to the music by the swaying of their bodies or by the patting of the foot or hand. Practically all their songs were accompanied by a motion of some kind..the weird and mysterious music of the religious ceremonies moved old and young alike in a frenzy of religious fervor...[80]

Many whites complained that blacks did not sing hymns "properly," or that they merely adapted field songs for religious use. These charges are correct, but what whites failed to realize was that blacks were not merely content with adopting white religion, they were also beginning to adapt it to fit their own requisites. Spirituals helped to do this by offering blacks an escape from the cruel and mundane white-dominated world. Spirituals gave them strength and solace and worked to

---

[79]Clifton H. Johnson, ed., God Struck Me Dead: Voices of Ex-slaves (1969; repr., Cleveland, Ohio: The Pilgrim Press, 1993), 10-11.

[80]Daisy Anderson Leonard, ed., From Slavery to Affluence: Memoirs of Robert Anderson, Ex-Slave quoted in Raboteau, 65,66.

44

bond slaves to one another and to God. Spirituals also provided a psychological release from the burdens of slavery.[81]

As more African Americans were attracted to evangelicalism this modification process developed greater momentum as they started to redefine the Christianity of their masters. Both black and white converts recognized the need for conversion, but for blacks conversion meant liberation and their first real taste of freedom. Being "born again" meant that they were no longer "things," as whites claimed, but rather human beings with worth and value, for after all had not Jesus suffered and died on the cross for them? Conversion was also egalitarian, for all people -- both black as well as white -- had to undergo it. Finally, being born again meant spirit possession, only now it was the Holy Spirit which seized the converted slaves rather than the African gods.

For blacks, conversion was a highly personal and emotional inner experience accomplished through the power of the Holy Spirit and often accompanied by visions.[82] One ex-slave, Jarena Lee, described seeing visions of hell and Satan until she was "convicted of her sins." Once saved she felt as if a "lightening bolt" [sic] had darted through her. Like most black conversions, hers was personal, emotional, and private. God spoke directly to her affirming her sense of worth, and empowered her with His spirit. Now she felt responsible to God alone and to no white person.[83]

For all evangelicals conversion was crucial, but blacks redefined this process in a unique manner. One convert named Sister Kelly described the role of the spirit in her conversion process in a way which would have left Philip Jacob Spener or John Wesley stunned and amazed when she said:

> I got upon my knees and prayed the Lord with a prayer tumbled from my lips, that the Lord had give me to pray himself -- ooh chile, I tell

---

[81] Levine, 7-10.

[82] Johnson, 65,91,111,114.

[83] Sernett, 160-179.

you it's a wonderful feeling when you feel the spirit of the Lord God Almighty in the tips of your fingers, and the bottom of yo' heart. I didn't know then what was the matter with me. I knows now I felt the spirit arising in my body, yessiree. I tell you, honey, you got to be touched from the inside, and be struck by his hand like I was 'fore you feel that holy uplifting spirit.[84]

Evangelicals generally repudiated dance for dance sake as sinful, but the slaves developed what they called the "ring shout" which they claimed was not dancing since they were careful not to cross their feet. Instead, this activity was called the "shout" which again has direct ties back to Africa, possibly coming from the West African Muslim term, *saut*, which means dance.[85]

Even black funerals were different, whites complained, for blacks buried the personal possessions along with the deceased. Unbeknownst, to them, this too was a direct folk religion carry over from Africa, for blacks believed that breaking up these items and interning them with the departed helped to release the person's soul.[86]

All of these features, shouting, ecstatic behavior, spirituals, spirit possession, dancing, and funerals, looked similar enough on the surface to Second Awakening practices that emerged from the camp meetings, but the infusion of the African heritage and slave experience meant that they were at heart very different. Evangelicalism proved quite compatible with Wet African rituals. While the traditional African world-view was never completely lost, it was made incoherent by the enslavement process. Ripped from their loved ones and their homes, punished for observing their religious and cultural heritage and treated like wild animals, blacks sought to carve out for themselves a new identity within the context of slavery. They did this based on what they remembered from Africa, and on things they found useful here in the new world, and from evangelicalism. Evangelicalism helped blacks

---

[84] Sernett, 72-7.

[85] Genovese, 233-234. Raboteau, 69-72.

[86] Ball, 265. Raboteau, 84. Johnson, 11.

46

develop a coherent world-view. The reason is that above all the other major religious expressions available to them in Protestant dominated North American, evangelicalism proved to be the most compatible with their African heritage. African religion was a "living, seeing, faith" similar to evangelicalism. Both shared an emphasis on experience. African religion stressed initiation rites that involved "dying" and rising again similar to the born again and baptismal practices of evangelicalism. Both stressed feeling and emotions. Therefore, they took the best from evangelicalism to form their own African American Christianity, similar to evangelicalism but different too because of the black folk religion element.

The Second Awakening also showed blacks that baptism meant that they were now incorporated into the body of Christ. They learned that Christianity was egalitarian for both blacks and whites stood in need of conversion. Conversion was the key in evangelicalism and through it blacks learned that they were free. By their acceptance of Christianity, blacks became part of a larger community which helped give them a sense of identity, purpose, and self-worth.

Whites eventually believed it necessary to reassert a measure of control, especially when blacks began "disrupting" worship services with their overzealous clapping, shouting, and the like. The following quotation from a former slave is quite illuminating:

> My grandma was a powerful Christian woman, and she did love to sing and shout. Grandma would get to shoutin' so loud and she would make so much fuss nobody in de church could hear de preacher and she would wander off from the gallery and go downstairs and try to go down to de white folkses aisles to get to de altar where the preacher was, and dey was always lockin' fer up for disturbin' worship, but dey never could break her from dat shoutin' and wanderin' 'round de meetin' house, after she got old.[87]

---

[87]Norman R. Yetman, <u>Life Under the 'Peculiar Institution": Selections from the Slave Narration Collection</u> (New York: Holt, Rhinehart and Winston, 1970), 64.

Blacks, naturally enough, resisted these efforts and fought back in different ways depending upon their location and status.

Southerners by no means held a monopoly on racism and discrimination as demonstrated in the journals of countless blacks. Leon F. Litwack has shown that Jim Crow practices began in the North before the Civil War in his fine book, *North of Slavery: The Negro in the Free States, 1790-1860.* Northern black church members were confined to the galleries contemptuously dubbed "negro heaven," or "negro pews." The latter were special seats located in the back of the church with high walls that formed virtual cages which served to separate them from whites. Despite these humiliations, Frederick Douglass called on blacks to remain in integrated churches and demand their equal rights, In 1848 he thundered these words in his *North Star*:

> Colored members should go in and take seats, without regard to their complexion, and allow themselves to be dragged out by the ministers, elders, and deacons. Such a course would very soon settle the question, and in the right way.[88]

Other northern blacks, however, decided to join with people like Richard Allen of Philadelphia, an earlier victim of northern church racism. Allen left the white controlled Methodist church to form the all black African Methodist Episcopal (A.M.E.) Church.

A few southern slaves resisted by creating their own churches, Methodist and especially Baptist, but they were carefully watched by whites who were afraid of insurrection. Therefore, blacks began forming what scholars now call the "invisible institution." There are many questions historians have concerning the invisible institution which cannot be answered due to a lack of written records and the secretive nature of these meetings. Apparently, though, the invisible institution acted as a parallel body that worked alongside the churches and plantation missions.

---

[88]Quoted in Leon F. Litwack, North of Slavery: The Negro in the Free States, 1790-1860 (Chicago: University of Chicago Press, 1961), 213.

Thus, regular Sunday services were supplemented at nights with secret services known only to the slaves. [89]

These meetings were held in secluded places like riverbanks, caves, and so forth, far away from the slave patrols and were called "brush harbors' or "hush harbors." These secret meetings also have their roots in West Africa where they were called the *indaba*. Here they were free to sing, pray, shout, dance, get "slain in the spirit" and generally worship in ways which met their needs unlike the plantation chapels where white ministers exhorted them to be good slaves, or where whites would sometime gather to laugh at their "outlandish" behavior.[90] These services gave strength to the slaves and helped them cope with their oppression. For instance, after being threatened with a beating one day by her master, one slave just smiled and replied:

> I'se saved. De Lord done tell me I'se saved. now I know de lord will show me the way, I ain't gwine to grieve no more. No matter how much you all done beat me and my chillen de Lord will show me de way. And some day we never be slaves.[91]

Her master beat her for this response but she never cried out, and forthwith went back to the fields singing.[92]

Slaves would receive clandestine notification of upcoming services at the hush harbor through spirituals like "Steal Away to Jesus." Services there revolved around an overturned washpot which was probably employed to absorb sound, although some scholars like George P. Rawick believed that it was yet another

---

[89]Raboteau, 212. Yetman, 75, 229, 312.

[90]Raboteau, 212. Yetman, 200-201, 262, 316.

[91]Yetman, 228, 312. George P. Rawick, ed., The American Slave: A Composite Autobiography, Volume 6 (New York: Greenwood Press, 1977), 202.

[92]Yetman, 228.

African vestige. John F. Szwed, on the other hand, maintained that the practice was utilized in order to sanctify the ground.[93]

Slave preachers "licensed only by the spirit" led the services which looked much different from the ones conducted by white ministers ordained by the church and hired by the planters. Slave preachers arose from within the slave community because of their special charismatic gifts, and a sense of calling by the Almighty. The slave participants believed that God empowered the preacher to serve which helped strengthen his resolve in the face of persecution. Another reason for the preacher's effectiveness was his ability to stay in touch with his people who knew and trusted him. Finally, these men, though illiterate for the most part, were quite intelligent and were able to memorize much of the Bible from the white services since it was illegal for them to read. Black preachers were special men and as Du Bois later wrote, the black "Preacher is the most unique personality developed by the Negro on American soil."[94]

The slave preachers that emerged in the invisible institution underwent a gradual evolutionary process. Initially they competed with the conjurer or cult leader. This latter group blended African religion, conjuration, witchcraft, and magic. Except in New Orleans, they died out because they could not deliver what they promised and were replaced by exhorters and slave preachers. Ex-slave Henry Bibb's account of seeking a love potion from a local conjurer provides a humorous illustration of this.[95] Some became exhorters or *de facto* preachers until several blacks received *de jure* recognition by white denominations. Many whites confessed that they enjoyed hearing black ministers' preach better than white ones, and all stood in awe of the power and sincerity of the blacks' prayers. Harry Hosier, who traveled

---

[93]Genovese, 236-237. Yetman, 229, 312, 335.

[94]Raboteau, 230-234. Rawick, 265-266. Yetman, 335. Lincoln, 65-67. Quoted in Sernett, 310.

[95]Sernett, 76-80. See also Rawick, 271, for the continuing influence of superstition.

with the famous Methodist minister Francis Asbury, is one example. But whether they had formal white approval or not, the bond they formed with their congregations was a powerful one made strong by a shared heritage and shared hardship.

As the scholar Henry Mitchell has written, the message these men delivered was "the product of two streams of culture, one West African and the other Euro-American."[96] They combined the best features of West African storytellers and evangelical preachers like George Whitefield and Charles G. Finney to form a unique triologue style in which God, the preacher, and the people communicated through the sermon.

Sermons typically consisted of three parts. The first part was an apology for the speaker's cold, hoarseness, or other ailment. The second part was the presentation of an argument or proposition and its application to life based on a scripture passage. Preachers during this "warming up" phase were feeling their way through until the spirit of God spoke directly to them. When the spirit contacted the preacher the sermon entered the third phase. The preacher's entire demeanor changed and he would begin to raise his voice oftentimes to the point of hysteria. The result was that black congregations participated in the worship service through repeating phrases uttered by the preacher or saying "Amen." Finally, the starting point was never the preacher's own opinion but rather the Word of God which was understood to be given to the preacher. He then delivered it to help them in their daily struggles.[97]

Unlike white sermons, the message blacks proclaimed never consisted of morality lessons of "do's and don't." The reason is twofold. First, neither West Africans not African Americans had a sense of original sin.[98] Therefore, the typical

---

[96] Quoted in Lincoln, 71.

[97] Lowe, 52. Johnson, 5-10.

[98] Original sin is a theological concept developed by St. Augustine and refers to Adam and Eve's violation of God's order not to eat from the Tree of Life (Genesis 3). Their disobedience led to estrangement from God, expulsion from the Garden of Eden, and ultimately death. The guilt of their crime was then passed on to their descendants. Only the redemptive work of Jesus Christ can restore

feelings of guilt associated with white evangelical Christianity were almost totally absent among blacks; instead blacks emphasized joy, dignity, self-esteem and a celebration of life in spite of the horrid conditions in which they found themselves. Second, white ministers often lamented that blacks claimed to be Christians and yet still stole from their masters. But as Albert Raboteau noted, slave religion was not centered on ethics but rather on the liturgy, worship experience, and spiritual aspects. When it came to morality, blacks formed a kind of situation ethics or dual code of sorts. They reasoned that because whites stole their freedom and sold their family members, that it was acceptable to steal from them.[99]

The very essence of their message was liberation, portraying the "conflict of the powerless with the powerful, the have-nots against the haves," the "just against the unjust."[100] But if this is the key, what exactly did slaves mean by liberation? Older scholarship asserted that black theology was escapist or otherworldly. With this presupposition, liberation meant only dying and going to heaven. Such a view was not only simplistic, but it also failed to take into account the heritage of blacks. Traditional African religion saw no distinction between the sacred and the secular and neither did African Americans. This close proximity between heaven and earth meant that such designations as "otherworldly" are irrelevant.[101]

African religion also sought to tie people to the past by this ever present spirit world. Thanks to evangelicalism, blacks now took on a progressive, linear dimension which offered hope and looked forward to a better future complete with freedom, rewards, and ultimate victory.[102] These rewards were hoped for in the *near*

---

humanity's relationship with God. See Romans 5.

[99]Raboteau, 295-300.

[100]Lowe, 56.

[101]Genovese, 249-250.

[102]Matthews, 195.

as well as distant future. Black Christianity saw God as immanent -- acting within history, and transcendent -- acting beyond history. Blacks sang frequently about heaven, but their understanding was quite sophisticated. As Eugene Genovese has written:

> If the lower classes cannot claim to be much, the idea of Heaven, with its equality before God, gives them a strong sense of what they are destined to become. It thereby introduces a sense of worth and reduces the stature of the powerful men of the world. The emphasis on Heaven metamorphoses from the otherworldly into the inner-worldly and creates its own ground for dissent in this world.[103]

Moses and Jesus received similar treatment. For antebellum blacks Moses and the Exodus story was *the* crucial event. Blacks came to identify with the Children of Israel in bondage in Egypt. They hoped and prayed that just as the Lord had freed ancient Israel under Moses, so too would he liberate them from their own bondage one day. Therefore, slaves saw Moses as a this world symbol for liberation.[104]

Meanwhile, Jesus was also extremely important for two reasons: first, he was revered as a close friend because he suffered like they did; second, he was thought of as their other world liberator complementing Moses. As one spiritual went:

> He have been wid us, Jesus,
> He still wid us, Jesus
> He will be wid us, Jesus,
> Be wid us to the end,
>
> In de mornin' when I rise,
> Tell my Jesus huddy [howdy] oh;
> I wah my hands in de mornin' glory
> Tell my Jesus huddy, oh.[105]

---

[103]Genovese, 251.

[104]Genovese, 252-253. Wilmore, 36-37. Raboteau, 311-312.

[105]Genovese, 252-253. Wilmore, 36-37. Raboteau, 311-312.

Black scholars and religious leaders today look back to their heritage for strength and have found inspiration in the faith of the slaves, and leaders like Nat Turner, Gabriel Prosser, Frederick Douglass, Harriet Tubman, and others. One of the most significant African American writers is James H. Cone. His 1975 book, *God of the Oppressed*, still stands today as one of the clearest expressions of black theology.[106] Cone wrote that the experience of suffering had given blacks special insight into the meaning of the Scriptures. White theologians from Jonathan Edwards on have missed a vital truth in the Biblical message because their understanding is from a context of dominance and power. In marked contrast, the message of the Bible is one of suffering, resistance, and liberation from oppression from the Hebrew's exodus from Egyptian slavery, to Amos' call for justice, to Isaiah's Suffering Servant, to Jesus' identification with the poor and oppressed, and to the first Christians' persecution by the Roman authorities. African Americans uniquely grasp and understand this message because, unlike whites, they have been the oppressed and not the oppressors.

Liberation was a key parameter of black theology for antebellum blacks, which continued through the Civil War and emancipation period. Liberation was a key theme espoused by Buffalo soldier chaplains as well. These chaplains believed that liberation meant more than the legal freedom brought by the Thirteenth Amendment. It meant freedom to be in relationship with God, self, and others. Liberation also meant freedom from fear and prejudice, and the chance for hope, strength, dignity, and respect as men and as Americans. Hence the message proclaimed was a positive one that was much needed by blacks who were beaten down but not broken by slavery. As blacks of that era saw it, God is on the side of blacks and will continue to be because they are oppressed. Not until whites end this oppression and greet blacks as equals can reconciliation between the two races or with God occur. As Gayraud S. Wilmore noted:

---

[106]James H. Cone, God of the Oppressed (New York: The Seabury Press, 1975).

Black religion, fluctuating between protest and accommodation, and protesting in the accommodating strategies, has contributed considerably to the ability of Afro-Americans to survive the worst forms of dehumanization and oppression. Beyond survival, as leaders and followers became more sophisticated about how to use religion, it helped them to free themselves, first from slavery, then from civil inequality and subordination, to go on to greater heights of personal and group achievement.[107]

---

[107]Wilmore, 221.

CHAPTER II

AFRICAN AMERICAN CHAPLAINS IN THE CIVIL WAR

Clergymen have provided ministry to the American military from the very beginning. Whenever and wherever there has been fighting -- from the Pequot War to the Mexican War -- chaplains were there. Despite this long association with American's armed forces, however, their status remained unclear. This ambiguity was particularity noticeable in the years before the American Civil War. Indeed, despite the impact of the Second Awakening, many opposed the chaplaincy on the grounds that it violated the principle of separation of church and state. Still others were antagonistic toward the chaplaincy because of the uncouth and overly aggressive way in which some ministers sought military assignments. It is not surprising, then, that between 1813 and 1856 only eighty chaplains received appointments.[1]

The American Civil War became a crucial turning point in the history of the chaplaincy in two ways. First, the war rescued the chaplaincy from possible extinction and helped establish its identity.[2] Second, the Civil War provided the

---

[1] Warren Bruce Armstrong, "The Organization, Function, and Contribution of the Chaplaincy in the United States Army, 1861-1865" (Ph.D. diss., University of Michigan, 1964), iii. See also Rollin W. Quinby, "Congress and the Civil War Chaplaincy, " Civil War History Vol. 10, No. 3 (1964): 246.

[2] Armstrong, iii. Rollin W. Quinby, "The Chaplains' Predicament," Civil War History Vol. VII, No. 1 (March 1962): 25.

opportunity for African Americans to become chaplains. This chapter begins with an examination of the professionalization of the army chaplaincy, which ensured that, by the time blacks were admitted into the military, only the best men were recruited. The second part is the story of the first fourteen black chaplains who blazed a trail for the Buffalo soldier chaplains of the Old West.

I

The Chaplaincy Comes of Age

There were no African American chaplains in the U.S. Army before the Civil War, and the possibility of recruiting any did not become an issue until there were sufficient black troops in the service beginning in early 1863. Fourteen black men eventually served as Union army chaplains before the war ended. They performed the same duties as their white counterparts, such as evangelism and caring for the spiritual needs of their men, but they also brought a unique perspective that was different from white chaplains. This distinctive point of view included African American Christianity, education of the freedmen, and a concern for fighting racism and injustice for their people.

Before the war began, chaplains were not fully integrated into the military organization and acted primarily as hired civilians. They were treated as officers but had no rank, no opportunity for promotion, nor any chaplain corps of their own. Few denominations provided army chaplains with any guidance or assistance beyond their initial ordination; basically, they were left on their own. Hired by the local commander, the chaplain's duties included conducting religious services and acting as school teacher for the post's youth. More often than not the command placed greater emphasis on their teaching, than on their preaching abilities.[3]

The American Civil War proved to be a turning point in the history of the United States Army chaplaincy. When Brigadier General P.T.G. Beauregard's Confederate artillery fired the first shots at Fort Sumter, South Carolina, on 12 April 1861, thereby launching the American Civil War, the United States Regular Army had twenty-six white chaplains on duty, with four additional authorized slots unfilled. Twenty-six chaplains were a small number but adequate to minister to a force of only 16,000 officers and men.[4] These clergymen served as schoolmaster-chaplains for a particular post -- not a particular regiment. Most of these posts were located in remote areas of the far West and the chaplains there played no major role in the Civil War. With President Abraham Lincoln's call for 75,000 volunteers to meet the rebel challenge, the need for more chaplains increased dramatically, as did their roles and responsibilities.[5]

On 4 May 1861, the War Department issued two orders: General Order Number 15 which outlined the plan of organization for the Volunteer forces called into service to supplement the Regular Army units; and General Order Number 16 which increased the size of the regular forces. Both orders contained the exact same provision for the recruitment of a different type of chaplain. One regimental chaplain "would be allowed to each regiment" who would:

> be appointed by the regimental commander on the vote of the field officers and company commanders on duty with the regiment at the time appointment is to be made. The chaplain so appointed must be

---

[3]Richard M. Budd, "Ohio Army Chaplains and the Professionalization of the Military Chaplaincy in the Civil War," Ohio History Vol. 102 (Winter-Spring 1993):6. Many soldiers were illiterate and needed to learn the basic arts of reading, writing, and arithmetic.

[4]This provided a ratio of one chaplain to about 615 soldiers.

[5]Herman A. Norton, Struggling for Recognition: The United States Army Chaplaincy, 1791-1865 (Washington, D.C.: Department of the Army, 1977), 83. Armstrong, 17, 18.

a regularly ordained minister of some Christian denomination, and will receive the pay and allowance of captain of cavalry.[6]

The actual process of becoming a regimental chaplain typically involved receiving an invitation by the commanding colonel to visit the troops, meet the men, and then win an election. Some clergymen joined the unit as an enlisted soldier first and then sought election from the ranks. Officers tended to respect this type of chaplain most of all.[7]

The establishment of regimental chaplains ensured that troops in the field would have access to chaplain services. But others, particularly Washington area clergymen who were stunned by the Battle of Manassas, were concerned over the lack of hospital chaplains to minister to the sick and provide last rites for the dying. Their petitions to Lincoln led the president to call on volunteer clergy to serve the hospitals without pay. Later he was successful in convincing Congress to commission army hospital chaplains. Initially one chaplain was assigned to each permanent army hospital. Subsequently, this was extended to include divisional field hospitals as well as mobile hospitals set up near the battle lines.[8]

Despite the issuance of these orders, confusion persisted among the various Volunteer units in several key areas. For instance, some Volunteer units followed the traditional commissioning method for new officers and required their chaplains to take the oath of office before a Regular Army officer who then sent a copy of the appointment papers to Washington. Some states, on the other hand, had their

---

[6] War of the Rebellion: A Compilation of the Official Records of the Union and Confederate Armies 130 vol. (Washington, D.C.: Government Printing Office, 1880-1901), Series III, 154, 157. Henceforth referred to as Official Records. Budd, 6. Chaplains had been assigned to regiments from colonial times through the War of 1812. After this conflict, chaplains were hired on a contract basis per fort.

[7] Gardiner H. Shattuck, Jr., A Shield and Hiding Place: The Religious Life of the Civil War Armies (Macon, Georgia: Mercer University Press, 1987), 57.

[8] Armstrong, 15-16. See also David Sabine, "The Fifth Wheel," Civil War Times Illustrated Vol. XIX, No. 2 (May 1980), 17-18. Quinby, "Congress and the Civil War Chaplaincy," 251.

governors commission the new chaplains; still others like Indiana and Maryland permitted their chaplains to serve without state or federal commissions. Some argued that the term "chaplain" represent a title and not a military rank. Therefore, they questioned whether chaplains should be treated as officers or as enlisted troops. General Order No. 44 helped clarify this issue by stating that volunteer chaplains "will in all cases be duly mustered into the service in the same manner prescribed for commissioned officers."[9] Once the clergymen learned that only properly commissioned chaplains were eligible to receive disability pensions of $20 per month, in contrast to the much lower rate of common privates for those not properly appointed, individual chaplains sought valid commissions in earnest.[10]

The issue of uniforms for chaplains was another source of concern and controversy throughout much of the war. *The Revised United States Army Regulations of 1861* stated the following:

> The uniform of chaplains of the army will be plain black frock coat with standing collar, and one row of nine black buttons; plain black pantaloons; black felt hat or army forage cap without ornament. On occasions of ceremony, a plain *chapeau de bras* may be worn.[11]

Many chaplains disliked this uniform, complaining that it looked unmilitary. Some of these men discarded the authorized uniform and substituted the uniform of a captain instead, including side arms. The War Department finally addressed this concern with General Order 247 which stated:

> The uniform for Chaplains in the Army, prescribed in General Orders, No. 102, of November 25, 1861, is hereby republished with modifications, as follows: Plain black frock-coat, with standing collar, one row of nine black buttons and button holes. Plain black pantaloons, Black felt hat, or army forage cap, with gold embroidered

---

[9]Official Records, Series III, Volume 1, 327. Quimby, "Congress and the Civil War Chaplaincy," 247.

[10]Norton, 84,85.

[11]Revised United states Army Regulations of 1861 (Washington, 1863), Appendix B, 524.

wreath in front, on black velvet ground, encircling the letters U.S. in silver, old English characters. On occasions of ceremony, a plain *chapeau de bras* may be worn.[12]

Pay was another problem facing the new chaplains. Post chaplains received $1,100 a year. General Orders 15 and 16 stated that regimental chaplains would receive the pay and allowances of a captain of cavalry which amounted to $1,746 per year. However, several legislators had second thoughts after learning how much the difference was. After considerable debate, the higher rate was allowed to stand for the time being because: (1) post chaplains were thought to face less danger and uncertainty than regimental chaplains, who were out on the battlefield alongside their units; (2) most regimental chaplains were volunteers and had interrupted their private lives; (3) finally, it was concluded that regimental chaplains needed to maintain a horse, like cavalry officers, thus justifying their higher pay. Later, hospital chaplains fought for and received the higher calvary officer's pay as well on the grounds that they were exposed to infectious diseases and the constant demands of dealing with the burdens of the sick and wounded.[13]

In spite of their victory, some lingering doubts continued to plague chaplains in the matter of pay. Officers received their pay based on their word of how much was due them. Chaplains were not afforded that trust. They had to get another officer to sign their pay vouchers. This convinced the skeptics that chaplains were not real officers, and the army's designation for chaplains -- "chaplain without command" -- did little to clarify the situation.[14]

---

[12]General Order Number 247, dated 15 August 1864, National Archives, Record Group 94.

[13]Armstrong, 18-20.

[14]Quinby, "Congress and the Civil War Chaplaincy," 253. An act of 9 April 1864 declared that chaplains had "rank without command" and that they were "borne on the field and staff rolls next after surgeons." A few chaplains like Henry Clay Trumbull felt that the lack of rank helped them to relate to all grades of soldiers better. Most, however, felt that it was a hindrance, and that it would one day hurt their chance of collecting pensions. Armstrong, 33-34. Henry Clay Trumbull, War Memories of a Chaplain (Philadelphia: J.D. Wattles and Company, 1898), 3.

Unfortunately for the chaplains, the skeptics were quite numerous. Chaplain John Hight of the 58th Indiana reported there was a "general feeling of distrust of army Chaplains...in the army. This feeling was especially shared by nearly all the officers." Chaplain James J. Marks of the 63rd Pennsylvania noted despairingly that "so far as the appointment of chaplains is concerned it was evidently a concession made to the religious sentiment of the country -- one of those formless, shapeless things thrown in to fill up a vacuum." Marks believed that most officers thought chaplains were a "great expense and annoyance" and only tolerated them because of their aid in securing enlistments.[15]

The negative sentiments expressed by some officers against chaplains came from two sources. The first was the inherent tension between war and religion. War was seen as organized death and destruction. Chaplains, on the other hand, represented a God who said: "Blessed are the peacemakers: for they shall be called the children of God."[16] This led many to question whether clergy should be in uniform at all. War also involved training and preparation. Many line officers felt that the soldiers' time would be put to better use drilling, rather than praying.[17]

The second issue was much more practical than philosophical. Despite the democratic tradition of electing chaplains, sometimes mismatches occurred between clergymen and units. John Chipman Gary, writing from Union-controlled Folly Island, South Carolina in September 1862, described the frustrations of just such a mismarriage between Chaplain Eben Francis, a Universalist minister, and the unit he was assigned to which was made up primarily of strict Calvinists and evangelical Christians. He noted that:

---

[15]Quinby, "The Chaplains' Predicament," 26.

[16]Matthew 5:9.

[17]Roy J. Honeywell, Chaplains of the United States Army (Washington: Office of the Chief of Chaplains, Department of the Army, 1958), 129.

this Chaplain who somehow slipped in has been a thorn in their side, the good officers, like true orthodox, hating him like Satan, and the wicked ones refusing to attend his services on the ground they could only support the preaching of evangelical preaching.[18]

The unpopular chaplain brought some of his troubles on himself by charging one cent per letter for carrying the mail for the troops. Soldiers nicknamed him "One cent by God," among other names. Gary reported that no sooner than the chaplain resigned than a religious revival broke out, "partly, I cannot help suspecting, with a grim delight to spite and mortify the old chaplain."[19]

Because the regulations regarding chaplains were vague, quality varied widely. For example, because no minimum age requirement was established, the youngest chaplain was in his late teens, while the oldest was seventy years old! Further, neither the initial War Department orders nor the subsequent Congressional acts established minimum education requirements for military chaplains. That resulted in the induction of men ranging from accomplished scholars to others who were actually illiterate. Some, with no formal association with any ecclesiastical body whatsoever, sought and received commissions as chaplains solely because of their political connections.[20]

Other chaplains were denounced as cowards and drunks, liars and cheats. For example, one chaplain sold items to his troops that had been donated by benevolent societies for free distribution to the men. Another chaplain from Wisconsin boarded in a brothel while his troops were in the field. An army major complained that his chaplain fled upon hearing the first sound of gunfire, which occurred just after the clergyman had delivered a sermon urging the troops to stand fast and firm in battle

---

[18] John Chipman Gray and John Codman Ropes, War Letters, 1862-1865 (Cambridge, Massachusetts: The Riverside Press, 1927), 217.

[19] Gray and Ropes, 217.

[20] Norton, 84-87. James I. Robertson, Jr., Soldiers Blue and Gray (Columbia: University of South Carolina Press, 1988), 176,177.

on the altars of patriotism. An army paymaster reported to a U.S. Senator that "Chaplains do not hesitate to draw pay for three horses, when it is known that they keep but one." A Maine private noted that "Our chaplain is not very popular; he hardly ever has any religious exercises and spends a great part of his time in New Orleans getting the mail, which generally takes longer than most of us think necessary." A Connecticut troop complained that his chaplain drank "whiskey in quantities -- in public too." Finally, one Yankee sergeant wrote:

> what drives the men to profanity and desperation is the ordeal of standing in hollow square and listening to our d--d old fool of a chaplain go thro' the miserable mockery of praying for the welfare of our country -- and then preach a sermon on God's love for his creatures. If the Almighty's love anything like the Chaplain's love for us? The old cuss is too indolent to ride over here to retail his wares -- so we have to be dosed with his ..[at headquarters], standing in the broiling sun, wearied, ill-tempered and mutinous. How often have I wished for the command to charge bayonets upon that reverend priest...I'd take care mine should find his vitals.[21]

Eventually the litany of complaints lodged against these bad chaplains grew so vocal that Washington was virtually besieged with grievances from the troops, good chaplains, the Young Men's Christian Association (Y.M.C.A.), and various denominational agencies. After several failed attempts at reform, Congress finally passed legislation on 17 July 1862 that prevented any individual from being commissioned a chaplain:

> who is not a regularly ordained minister of some religious denomination and who does not present testimonials of his present good standing, with recommendations for his appointment as an army chaplain from some authorized ecclesiastical body or from not less than five accredited ministers belonging to said religious denomination.[22]

---

[21]Bell Irvin Wiley, "'Holy Joes' of the Sixties: A Study of Civil War Chaplains," Huntington Library Quarterly 16 (May 1953), 295. Robertson, 177.

[22]Norton, 89.

Next, they issued General Order No. 91 which called for commanders to evaluate all chaplains within 30 days and to dismiss those deemed unfit.[23] Finally, Congress moved to lower the pay of chaplains to $1,200 a year in order to discourage those in it for the money alone.[24]

With most of the riff-raff and undesirables weeded out, the good chaplains were able to perform their duties effectively. Sometimes these duties involved responsibilities beyond the spiritual realm such as serving as regimental postmaster, banker, librarian, manager of the officers' mess, or social worker for the freedmen who escaped to the army camps. Occasionally they even took up arms as combatants.[25]

Most of the time chaplains just served as ministers. In between battles, the clergy converted many to Christianity, but they also encouraged their troops, counseled them, and even wrote letters home for those unable to read or write. Worship services were held in buildings or tents when available, under an open sky when necessary. Sermons citing Biblical texts with martial overtones were quite popular, but hellfire and brimstone sermons were not. During battle, a chaplain's presence often strengthened the men's resolve; after the fighting, chaplains visited the wounded and buried the dead. Often they were aided by the United States Christian Commission and the American Tract Society. These agencies were particularly helpful by providing free reading material for soldiers. At all times, effective chaplains endured the same hardships as the troops which helped form a bond between them.[26]

---

[23]Norton, 90.

[24]Shattuck, 53.

[25]Budd, 14-17.

[26]Trumbull, 4,5,15,107,110,141. Emil and Ruth Rosenblatt, eds., Hard Marching Every Day: The Civil War Letters of Private Wilber Fisk, 1861-1865 (Kansas: University of Kansas Press, 1992), 167, 200, 201, 315. Robertson, 178, 181, 182.

The very best way for a chaplain to win the support of his troops was to face the same dangers to which the men were exposed, and the good chaplains never shirked. A soldier of the 100th Indiana Regiment wrote of his chaplain, John A. Brouse, that: "Without a thought of his personal safety he was on the firing line assisting the wounded, praying with the dying, doing all that his great loving heart led him to do. No wonder our boys love our gallant Chaplain." A New York lieutenant offered the following concerning his chaplain: "I am particularly proud & thankful for him as some officers (nonprofessors) used to think & even say that a chaplain was a sort of fifth wheel...and even voted against having one, but now all are ready to admit that we could not get along without our Chaplain."[27]

It was a fortunate turn of events that at this point the first African American chaplains began to enter the U.S. Army. Spared the confusion, controversies, and turmoil of the early years, the professionalization of the chaplaincy meant that those African American clergy selected to become chaplains were some of the best men available. That is important for all black soldiers were "on trial" and none more than the fourteen black clergy who were also commissioned officers.

II

The Emergence of African American Chaplains

Though blacks had fought and died in America's colonial wars, Revolutionary War, and the War of 1812, none had been members of the United States Army. The Civil war changed this.[28] The start of hostilities convinced many blacks that the long

---

[27]Bell Irvin Wiley, The Life of Billy Yank: The Common Soldier of the Union (Indianapolis: The Bobbs-Merrill Company, 1951),267.

[28]Available records indicate that no blacks fought in the Mexican War. For a thorough bibliography on the role of blacks in the American Civil War to 1983 see: Lenwood G. Davis and

predicted biblical day of Jubilee had finally come, thus encouraging them to escape their bondage and seek asylum with the Union armies. Unfortunately, most were taken into custody as fugitives or sent back to their masters. Union General Benjamin F. Butler reversed this trend on 24 May 1862 by arguing that the Fugitive Slave Act did not apply to Virginia which was now a "foreign country" since its secession. Soon other runaway slaves, or "contraband of war" as they were now called, showed up in Yankee camps all over the South and were quickly put to work as laborers for the U.S. Army.[29]

Abolitionists and black activists like Frederick Douglass demanded that African Americans be permitted to serve as soldiers and not just laborers. Douglass sarcastically noted, "Colored men were good enough to fight under [George] Washington, but they are not good enough to fight under McClellan." He also predicted that: "The side which first summons the Negro to its aid will conquer."[30]

Many Union generals in the field like John W. Phelps and Rufus Saxton agreed and led the way in recruiting African American troops, even while the official policy of the federal government still opposed black participation. The fears of enlisting blacks were many, including: the belief that African American were too docile to become soldiers; that they would demand racial equality; that white soldiers would refuse to enlist or desert rather than fight alongside them; that such a move would lead to bloody slave insurrections; and that it would cause the vital Border States to join the Confederacy. But politician-turned-general Benjamin Butler, another early advocate of black participation, proved more successful in overcoming

---

George Hill, Blacks in the American Armed Forces, 1776-1983.

[29]Official Records, Series III, Volume I 243. Charles Wesley and Patricia Romeo, African-Americans in the Civil War: From Slavery to Citizenship (Cornell Heights, PA: Publishing Agency, 1978), 26-27. Alfred H. Guernsey and Henry M. Alden, eds., Harper's Pictorial History of the Civil War (New York: Harper and Brothers, 1866; reprint, Fairfax Press), 201.

[30]Jack D. Foner, Blacks and the Military in American History (New York: Praeger Publishers, 1974), 33. See also: Official Records, Series III, Volume I, 77-78, 107, 609, 626 for other early calls for enlisting African American troops.

Washington's objections by demonstrating that he had lost none of his political shrewdness by putting on a blue uniform. In August of 1862 Butler made no general appeal for the recruitment of blacks to avoid controversy. Instead, he accepted only free blacks who had just recently been a part of the Louisiana militia fighting for the Confederacy which he mustered into service as the 1st, 2d, and 3d Native Guards. Butler's move was a bold but clever one because he lacked approval by the War Department. As a contemporary noted, "By accepting a regiment which had already been in Confederate service, he left no room for complaint that the [U.S.] Government was arming negroes. But, in enlisting, nobody inquires whether the recruit is [or has been] a slave."[31]

Meanwhile others were trying to do the same thing, such as Kansas senator and now general, James H. Lane, who established the 1st Kansas Colored Regiment. Like Butler, Lane did not have federal recognition and even faced outright opposition by Secretary of War Edwin Stanton. Lane's regiment earned the first "red badge of courage" of any black Civil War unit when it took casualties at a skirmish fought near Butler, Missouri on 28 October 1862.[32]

Important as they were, both Butler's and Lane's efforts were small scale. The first large, systematic effort to create an all black regiment was conducted in May 1862 by General David Hunter aat/Port Royal, South Carolina. Hunter faced a multitude of problems, some brought on himself, others caused him by his own officers and by his Washington, D.C.'s political foes. Eventually these obstacles led the War Department to disband "Hunter's Regiment," save for one company. Hunter was later vindicated, however, when the War Department reversed its position on

---

[31]Dudley Taylor Cornish, The Sable Arm: Black Troops in the Union Army, 1861-1865 (Kansas: University of Kansas Press, 1987), 82-86. Butler did oppose his subordinate Phelps' enlistment of black troops initially which led Phelps to resign in July 1862. Butler changed his mind the next month, however, and became a strong promoter of African American participation.

[32]Glenn L. Carle, "The First Kansas Colored" Civil War Chronicles Volume 3, Number 3 (Winter 1994), 55-60.

black troops. His surviving company became the nucleus of the 1st South Carolina Volunteers which was officially mustered into federal service in January 1863, coinciding with the Emancipation Proclamation. The 1st S.C. Volunteers was headed by New England abolitionist and former John Brown supporter, Thomas Wentworth Higginson, and was made up of liberated slaves from the Union-held islands off the coast of South Carolina. Technicalities aside, this unit deserves the title of the first African American regiment in the U.S. Army.[33]

Despite these successes, the fight to permit blacks to join the army was almost as intense as the actual battles being waged on the front. Eventually, northern defeats and reports that the South was utilizing slaves in their war effort gradually worked to change the minds of government officials and the northern public. On 17 July 1862 Congress passed two acts which eased recruitment efforts and permitted African Americans to join the U.S. Army officially.[34]

Recruitment of blacks for the army was conducted in the North and South among free blacks and runaway slaves. Soon the 54th and 55th Massachusetts Regiments, the 29th Connecticut, and the 5th Massachusetts Cavalry were established as state units, with all black federal units designated as United States Colored Troops (U.S.C.T.). Not counting blacks employed as military laborers and sailors, over 180,000 African Americans served the Union cause as soldiers in 166 regiments.[35]

---

[33]For more details on who can claim rights to being the first black unit, see Cornish, 92. Thomas Wentworth Higginson, Army Life in a Black Regiment (1869; repr. New York: W.W. Norton, 1984), 27, 260-264. For a fascinating view from a black female's perspective see Susie King Taylor's Reminiscences of My Life in Camp (Boston; Privately printed, 1902; reprint, New York: Arno Press, 1968).

[34]James McPherson, The Negro's Civil War (New York: Pantheon Books, 1965), 161, 164-165. Dudley Taylor Cornish, The Sable Arm: Black Troops in the Union Army, 1861-1865 (Kansas: University of Kansas Press, 1987), 7-13, 24, 34-44, 65-66. For the North's fear of the South enlisting black troops, see: Official Records, Series III, Volume I, 340, 348, 524.

[35]Wesley and Romeo, 27, 68. Norton, 94. John Blassingame "Negro Chaplains in the Civil War" Negro History Bulletin 37 (October 1963), 1. Other sources list 158 black units and nearly

As these units were being manned and outfitted, the need for leadership emerged. Many in the black community had long argued that African Americans should spearhead these new units. The selection of black noncommissioned officers was accomplished with little opposition, but calls for black commissioned officers met with heavy resistance, because many whites feared that one day these same black officers might have authority over white troops. The commissioning of African American chaplains seemed to be a compromise of sorts between the two camps, because the clergymen would be officers but have no command authority.[36] Further, white chaplains assigned to the black units found that the religious needs and worship styles of the troops too different from their own because of the uniqueness of African American Christianity. For example, Chaplain George N. Carruthers criticized the worship of his black soldiers noting that it consisted "more in emotional exercises than a conscientious performance of duty and trust in God." Another white chaplain, Thomas Stevenson of the 114th U.S.C.T. stated of blacks, that "their literary and theological attainments are narrow and superficial, and often preposterously absurd."[37] Therefore, many argued that black chaplains would be better able to meet the spiritual needs of black troops.[38]

By the war's conclusion 133 chaplains served the all-black units, but only fourteen of these men were African Americans. Because of the reforms made in the

200,000 black soldiers. Some 20,000 blacks served in the Union navy.

[36]Ira Berlin, ed., The Black Military Experience, Series II, Freedom: A Documentary History of Emancipation, 1861-1867 (Cambridge: Cambridge University Press, 1982), 303. Redkey, 331. Joseph T. Wilson, The Black Phalanx: A History of the Negro Troops in the War of the Rebellions, 1861-1865 (New York, 1888), 176-179.

[37]Quoted by Anthony L. Powell, "Black Chaplains in the United States Army, 1863 to 1945" No date. An unpublished paper presented at the U.S. Army Chaplain Center and School, Fort Jackson, S.C., 7.

[38]Colonel Thomas Wentworth Higginson wrote numerous articles in The Atlantic Monthly concerning religious life amongst his black troops. See William Wells Brown's The Negro in the American Rebellion Chapter XVII, Thomas Wentworth Higginson's Army Life in a Black Regiment, and Reid Mitchell's Civil War Soldiers. Reid Mitchell, Civil War Soldiers: Their Expectations and Their Experiences (New York: Simon and Schuster, 1988), 120, 121.

army chaplaincy earlier, the quality of the black chaplains was very admirable. An examination of the careers of a few of the men illustrate this point well.[39]

Governor John A. Andrew of Massachusetts was an early advocate for African American participation in the war and worked hard to establish the North's first black volunteer regiment, the 54th Massachusetts, despite facing much opposition. He was also ahead of his time in pursuing the commissioning of black chaplains even before the federal government would permit it. Andrew was persistent, though, and appointed William Jackson, a Baptist, and William Grimes, a Methodist, "post chaplains" at Camp Meigs, Massachusetts. Grimes and Jackson were apparently popular with both officers and the men. Jackson even performed eight weddings during this period. After receiving assistance from important abolitionist supporters like Secretary of the Treasury Salmon P. Chase, Andrew made Jackson regimental chaplain of the 55th Massachusetts on 23 March 1863 making him the first African American chaplain to serve in a state regiment, and, paving the way for others to follow.[40]

Another black clergyman who overcame the odds to become an army chaplain was Samuel Harrison, a Congregationalist minister from Pittsfield, Massachusetts. He had written to Governor Andrew in the early part of 1863 about the possibility of becoming a regimental chaplain in one of the new black units being formed. The War Department was still hindering Andrew's efforts in this area and so no decision was made at the time. Meanwhile, the 54th Massachusetts was deployed south and eventually wound up fighting a battle at Fort Wagner near Charleston, South Carolina on 18 July 1863. The regiment took heavy casualties as

---

[39]Edwin S. Redkey, "Black Chaplains in the Union Army" Civil War History XXXIII, No. 4 (1987), 331-332.

[40]Virginia M. Adams, ed., On the Altar of Freedom: A black Soldier's Civil War Letters from the Front, Corporal James Henry Gooding (New York: Warner Books, 1991), 6, 8, 10-11. Redkey, 332. Russell Duncan, ed., Blue-Eyed Child of Fortune: The Civil War Letters of Colonel Robert Gould Shaw (Athens, GA: University of Georgia Press, 1992), 33-34, 310.

the lead assault unit, including the death of its commander, Colonel Robert Gould Shaw. The 54th had no chaplain at the time and so Andrew asked Harrison to act as an emissary to the 54th. Once in South Carolina, Harrison found that he has been elected chaplain, a position which he promptly accepted, and on 8 September 1863 he was commissioned.[41]

Some African American ministers did not want to wait as long as Harrison. The Reverend William J. Hodges enlisted in the 36th U.S.C.T. with the hope of being elected chaplain. The officers of the unit named David Stevens chaplain instead and Hodges eventually rose to the rank of sergeant major. Francis A. Boyd was also told he stood a greater chance of becoming regimental chaplain if he enlisted in the 109th U.S.C.T. first. When no such opportunity came, Boyd wrote to General Benjamin Butler who was convinced by the clergymen's argument that he should be commissioned. Boyd's success was short-lived, however, for the 109th's commander was highly irritated over this breach of the chain of command and worked against him at every opportunity. Three months after his commissioning, Boyd was stripped of his chaplain's title and returned to the rank of private.[42]

Garland H. White was the man who eventually became chaplain for the 28th U.S.C.T. White was born a slave in Hanover County, Virginia in 1829. He was sold at a young age to Robert Toombs of Georgia and trained as Toombs' personal servant. In the 1850s, Toombs became a U.S. congressman and later senator representing Georgia and he took White with him to Washington. White met many influential people in the capital including men like William Henry Seward. Many

---

[41]Adams, 11. Redkey 334-335.   Sgt. William H. Carney of the 54th became the first black to receive the Medal of Honor for his role at Fort Wagner. See Luis F. Emilio, A Brave Black Regiment (1894; repr., New York: Bantam Books, 1991) for an account of the battle at Fort Wagner.

[42]Redkey, 335-336. Berlin, 351-353.

of these people were abolitionists who encouraged White to escape and in 1859 he fled to Canada.[43]

In October 1861, White was appointed "to the Pastoral Charge" of the London A.M.E. Mission in Ontario, Canada. It was from this post that he began a letter writing campaign to Secretary of War Edwin Stanton urging that he be permitted to serve in the U.S. Army. He based his appeals on the then commonly accepted theory that blacks were more fit than white troops to serve in semi-tropical regions like the Deep South. Stanton never replied, but White did not give up hope. By January 1863, he moved with his family to Ohio where he became actively involved in recruiting African Americans as soldiers for the new all-black units that were now being formed. [44]

White eventually joined the 28th U.S.C.T. as a private on 4 January 1864 but continued serving as recruiter as well as unofficial chaplain. The commanding officer of the regiment, Lieutenant Colonel Charles E. Russell, recommended that White be appointed as the official chaplain, but the request was turned down because regulations required that no chaplain's position be established until a regiment had reached full strength. Therefore, White continued to serve as a common soldier and even participated in the Battle of the Crater outside of Petersburg, Virginia.[45]

Finally on 25 October 1864, White was commissioned as chaplain for the 28th U.S.C.T. Meanwhile, he took the opportunity to write several letters to the *Christian Recorder* addressing various related topics. In an interesting letter to the editor he wrote a response to the black troops of the 54th Massachusetts who had complained at not receiving pay equal to that of white troops. White wrote:

---

[43]Edward A. Miller, Jr. "Garland H. White, Black Army Chaplain," <u>Civil War History</u> Volume 43, No. 3, (September 1997), 204.

[44]Miller, 204-205.

[45]Miller, 206-208.

Up to the present time, under the present Administration, no colored man has any right to complain; and I am happy to say, as yet, none of the colored troops make any complaint, except those from Massachusetts.... Those few colored regiments from Massachusetts make much fuss, and complain more than all the rest of the colored troops of the nation. They are doing themselves and their race a serious injury. I sincerely hope they will stop such nonsense, and learn to take things as soldiers should, it is not that they are undergoing any more than we are. [46]

There is no doubt that White desired that black troops be paid the same as white ones. But White, the former slave, presented a much more patient attitude in contrast with those mostly free black recruits from Massachusetts. In this regard he was much like Booker T. Washington, and, Chaplain Allen Allensworth of the later Buffalo soldier era.

An interesting event occurred soon after White entered the Confederate capital at Richmond, Virginia as part of the lead element in April 1865. While there, an elderly black lady approached the African American troops wishing to see Garland H. White. When the woman was brought to Chaplain White, it was discovered that she was his mother whom he had not seen since he was sold to Robert Tombs as a small boy. The reunion must have been a joyous one but unfortunately we are told nothing else by White.[47]

Chaplain White worked hard in ministering to the men in the 28th U.S.C.T. In addition to Sunday services, he also conducted two prayer meetings a week. An average of 131 troops attended his services and he eventually baptized 40 soldiers. His only complaint was that both the troops and officers used far too much profanity.[48]

---

[46]Quoted in Miller, 211.

[47]Miller, 212, 213.

[48]Miller, 214.

In October 1865, just three months before White and the men of the 28th were mustered out of service, Lieutenant Colonel Logan and the white officers of the regiment wrote "A Tribute of Regard to Chaplain White." In it they noted that:

> he has had charge of the spiritual interests of this regiment, and during that time up to the present day, we here find him a gentleman, a soldier, a patriot, and a Christian. [49]

Hiram Rhodes Revels was another interesting black who became a Union chaplain in the Civil War. Revels was born free of mixed ancestry in Fayetteville, North Carolina in 1827. He was educated at a local school run by a free black woman. Later he worked as a barber and school teacher. In 1844, he continued his education by attending a Quaker seminary in Liberty, Indiana and later Drake County Seminary for African Americans at Miami University in Ohio, and Knox College in Galesburg, Illinois. [50]

Revels eventually ended up in Baltimore, Maryland and became an ordained minister in the A.M.E. Church. Over the next several years, the church sent him out teaching and preaching to congregations in Maryland, Illinois, Indiana, Ohio, Missouri, Tennessee, Kentucky, and Kansas. [51]

After the Civil War broke out, Revels worked to recruit the first two black regiments in Maryland, and later a black regiment in Missouri. Later Revels became an army chaplain and worked with the Freedman's Bureau to establish schools in Mississippi. After the war, Revels went on to become the first black elected to serve as a U.S. Senator, and as the first president of Alcorn University in Mississippi. [52]

---

[49] Quoted in miller, 216.

[50] Julius E. Thompson, "Hiram Rhodes Revels, 1827-1901: A Reappraisal," The Journal of Negro History Vol 79, No. 3 (Summer 1994), 297.

[51] Thompson, 298.

[52] Thompson, 297, 298.

One of the most interesting black chaplains of the American Civil War was the Reverend Henry McNeal Turner, who had been born free on a farm near Newberry, South Carolina on 1 February 1834. Tradition says that he was the grandson of an African prince who was brought to America in the late eighteenth century and subsequently set free because British law forbade the enslavement of royalty. Turner was first licensed to preach in the African Methodist Episcopal Church (A.M.E.) in 1853. By the beginning of the Civil War, he was pastor of the Israel Methodist Episcopal Church (A.M.E.) in Washington, D.C. His pastorship in the capitol provided him with the opportunity to befriend important Republican politicians like Thaddeus Stevens, Salmon Chase, Benjamin Wade, and Charles Summer. These men would later prove invaluable in aiding Turner's political and professional career.[53]

When the war broke out Turner found himself in a strategic position to provide crucial leadership to the black community both as an African American minister and a pastor of a Washington, D.C. church. African American churches were always at the forefront of the black freedom movement, and like other black preachers, Turner used his church both as a refuge for blacks in a hostile white world and as a center for education and political involvement. Nevertheless, the young pastor struggled in the early days of the fighting to make sense of the war in theological terms.[54]

Turner was opposed to war in general as were many men of the cloth. But he believed that the present conflict was the means by which God would work His will to free the oppressed and downtrodden slaves just as He had done for the Hebrews during the Exodus event. He even thought that Lincoln would be "a Moses waving a mace of independence" calling on southerners to "Let my people go," or the

---

[53]Stephen Ward Angell, Bishop Henry McNeal Turner and Afro-American Religion in the South (Knoxville: University of Tennessee Press, 1992), 33, 35. Bishop R. R. Wright, Jr., The Bishops of the African Methodist Episcopal Church (The A.M.E. Sunday School Union, 1963), 329.

[54]Angell, 40.

"Jesus of Liberty coming to dethrone the Herod of tyranny." The president's slow conversion to the abolitionist cause disappointed him, as did the early Union Army defeats, but Turner believed that these losses were the result of the North's sins for its complicity in regard to slavery. He often stated that "the head of this rebellion was in the South and its tail was in the North and that God intended to punish the whole due to its unnumbered crimes." Therefore, the conflict served a redemptive purpose, bringing suffering in the short run but ultimately resulting in a victory which would far outweigh the anguish of war.[55]

Turner also drew inspiration from nonbiblical writers like William Miller, the Adventist, and Hollis Read, author of *The Coming Crisis of the World* (1861). Turner acknowledged that Miller's date was wrong for the end of the world, but he believed Miller was correct in believing that a new dispensation was about to begin for humanity. Likewise he agreed with Read's prediction that 1866 was going to be a crucial year and that the seven vials of the Book of Revelation were critical to understanding the events leading up to this time.[56] But unlike Read, Turner identified the signs of the times with freedom for the slaves, and especially with Lincoln's Emancipation Proclamation and decision to utilize black troops. Finally, while white theologians like Horace Bushnell and Philip Schaff saw the Civil War as a God-ordained event designed to bring about the rebirth of the nation and unification of all Americans, Turner rejected this notion and began to formulate his views of a separate black homeland. This was an idea which would gain momentum, later, especially during the Buffalo soldier era of the 1890s.[57]

When the capitol was threatened by a Confederate invasion in 1862 the war suddenly struck even closer to home for the young pastor. Turner, along with the

---

[55]Angell, 42-45.

[56]Revelation 15. Modern translations render the term vial as bowl.

[57]Angell, 44-47.

city's other blacks, was forced to perform corvee' labor to strengthen its defenses. Turner is reported to have said to the authorities:

> Gentlemen, all that is necessary is to let us know what you need, and you will have five thousand of us before sundown. All I want is somebody to preach for my people tomorrow morning, and here I am.[58]

True to his word, blacks turned out the next day in droves, due in large measure to Turner's leadership.[59]

Turner's role in the defense of Washington, along with his tireless calls for the use of black troops, his endeavors at recruiting African American soldiers, and his permitting his church to be used as a rallying point and sign-up station for the new regiment, went a long way in helping him gain appointment as an army chaplain. But perhaps the greatest help was the assistance he received from his prominent abolitionist friends, including Secretary of the Treasury Salmon Chase and Congressman Owen Lovejoy among others. Turner's wish finally came true and on 10 September 1863 he was appointed chaplain of the 1st U.S.C.T.[60]

Turner faced discrimination from whites, as Thomas Morris Chester, a black Civil War correspondent for the Philadelphia *Press* reported. A steward aboard the steamer *Manhattan* refused to permit Chaplain Turner to enter the dining facility through the front entrance like the white officers, and, instead, compelled him to reach the mess facilities through the lower decks upon threat with a knife. The chaplain complained and much to Chester's satisfaction the steward was arrested and brought up on charges, which led the black reporter to write:

---

[58]Wesley and Romeo, 198-199.

[59]James McPherson, The Negro's Civil War (New York: Pantheon Books, 1965), 178. Blassingame, 1. Angell, 46, 53, 55.

[60]Redkey, 334. Turner, then, was the first black chaplain to serve in the federal army; Grimes and Jackson were member of a state supported unit.

These negro-haters do not incur much risk in their ill-treatment of unprotected colored persons; but when they insult, on a Government boat, a chaplain, though he may happen to be a little darker than themselves, they become involved in a difficulty which is rendered worse by the prospect of being summoned before Gen. Butler.[61]

Becoming a chaplain was just the first of many hurdles for aspiring African American clergymen for they soon found, like Chaplain Turner, that being a commissioned officer was not enough to spare them the frustrations of racism. For example, even though Congress had authorized a chaplain's salary to be set at $1,200 per year, army paymasters refused to pay them this rate; instead, they interpreted the regulations to mean that black chaplains should be paid the same as black common laborers. After Chaplain Samuel Harrison complained to the Massachusetts governor, Andrew wrote President Lincoln who put the matter to the attorney general for a ruling. He ruled on 23 April 1864 that Harrison had been commissioned and mustered the same as any other chaplain and should receive equal pay and benefits. Later the U.S. Senate upheld this decision.[62]

Chaplain William Hunter, whom one white soldier called "a colored man of remarkable ability," fought a similar battle for his troops of the 4th U.S.C.T. Black soldiers were paid seven dollars a month despite being told at their enlistment that they would receive the same pay as white troops. The chaplain complained that many of the men had families back home and that this dual pay system was unfair. Finally Congress rectified this pay difference in 1864.[63]

African American chaplains also faced many of the same dangers and opportunities that challenged their white counterparts. The dangers were many, including sickness and disease, as well as threat of hostile fire. Chaplain Samuel

---

[61]R.J.M. Blackett, ed., Thomas Morris Chester, Black Civil War Correspondent: His Dispatches From the Virginia Front (Baton Rouge: Louisiana University Press, 1989), 153-154.

[62]Emilio, 192. Norton, 95, 96. Angell 7, 56, 57. Blassingame, 8.

[63]Rosenblatt, 231. Wiley, 315.

Harrison of the 54th Massachusetts contracted malaria shortly after arriving in South Carolina and was discharged from service after only four months on duty. Chaplain Stevens of the 36th U.S.C.T. tried to resign because of prostate and intestinal problems but had his request denied by General Butler. Henry M. Turner spent time in the hospital due to smallpox, and later from injuries sustained from being thrown from a horse while facing Confederate troops. Jeremiah Asher of the 6th U.S.C.T. was the only black chaplain to die on duty, falling victim to disease on 27 July 1865.[64]

Fortunately, chaplains' spirits were boosted by plenty of opportunities for ministry. Chaplain Benjamin Randolph reported seventy-six members in his regimental church. Chaplain Garland White noted, "I have organized a church system in my regiment, and large numbers are coming in every day."[65] No full sermons remain from this period, but most of the evidence shows that black chaplains were very concerned with evangelism just like their white counterparts. Soldiers could be quite blunt in their opinions of the sermons preached, but most reports show that the African American chaplains' words were warmly received. Colonels Robert Gould Shaw and Thomas Wentworth Higginson and other white officers always commented on the importance of religion to the black troops in motivating and inspiring them. Therefore, chaplains proved themselves to be quite valuable in raising troop morale and, hence, combat effectiveness.[66]

Sometimes the chaplain's duties were less pleasant, however, especially when they had to minister to the casualties among the black troops killed and wounded in battles that included Port Hudson, Milliken's Bend, Fort Wagner, Olustee, Fort

---

[64]Redkey, 338.

[65]Redkey, 340.

[66]For an insightful article on the role of religion as a combat motivator in the Confederate Army, see Samuel J. Watson, "Religion and Combat Motivation in the Confederate Army," The Journal of Military History Vol. 58, No. 1 (January 1994): 29-55.

Pillow, Brice's Cross Roads, and Nashville, to name a few. Black chaplains were expected to conduct funerals for their troops, which were always an emotional time as soldiers said farewell to their friends and comrades. In addition, another 60,000 black soldiers were so injured or debilitated that they eventually died of wounds or disease. Chaplain Jeremiah Asher reported from the army hospital at Portsmouth, Virginia that "There are in the hospitals here about five hundred sick and wounded colored soldiers...some few are without arms and legs." A chaplain's prayers and ministry of presence often made an important difference to wounded troops far from home.[67]

Chaplain George LeVere of the 20th U.S.C.T. gave readers of the *Christian Recorder* a glimpse into another not so pleasant aspect of an African American chaplain's duty: participation in an execution. LeVere spent three hours with a remorseful condemned man before the order was given to the firing squad to shoot. White remarked that "It was the saddest spectacle I ever witnessed."[68]

Some duties were more rewarding though. For instance, many chaplains served as recruiters for their units. Black troops of this era wrote constantly of the sense of pride and the feeling that they were "men," thanks to being able to wear a uniform and lending a hand in freeing their people. Black Chaplains were pleased to help those of their race to share in this liberating experience.[69] They also welcomed the opportunity to aid the freedmen. One of them, Chaplain Garland

---

[67]Redkey, 340. Black soldiers' fatality rates of killed in action or death from wounds or disease were approximately 62, 751 out of almost 200,000 which was 31 percent. This percentage was higher than for many white regiments.

[68]Redkey, 342. Wiley, 314. Chaplain (LTC) John Brinsfield, "'Better Men Were Never Led:' The Battle of New Market Heights, Virginia, 29 September 1864" No date. An unpublished paper presented by Chaplain Brinsfield, U.S. Army Chaplain Center and School, Fort Jackson, South Carolina.

[69]Redkey, 344, 345, 348. Berlin, 564.

White, wrote the secretaries of war and of state urging them to put the freedmen to more efficient use, especially as soldiers.[70]

Still other black chaplains focused on educating their troops in the basic arts of reading and writing. Most believed that education was the best way to improve the status of the black race and so a great deal of emphasis was placed on teaching and learning. Indeed, it was reported that in just one regiment, the 62nd U.S.C.T., over two hundred troops could finally sign their own names by the end of their enlistments, thanks to their efforts of their chaplain. Henry M. Turner wrote that he hoped to leave his "regiment with every man in it reading and writing. If I can accomplish that I shall say to myself, Well done!" This sense of accomplishment was particularly rewarding when the black soldiers could write their own letters home for the very first time.[71]

But one of the greatest tests for black chaplains personally, and in the eyes of the troops, was whether they stood their ground when the bullets starting flying. Black units fought in 198 battles and skirmishes during the Civil War, but the 29 September 1864 Battle of New Market Heights, Virginia was unique in that four black army chaplains were present. Earlier in the month, Union General Ulysses S. Grant concentrated forces from the Army of the Potomac and the Army of the James in an effort to destroy Confederate General Robert E. Lee's Army of Northern Virginia near Petersburg, Virginia. General Benjamin Butler commanded the Union X Corps, which included a large number of black troops and black Third Division chaplains: Henry M. Turner of the 1st U.S.C.T., William H. Hunter of the 4th U.S.C.T., Jeremiah Asher of the 6th U.S.C.T., and David Stevens of the 36th U.S.C.T. No complete sermons have been preserved from this or any other battle in which black chaplains participated, but Chaplain Turner did tell his men that "Those

---

[70]Berlin, 141.

[71]Redkey, 344, 345, 348. Blassingame, 23. Berlin, 630. See also "The Union Army as a School for Negroes" in The Journal of Negro History 37 (1952), pages 368-381.

heroes who have fallen on many battlefields...will rise before your face to recount the fruits of their labors and join in the chorus of the anthem, forever to sing, 'The world is redeemed, the slaves are free.'"[72]

The black troops went on to suffer terrible losses during the Petersburg-Richmond campaign, including the deaths of 6,000 of the 20,000 black troops engaged, but both they and the black chaplains who stood by them proved themselves. Charles E. Bolton, an Amherst College student who tended to the wounded after the Battle of the Crater, reported that he heard several black casualties sing:

> Times going away, why don't you pray,
> And end this cruel suffering in heaven,
> Oh my blessed Lord.
> I wish my Lord would come down
> And take us to wear the crown,
> Oh my blessed Lord.[73]

General Butler was so pleased by the gallantry of the African American soldiers that he recognized more than 109 individuals for their outstanding efforts, as well as ordering, at his own expense, 197 special Tiffany designed silver medals. On 21 August 1993, the first monument dedicated to black soldiers at a national park was erected in Petersburg bearing these words: "In memory of the valorous service of regiments and companies of the U.S. Colored Troops, Army of the James and Army of the Potomac."[74] A monument honoring the memory of the black troops was quite appropriate, but it is a sad commentary that it took 129 years before one was finally erected.

---

[72]Brinsfield, 7. Robert Mullen, <u>Black's in America's Wars: The Shift in Attitudes from the Revolutionary War to Vietnam</u> (New York: Monad Press, 1973), 23.

[73]Wiley, <u>The Life of Billy Yank</u>, 168.

[74]Brinsfield, 16-19.

The Civil War was an important transition period in the story of black U.S. Army chaplains, 1884-1901, in two ways. First, the war forced the army to professionalize the chaplaincy and improve that standards for the clergymen called into this unique ministry. That meant that future chaplains were of much higher quality. Second, the successful participation of black troops, and especially the fourteen black chaplains, paved the way for more opportunities for African American soldiers of the Indian War era of 1865-1890.

Only fourteen black chaplains participated in the Union cause in the Civil War, a small number given the fact that 2,300 men altogether served as Union army chaplains.[75] The small number of black chaplains was due to several factors, including the high standards set by the army after the reform of the chaplaincy. These high qualifications, however, ensured that those African Americans who did participate were men who established a solid and respectable reputation. Like their white counterparts, black chaplains engaged in evangelism and worked to care for the spiritual needs of their troops, but black chaplains brought another perspective to the chaplaincy. They saw the redemptive hand of God using the war to free the African American people and they shared this view with their soldiers. They helped to provide a basic education for the troops which enabled the men to have a better change for success after their service to the army had ended. They fought racism in the form of the segregated officers' dining hall, and unequal pay for themselves and for their troops. African American chaplains were an important factor in raising morale and hence combat effectiveness.[76]

---

[75]These fourteen include the following: Jeremiah Asher, 6th USCT; John H. Bowles, 55th Mass.; Francis A. Boyd, 109th USCT; Samuel Harrison, 54th Mass.; William H. Hunter, 4th USCT; William Jackson, 55th Mass.; George LeVere, 20th USCT; Chauncey Leonard; Benjamin Randolph, 26th USCT; David Stevens, 36th USCT; Henry M. Turner, 1st USCT; James Underdue, 39th USCT; William Waring [Warring], 102nd USCT; Garland White, 28th USCT, Redkey, 350.

[76]George Washington Williams, A History of the Negro Troops in the War of the Rebellion, 1861-1865 (1888; reprint, New York: Bergman, 1961), 143, 144. Joseph T. Wilson, The Black Phalanx: A History of Negro Soldiers of the United state in the Wars of 1775-1812, 1861-1865 (Hartford, Connecticut: American, 1890), 175.

These men proved that African Americans could serve effectively as chaplains in the United States Army. The solid reputation they earned and the precedent they established were important for opening a door for the five Buffalo soldier chaplains during the period between 1884 and 1901.

CHAPTER III

CHAPLAINS OF THE NINTH REGIMENT OF U.S. CAVALRY:

HENRY V. PLUMMER AND GEORGE W. PRIOLEAU

The conclusion of the American Civil War led to two pivotal changes for black soldiers. First, the entire military underwent significant modifications due to rapid downsizing and reorganization which meant that the grand army of 180,000 black men was severely reduced as well. The new role they assumed in the following years was different, but it proved just as significant as the one played during the Civil War. Second, by the end of 1865 all fourteen black chaplains had resigned their commissions to either start new churches for the freedmen, work with the Freedman's Bureau, enter Reconstruction politics, or simply return to their parishes in the North.[1] In fact, no black clergyman served as a federal army chaplain from the end of the Civil War and early Reconstruction era until Henry V. Plummer accepted a Regular Army commission in 1884 and began his work with the Ninth Regiment of U.S. Cavalry.

---

[1]Edwin S. Redkey, "Black Chaplains in the Union Army," Civil War History XXXIII, No. 4 (1987), 349. Ernest L. Wiggins, "Group trying to preserve cemetery history," The State, 2 May 1992, 12B. Henry M. Turner and Benjamin Randolph are two excellent examples of black chaplains who got involved in Reconstruction politics. Randolph was assassinated in South Carolina in 1868 because of his efforts in this area.

The first part of this chapter acts as a transition from the Civil War army to the army in which the Buffalo soldiers served. It does this by exploring the restructuring of the post-Civil War army undertaken to meet the new "threat" posed to the United States, the Plains Indians. The chapter then provides a brief history of the black troopers of the Ninth Cavalry Regiment, which establishes the setting for the role Chaplain Henry V. Plummer played in this unit. Plummer's historic commission as the first Regular Army chaplain in nearly twenty years began with much hope and expectation, but was cut short prematurely. By battling racism within the army, he made many enemies, which resulted in his court-martial and dismissal from the service. An analysis shows that his main crime was that he was too assertive for a black man of the 1890s.

A concluding section presents the story of Chaplain George Prioleau, Plummer's replacement. Prioleau's tour as the Ninth Cavalry's chaplain was more successful than Plummer's, but he, too, had to deal with the theme of "doubleness" first mentioned by W.E.B. Du Bois. Prioleau's struggle was different from that of the other four black chaplains, for he was the only Regular Army chaplain to spend any length of time in the Jim Crow South.

I

Buffalo Soldiers of the Ninth
Regiment of U.S. Cavalry

The end of the American Civil War led to the demobilization of the Volunteers and the Regular Army's return to preeminence. On 1 May 1865 there were 1,034,064 Volunteer troops in service to the United States. One year later only 11,043 remained, with most of these belonging to the United States Colored Troops.[2]

By March 1866 the U.S. Senate was engaged in debate over the precise organization and role of the new army. The result was that 40 percent of the army served Congress on Reconstruction duty in the South, and the rest served the president in the West. Most generals agreed that the major role for the military was to be in the West. Events proved them correct, for by 1876 only 15 percent of the army was still in the South.[3]

Therefore, an impressive amount of attention was given to how the military units in the West were to be administered. For greater efficiency, that region was separated into two sections roughly split by the continental divide. Major General Henry W. Halleck commanded the Division of the Pacific. Lieutenant General William T. Sherman commanded the Division of the Missouri that included most of the more important areas to which black troops were assigned. Sherman's Division was further broken down into four parts: the Department of Missouri (Missouri, Kansas, Colorado, and New Mexico); the Department of the Platte (Iowa, Nebraska, Utah, and part of Dakota and Montana); the Department of Dakota (Minnesota and the rest of Dakota and Montana); and the Department of Arkansas (the Indian Territory). Texas fell into the Department of the Gulf. The plan helped matters but efficiency often broke down due to changing boundaries, miscommunication, and the limits on authority.[4]

---

[2]Maurice Matloff, ed., American Military History (Washington: U.S. Printing Office, 1969), 282. Many of these black federal troops were utilized on occupation duty in the Reconstruction South which was highly unpopular with white southerners. See Otis A. Singletary's Negro Militia and Reconstruction. For another interesting article on the role of black militia units in the New South and their demise after the end of Reconstruction, see Alwyn Barr, "The Black Militia of the New South: Texas as a Case Study," The Journal of Negro History Vol. LXIII, No. 3 (July 1978): 209-219.

[3]Robert Wooster, The Military and the United States Indian Policy, 1865-1903 (New Haven: Yale University Press, 1988), 14.

[4]Robert M. Utley, Frontier Regulars: The United States Army and the Indian, 1866-1891 (New York: Macmillan Publishing Co., 1973), 13, 14,. Wooster, 17, 18.

Serious consideration was also given to establishing to a force composed of 57,000 men in sixty-seven regiments: five artillery, twelve cavalry, and fifty infantry. Eight of these units were to be made up of black soldiers. Radical Republican Senator Benjamin F. Wade also called for two black cavalry units. The final plan established a peacetime force of 54,302 men which included six black regiments: the Ninth and Tenth Cavalry and the Thirty-eighth, Thirty-ninth, Fortieth, and Forty-first Infantry.[5]

A few years later the Senate decided to reorganize the army again by decreasing the total number of troops to 27,442, with most of the reduction affecting the infantry units. In the shuffle, the eight black infantry units were merged into two: the Twenty-fourth and Twenty-fifth Infantry Regiments. These two infantry regiments, plus the two cavalry regiments, were significant for they were the first all black Regular Army units, as opposed to the Volunteer regiments of the Civil War.[6]

Many African Americans who opted for service in the Regular Army were Civil War combat veterans who had formerly served with Volunteer units. Others were freedmen straight from the farm. All the men were volunteers who signed up for five-year terms of enlistment. The army's requirements at the time were not very stringent: the men simply had to be unmarried, between eighteen and thirty-five years old, and in good physical condition. Even the ability to read and write was not required in the early years. The average black soldier was an illiterate farmer or laborer approximately twenty-three years old.[7]

A young black male enlisted for several reasons. First, in an era of few economic opportunities for African Americans, the army offered food, clothing,

---

[5]Jack D. Foner, Blacks and the Military in American History (New York: Praeger Publishing, 1974), 52. Matloff, 301. Allan R. Millet and Peter Maslowski, For the Common Defense: A Military History of the United States of America (New York: The Free Press, 1984), 233. Utley, 10.

[6]Foner, 52. Matloff, 301. Millet and Maslowski, 233.

[7]Foner, 55.

90

shelter, and a steady income. The post-Civil War common private was paid $13 a month with an annual increase of a dollar a month, followed with a bonus for reenlisting every five years. Many black men found this offer quite enticing, and later, the service also provided a basic education which appealed to others as well. Another incentive was less tangible but just as alluring: a sense of pride and accomplishment. Chaplain George M. Mullins of the Twenty-fifth Infantry wrote in 1877 that black soldiers were "possessed of the notion that the colored people of the whole country are more or less affected by their conduct in the Army." This feeling of pride was not unwarranted. Indeed, while many in the white community looked upon common soldiers with contempt, the black community proudly hung their pictures upon their walls and held these men up as symbols of accomplishment. As one African American contemporary noted: "We Negroes had little, at the turn of the century, to help sustain faith in ourselves except the pride that we took in the Ninth and Tenth Cavalry, the Twenty-fourth and Twenty-fifth Infantry." Thus, it is no wonder that the *Army and Navy Journal* reported that there were "seldom any vacancies in the colored regiments," as opposed to the all white units.[8]

The young black men who enlisted had to first make the transition from civilian to soldier, however. For the initial enlistees of the Ninth Regiment of U.S. Cavalry, this odyssey began in New Orleans on 3 August 1866 after Major General Philip H. Sheridan was given authorization to raise this unit. By the winter of 1866-1867, 885 individuals had been recruited, their mounts purchased, and the regiment's leadership launched into the task of transforming the raw recruits into soldiers.[9]

Training the men of the Ninth proved a demanding task. As the unit's first historians noted, "It is difficult nowadays to fully appreciate all the work and labor

[8]Foner, 53-55. William Loren Katz, The Black West (Seattle, Washington: Open Hand Publishing Company, 1987), 201. The desertion rate for white units was 20-30 percent, while that of black units was only five percent. Fletcher, 26.

[9]John M. Carroll, ed., The Black Military Experience in the American West (New York: Liveright, 1971), 66, 67.

devolving upon the officers in those days. The men knew nothing, and the noncommissioned officers but little more."[10] The main problem this and other black regiments faced was that there were so few white officers willing to serve in black units. Throughout the Indian War period (1865-1890) army officers typically remained with the same unit until they reached the rank of colonel. Officer morale was low after 1865 due to the tremendous downsizing of the force which meant that many Civil War generals were now reduced to colonels, captains, and in a few cases, sergeants. Petty jealousies and unhealthy rivalries flourished in this environment. Thus, many white officers believed that service in an all-black unit would hurt their long-term career aspirations even more.[11]

Some of these officers doubted the ability of the black soldiers to perform, while most also realized that because of the lack of literary skills among black troops in the early days, the majority of clerical work would have to be performed by officers. It also did not escape notice that the black units were going to be assigned to the most rugged, desolate posts far from whites and any comforts of civilization. Therefore, George Armstrong Custer was not unusual when he turned down the colonelcy in a black unit to take a lower-ranking position in an all-white unit instead.[12]

The man the army finally found to accept the position of commander of the Ninth was Colonel Edward Hatch. Hatch was born in Bangor, Maine in 1832 and attended Vermont's Norwich University for time. Later he worked in the lumber business in Pennsylvania and Iowa, and as a merchant seaman. Shortly after the

---

[10]Theodore F. Rodenbough and William J. Haskin, The Army of the United States (New York, 1896), quoted in Carroll, 68.

[11]Marvin Fletcher, The Black Soldier and Officer in the United States Army, 1891-1917 (Columbia, MO: The University of Missouri Press, 1974), 21. Foner, 60. William Leckie, The Military Conquest of the West (Norman: University of Oklahoma Press, 1963), 27. Edward M. Coffman, The Old Army: A Portrait of the American Army in Peacetime, 1784-1898 (New York: Oxford University Press, 1986), 217, 218.

[12]Fletcher, 21. Foner, 60. Leckie, 27.

outbreak of the Civil War, he was appointed captain in the Second Iowa Cavalry. His unit saw action right from the start and Hatch rose rapidly up the ranks. In December 1863, he was shot through the lungs and had a shoulder shattered at Moscow, Tennessee. Nevertheless, he recovered and went on to be cited for bravery at the Battles of Franklin and Nashville. His commander, Brigadier General Benjamin H. Grierson, recommended him for promotion to brigadier general which was done on 27 April 1864. By the time of Appomattox, he had risen to the rank of brevet major general of volunteers, and colonel in the Regular Army. Hatch had never commanded black troops, but because of his courage and non-racist views, he was given command of the Ninth in 1866 and stayed with the unit for the next twenty years.[13]

In an unusual move, a regimental chaplain was assigned to the Ninth Cavalry. When Congress reorganized the army after the Civil War, it made a special provision for regimental chaplains to be assigned to each of the all-black units. This was unique for after the war the army resorted to its old practice of utilizing only post chaplains. Race or religious concerns did not play a role in the decision. The reason was that Congress recognized the special educational needs of African American recruits, so teaching the new soldiers reading, writing, and arithmetic was viewed as major role for these men of the cloth.[14]

John C. Jocobi and Manuael J. Gonzales were the first chaplains to serve the Ninth, but ironically, neither were black. Both men also shared something else in common: each proved physically unfit to endure the rigors of hard campaigning

---

[13]Monroe Lee Billington, New Mexico's Buffalo Soldiers, 1866-1900 (Niwot, CO: University of Colorado Press, 1991), 46. Frank N. Schubert, Black Valor: Buffalo Soldiers and the Medal of Honor, 1870-1898 (Wilmington, DE: Scholarly Resources, 1997), 11. Patricia L. Faust, ed. Historical Times Illustrated Encyclopedia of the Civil War (New York: Harper and Row, 1986), 349.

[14]William Leckie, The Buffalo Soldiers (Norman: University of Oklahoma Press, 1967), 6. Roy J. Honeywell, Chaplains of the United States Army (Washington: Office of the Chief of Chaplains Department of the Army, 1958), 126, 1159. The army kept the post chaplain system until the Spanish-American War demonstrated that the regimental chaplain was much more effective.

experienced by this unit for both were either ill or on disability leave a full two-thirds of their total fifteen years of active duty. The next chaplain, another white, Charles C. Pierce, was in much better physical condition. He arrived with great hopes of improving the moral condition of the cavalrymen but was shocked to find rampant gambling, prostitution, and drunkenness.[15]

Vice and debauchery were not the only problems facing the Ninth Cavalry. The unit's first home, New Orleans, was rife with racial tensions and resentment of Reconstruction and in July 1866 exploded into a race riot. Then a cholera epidemic broke out. And to add to their misery, the troopers of the Ninth were jammed into unsanitary and unvented buildings. There is not much doubt that the soldiers were glad to leave the city to head west, but before this mob of raw, new recruits even reached San Antonio, Texas a mutiny broke out. Upon arrival in San Antonio, troopers and local white citizens, many of them ex-Confederates, clashed on an almost daily basis. In one incident, Lieutenant Seth Griffin was mortally wounded, and another officer, Lieutenant Fred Smith, was forced to shoot two of his own men. Both Colonel Hatch and an outside investigating officer blamed much of the turmoil on the lack of officers. In time these discipline problems were worked out, but in the early days Hatch much have wondered whether accepting the command was a wise decision.[16]

Despite the regiment's need for more discipline, training, and preparation, the Ninth was soon deployed to west Texas and ordered to defend the territory from Fort Clark to El Paso, and from the Rio Grande to the Concho River. In order to cover such a large area the regiment's twelve companies had to be divided. Hatch took personal command of the Headquarters and Troops A, B, E, and K at Fort Stockton; while his second in command, Lieutenant Colonel Wesley Merritt, led Troops C, D,

---

[15]Earl F. Stover, Up From Handymen: The United States Army Chaplaincy, 1865-1920, Volume III (Washington, D.C.: Office of the Chief of Chaplains, Department of the Army, 1977), 88.

[16]Leckie, The Buffalo Soldiers, 11. Schubert, Black Valor:, 9-12.

F, G, H, and I at Fort Davis. Troops L and M were deployed to nearby Brownsville. This meant that the regiment was spread out over a vast expanse much too large for a single regiment to control, especially in light of the numerous hostile Indians present.[17]

Soldiers stationed in remote spots far from the regimental headquarters appreciated a visit by their chaplain even if conditions made such opportunities infrequent. Chapel services were held in such circumstances whenever and wherever possible. As Chaplain Pierce noted, "we were carrying the ministrations of the Church to a garrison where Sunday is as any other day, and where no religious service has been held for many months," therefore, "all seats were filled" and no one could ask for "a more attentive body of listeners than those the Chaplain had journeyed more than a hundred and twenty-five miles to reach."[18]

Another top priority the soldiers confronted was to build a roof over their heads. Forts Stockton and Davis had become so completely dilapidated during the Civil War years that they required months of hard, backbreaking labor just to become bearable. This arduous task was even more burdensome because half the troops had to remain on constant patrol. Living conditions were miserable in the run down posts: the men were constantly exposed to wind, sand, dust, heat, cold and rain; and food consisted of coffee, bread, beans, beef, molasses, corn bread, and sweet potatoes, usually in poor quality and quantity. At the end of the day the tired soldiers slept on straw mattresses placed across iron bunks.[19]

The Ninth's primary responsibility in west Texas was protecting the mail and stage route from San Antonio to El Paso, and defending settlers from bandits and marauding Indians. This meant constant patrolling and the Ninth Cavalry's chaplain

---

[17]Leckie, 84.

[18]Steward, 74, 75.

[19]Leckie, 84.

often accompanied the soldiers on their missions. Chaplain Pierce wrote of traveling eighty miles in one day with the cavalry while hauling "prayer-books and bedding, vestments and victuals" on the back of a pack-mule. The trip included swimming across swollen rivers which left the men's clothes soaking wet, and crossing mountains so rugged that Pierce noted, "it was mercy to the beasts and safety for the riders to dismount and walk."[20]

Another problem confronting the chaplain and soldiers of the Ninth Cavalry involved hostile Native Americans. Ironically, rather than avoiding the army posts, the local Kickapoo, Kiowa, Apache, and Comanche Indians often found the forts inviting targets to raid in order to steal horses and cattle. The resulting firefights severely tested the mettle of the new black troops. Despite the army's obvious material advantage, the Indians had several points in their favor. For example, the Native Americans had no towns to defend, could live off the land, and were fast and highly mobile on their ponies, especially during the spring and summer months when there was plenty of grass for the animals to feed on. The army, in contrast, was responsible for protecting vulnerable pioneers, wide-open settlements, and cumbersome, slow-moving supply trains.[21]

For soldiers accustomed to the linear tactics of the Civil War, the Indians' hit-and-run guerrilla warfare proved quite frustrating, especially when combined with the extreme variations in climate and rugged terrain of the American West. One veteran army colonel expressed this well in a report:

> To act against an enemy who is here to-day and there tomorrow; who at one time stampedes a herd of mules upon the headwaters of the Arkansas, and when next heard from is in the very heart of the populated districts of Mexico, laying waste to haciendas, and carrying devastation, rapine and murder in his steps; who is every where without being any where; who assembles at the moment of combat,

---

[20]Theophilus G. Steward, ed., <u>Active Service: or Religious Work Among U.S. Soldiers</u> (New York: United States Army Aid Association, 1897), 3.

[21]Millet and Maslowski, 238.

and vanishes whenever fortune turns against him; who leaves his women and children far distant from the theater of hostilities, and has neither towns nor magazine to defend, nor lines of retreat to cover; who derives his commissary from the country he operates in, and is not encumbered with baggage wagons or pack-trains; who comes into action only when it suits his purpose, and never without the advantage of numbers or position -- with such an enemy the strategic science of civilized nations loses much of its importance.[22]

The army's tactical manuals were of no help to army officers for they were based on European models. Most commanders simply had to learn as they went along -- the hard way. In the end, the majority resorted to the use of Native American scouts and widely spaced converging columns which worked like a giant dragnet to force the elusive Indians into battle. These thinly spread columns were fairly effective, unless the Indians concentrated their total numbers against any one of them. That is precisely what happened to George Armstrong Custer at the Battle of Little Big Horn on 25 June 1876.[23]

Not only were the Indians' tactics superior, sometimes the Native Americans were better armed, too. The army adopted the single-shot, breech loading, .45-caliber, black-powder Springfield rifle as its standard arm in 1873 and kept it until the smokeless Krag-Jorgensen finally replaced it in 1892. Meanwhile, many Indians had long since acquired fast action Winchester repeating rifles. Soldiers in black units also complained that they received nothing but broken-down horses and worn-out equipment.[24]

Eventually, the same concept of total war that has been successfully used by Ulysses S. Grant, William T. Sherman, and Philip H. Sheridan to defeat the

---

[22]William H. Leckie, The Military Conquest of the Southern Plains (Norman, Oklahoma: University of Oklahoma Press, 1963), 9, 10.

[23]Millett and Maslowski, 238. Matloff, 309, 310.

[24]Millett and Maslowski, 238. Katz, 203, 204. Some cavalry troops did have Spencer repeating rifles.

Confederacy was applied to conquering the Native Americans. Total war meant bringing the war to the civilian population in order to deprive them of resources (e.g., food, fuel, etc.) and break their will to fight. Sheridan summed up this approach by noting: "The proper strategy consists in the first place in inflicting as telling blows as possible upon the enemy's army, and then causing the inhabitants so much suffering that they must long for peace, and force their government to demand it. The people must be left nothing but their eyes to weep with over the war."[25]

Unable to defeat the highly mobile and elusive Native Americans in open battle, the army concentrated on destroying their base camps in winter campaigns when the Indians were most vulnerable, and, in slaughtering their "commissary," the buffalo, much as Sheridan had done to the Confederates in the Shenandoah Valley, and Sherman in his March to the Sea in 1864.[26] Sheridan justified the tactics to total war against the Native Americans in a letter he wrote to Sherman in 1873.

> In taking the offensive, I have to select that season when I can catch the fiends; and if a village is attacked and women and children killed, the responsibility is not with the soldiers but with the people whose crimes necessitated the attack. During the [Civil] war did any one hesitate to attack a village or town occupied by the enemy because women or children were within its limits? Did we cease to throw shells into Vicksburg or Atlanta because women or children were there?[27]

As encroaching white settlers moved west en masse, confrontations with the Native Americans became quite frequent. In January 1868, Troop F was attacked at Fort Quitman sixteen times by the Apaches. Later that year sixty troopers were

---

[25]Quoted in Lance Janda, "Shutting the Gates of Mercy: The American Origins of Total War, 1860-1880," The Journal of Military History, Vol. 59, No. 1 (January 1995): 7-26. Native Americans were vulnerable to attack in winter for two reasons: first, they left the field and remained in their camps with their women and children; and second, because both they and their ponies were weakened by the lack of food during the cold months.

[26]Janda, 25, 26. Paul Andrew Hutton, Phil Sheridan and His Army (Lincoln: University of Nebraska Press, 1985), 53-55.

[27]Quoted in Janda, 21.

assaulted by a large Indian force at Horsehead Hills which resulted in the deaths of twenty-five braves and the capture of all their horses and supplies. The black soldiers suffered only one man wounded.[28]

Sergeant Jacob Wilks, an ex-slave from Kentucky, related the following dramatic story about a skirmish he participated in while on a mail run to Fort Bliss:

> At Eagle Springs we were attacked by about one hundred Apaches. The fight lasted several hours, during which the Indians made repeated charges. We were on an open plain without any protection whatsoever, but we dismounted, held our horses by the halter-reins, kept close together, and withheld our fire until the Indians charged up within close range. Our rapid fire from log range guns wrought such havoc that in the evening they drew off, after killing one of our men. During the fight they made six charges, and it was after a repulse of one of these charges that our man Johnson was killed.[29]

In another episode, Charleston, South Carolina native Sergeant Emanuel Stance and nine Company F troopers were out looking for two kidnaped white children taken during a recent Indian raid. Stance had joined the regiment on 2 October 1866, less than two months after it was first organized, and as one historian has written, he "and the Ninth Cavalry grew up together." [30] Fourteen miles from Fort McKavett, Stance and his men ran into a band of Indians with eight stolen horses. The soldiers fought a running firefight for eight miles before the Native Americans finally released the animals. Later that evening, they were ambushed by twenty other Indians who were successfully beaten off only after numerous attacks and counterattacks. Sergeant Stance won the Medal of Honor for his actions during these two engagements making him the first black soldier to earn this coveted medal during the Indian Wars. Seventeen other African American soldiers would

---

[28]Carroll, 71.

[29]Quoted in Carroll, 336.

[30]Schubert, 9.

eventually go on to earn this distinction. Such actions helped the men establish a name for toughness among whites as well as Native Americans.[31]

Army chaplains adopted a variety of views concerning the Native Americans, but most reflected the same negative attitudes of other whites who lived in the West, especially toward those Native Americans who refused to convert to Christianity. Ironically few blacks sympathized with the Native Americans either probably because of their Christian background which led them to dismiss the Native Americans as heathens. Chaplain Charles A.M. Blake believed that the struggle between whites and Indians was "pure self-defense" for whites. In his 1868 Thanksgiving Day sermon, he told his Fort Whipple, Arizona soldiers that God never intended "the earth for a few hordes of wandering, murdering savages." Therefore, he admonished the soldiers to use the "sternest measures...because they are the most humane and in a short period the Indian question will be finally and forever settled; and in no other way can it ever be disposed of."[32] Chaplain Gamaliel Collins of Fort Lyon, Colorado agreed and instructed his men to wage continuous war until the Native Americans "believe and feel that the white man is...[the] superior, the conquering, and therefore, the ruling race."[33]

Other chaplains displayed a more humane view toward Native Americans despite having reasons to feel otherwise. Chaplain David White had been wounded and nearly killed by Indians at one point early in his army career. On 21 July 1866 he and his party were attacked by a large number of Lakota Sioux while on the Bozeman Trail between Fort Reno and Fort Phil Kearny. White and numerous other soldiers and civilians were wounded which led some ladies in the group to begin

---

[31]Donna Miles, "Buffalo Soldiers," Soldiers (July 1990): 44. Leckie, 10.

[32]Stover, 34.

[33]Stover, 34. Ironically, white antebellum slave holders had made similar arguments that slaves needed to be Christianized and domesticated.

100

praying loudly. The chaplain told them, "Ladies and gentlemen, there is a time for praying, and...as we may gather from Holy Writ, a time for fighting. This is a time for fighting! God aids whose who are willing to help themselves. Now, stop praying and turn in to make some 'good Indians'." Reportedly the chaplain's words stirred the party to fight back ferociously. White and a private named Fuller then went into the ravine where their attackers were hiding and the two held the Indians at bay until the other soldiers and civilians could escape. Despite these unpleasant incidences, a few months later the Chaplain White intervened in order to prevent the massacre of nine friendly Cheyennes at the hands of some angry soldiers near Fort Phil Kearny, Wyoming, and then went on to establish a mission on nearby Verde Reservation.[34] Unlike many whites, Chaplain White seemed to avoid prejudice and blanket judgements of all Native Americans by the actions of a few.

Chaplain Charles Pierce, Henry Plummer's immediate predecessor in the Ninth Cavalry, used to conduct worship services for local Native Americans on Sunday afternoons. Pierce noted that it was a joy "to tell the old, old story to those whom it seemed so very, very new." One Sunday an elderly Native American interrupted the chaplain during his sermon by saying "You are telling us about God's Book...we never heard it before. Now tell us everything you know." Later the same man told Pierce that he believed the whites had deliberately kept the Bible from the Native Americans and that he hoped that they would soon be able to obtain their own copies. Reportedly, Pierce felt ashamed at the neglect the Native Americans received when it came to mission work, and hoped that more could be done in the future.[35]

The Ninth Regiment remained in Texas for eight years and continued to earn a reputation for bravery in numerous clashes with local Indians (as in the Red River War), and with bandits, cattle rustlers, bootleggers, Mexican revolutionaries, and other threats to the nation. The unit was transferred to New Mexico during the winter

[34]Stover, 38, 39.

[35]Stover, 43.

and spring of 1875-1876. Soldiers who had complained about the nasty environment in west Texas probably looked back to their time in the Lone Star state as the "good ole days." New Mexico's terrain was unbelievably hostile and once again the unit was spread out, this time to nine forts and one camp. Such distances meant that the troopers were on constant patrol. In one year, 1876, the Ninth rode 8,813 miles.[36]

The local Indians encountered by the soldiers had just been forced onto reservations as reluctant wards of the federal government. Added to this unhappy situation was the fact that the Bureau of Indian Affairs failed to provide the tribe with adequate food and yet expected the army to punish the starving Indians if they wandered off the reservations in search of something to eat. This situation was bound to produce trouble; and, if problems with New Mexico's Indian were not enough, the Ninth was also called out to quell two civil disturbances, the Colfax Country War and the Lincoln County War, which at one point included chasing the infamous Billy the Kid.[37]

The regiment was next transferred to Kansas and the Indian Territory in June 1881 where they were tasked with the thankless duty of keeping out illegal settlers, or "Boomers."[38] In 1885 the Ninth was moved again, this time far north to the Department of the Platte. The Headquarters was established at Fort McKinney, Wyoming. Eight troops were garrisoned at Fort Robinson, Nebraska with Troops B and F deployed to Fort Duchesene, Utah. Eighteen years of hard fighting in the Southwest had finally taken its toil, and the move to the Department of the Platte was seen as a much deserved respite.[39]

---

[36]Billington, 47.

[37]Billington, 61, 62, 67, 68. These civil disturbances were fought over land and money between rival power groups.

[38]Leckie, 245-251.

[39]Carroll, 74.

102

The Ninth Cavalry Regiment that departed for the Northern Plains in 1885 was a much different unit than the motley crew which had first arrived in West Texas. The men were now well-disciplined, seasoned veterans. They had also picked up a new nickname along the way: Buffalo soldiers. The Native Americans honored them with this name for their fighting ability, but the particulars of when and how they first acquired it vary. One interesting story tells of an Indian brave, who cut up a buffalo hide to resemble "scalps" taken from the black troopers until he was exposed and himself scalped by the chief! The most commonly accepted explanation, though, is that the troopers' dark skin and hair reminded the Indians of the buffaloes that they revered and so the name was bestowed upon the African American soldiers out of respect.[40] Whatever the case, both friends and enemies alike agreed that the black troopers had earned the right to wear the uniform of the United States Army.

Therefore, by 1884 the Ninth Cavalry's reputation was well-established thanks to the excellent leadership of officers like Edward Hatch and Wesley Merritt, and the courage of the Buffalo soldiers. What the Ninth needed now was an effective chaplain. Chaplains Jacobi and Gonzales both had lackluster careers. Chaplain Pierce, despite some successes, never seemed to get over his initial shock at the vice and debauchery he found in the unit. Apparently, he was more successful working with the Native Americans than the Buffalo soldiers for he resigned in 1884 noting that he had accomplished "very little."[41] Henry V. Plummer was Pierce's replacement and time would tell what he would achieve with the Ninth Cavalry.

---

[40]Miles, 43.

[41]Letter from Chaplain Charles Pierce to the Adjutant General, U.S. Army, Washington, D.C., dated 5 April 1884, Record Group 94, National Archives.

Chaplain Henry V. Plummer

Henry Vinton Plummer was the fourth Chaplain appointed to the Ninth Cavalry, following in the footsteps of John C. Jacobi, Manual J. Gonzales, and Charles C. Pierce. Plummer's commission made history for he was the first African American chaplain to serve in the army since the end of the Civil War, and the first black to minister to soldiers in the Regular Army since Henry McNeal Turner's brief tour in the Reconstruction era.

Plummer was born into slavery on 30 June 1844 at the Calvert Plantation in Prince George's County, Maryland. He worked as a field hand in that state until the Civil War presented him with the opportunity to escape and join the U.S. Navy. He served aboard the gunboat, U.S.S. *Coer de Leon*, which for sixteen months was part of the Potomac Flotilla, and was later assigned to the Washington Navy Yard. It was during his time in the navy that he learned to read and write. After the war he worked as a night watchman at a Washington, D.C. post office saving his money until he was able to attend the city's Wayland Seminary. While attending school, he served as a Baptist pastor and missionary in Washington and Charles and George's County, Maryland. He also met his future wife, Julia Lomax, and on 22 June 1867 the two were married. They went on to have six sons and two daughters. The busy young Plummer finally graduated from Wayland in 1879.[42]

By early 1881, Plummer decided that he wanted to become an army chaplain and began what turned out to be a four-year campaign by writing to Secretary of War

---

[42]Earl F. Stover, "Chaplain Henry V. Plummer, His Ministry and His Court-Martial," Nebraska History Volume 56, Number 1 (Spring 1975), 21. Frank N. Schubert, On the Trail of the Buffalo Soldiers: Biographies of African-Americans in the U.S. Army, 1866-1917 (Wilmington, DE: Scholarly Resources, 1995), 338. Rayford W. Logan and Michael R. Winston, eds. Dictionary of American Negro Biography (New York: W.W. Norton and Company, 1982), 498.

Robert T. Lincoln.[43] Many notable figures vouched for his abilities, including Frederick Douglass who wrote President Chester A. Arthur on his behalf. The great black spokesman noted that Plummer was "well known to me as an honest man, well fitted by character and attainment to fill credibility the position."[44] Plummer's application was accepted, and, on 1 July 1884, he became the first African American commissioned as a Regular Army chaplain.[45]

When Plummer reported for duty with the Ninth Cavalry, the unit had one year left to serve at Fort Riley, Kansas. His arrival was welcomed by the local newspaper which stated that he "well merits the office." There is little doubt that the troops of the Ninth welcomed this black minister as well especially after the less than spectacular performance of the three previous clergymen. In general, white chaplains, like their fellow white line officers, were not overly enthusiastic about serving in African American regiments, something which was noticed by the men. Indeed, as one such clergyman, Chaplain George Mullins, noted in one of his early reports:

> They who sentimentally contend that there is no reason why the colored soldier should be considered inferior to the white not only overlook that God made differences of races, but do ignore all that is loudly proclaimed for the influence of freedom, education, and society. I find these colored soldiers of the 25th Inf. Reg. and 10th Cav., generally of that abject servile disposition which does just what is absolutely necessary, and nothing more....[46]

---

[43]Letter from Henry V. Plummer to Secretary of War Robert T. Lincoln, Washington, D.C., 1881, RG 94, National Archives.

[44]Letter from Frederick Douglass to President Chester A. Arthur dated 14 May 1884. Courtesy of the Rene Klish, Director, U.S. Army Chaplain Museum, Fort Jackson, S.C.

[45]Stover, "Chaplain Henry V. Plummer: His Ministry and His Court-Martial," 22.

[46]Report of Chaplain George G. Mullins, Fort Davis, Texas, 12 July 1875. Record Group 94, National Archives. Powell, 19.

The command of the Ninth greeted Plummer with a show of trust by putting him to work immediately as chaplain, post school superintendent, and post bakery manager. Plummer accepted the positions and conducted himself without incident save for one seemingly trivial occurrence. One morning the soldiers assigned to the bakery failed to produce the bread on time. Plummer's subsequent investigation found that one soldier, a Private Robert Benjamin, had a "little social gathering" the night before which was the reason for the delay. Plummer put Benjamin on report and forgot about the incident. Later events proved, on the other hand, that Benjamin never did.[47]

Plummer and the Ninth were soon transferred to the Department of the Platte which included Utah, Wyoming and Nebraska. As usual the troops were spread out with the headquarters at Fort Robinson, Nebraska. The twenty-year old fort had only two chaplains prior to Plummer's arrival, and neither man had remained for very long. The Platte Department commander, Brigadier General Oliver O. Howard, was a pious and deeply religious man who was also known to be a friend of African Americans. He had demonstrated that concern after the Civil War by heading the Freedmen's Bureau, and by helping to establish Howard University in Washington, D.C. for blacks. Now he was troubled for the welfare of the entire Platte region and the Buffalo soldiers of the Ninth at Fort Robinson in particular. He remarked that the soldiers and their families at the isolated post were "cut off from ordinary religious and social privileges" and needed a chaplain.[48]

Despite years without a clergyman, Fort Robinson did have a chapel which also served as an amusement hall, boxing ring, ballroom, and Grand Army of the Republic meeting place. Upon his arrival, Plummer wasted little time in putting the building to use for religious purposes and soon chapel services included up to 187

---

[47]Stover, "Chaplain Henry V. Plummer: His Ministry and His Court-Martial,"22.

[48]Frank N. Schubert, Buffalo Soldiers, Braves and the Brass: The Story of Fort Robinson, Nebraska (Shippensburg, PA: White Mane Publishing, 1993), 126.

participants. He also initiated Thursday evening services, which drew as many as 130 men, and periodic revival meetings. In addition, he established a Sunday School for the children of the post which included twenty-one of the forty children who lived at Fort Robinson.[49]

His efforts did not go unnoticed by his superiors who were well pleased by his energy and initiative. All indications are that Colonel Hatch seemed satisfied with the new chaplain, and, after his death at Fort Robinson in 1889, so did his subsequent replacements. In 1890, the army began issuing monthly efficiency reports on chaplains covering the following categories: professional ability, attention to duty, general conduct and habits, condition and discipline of men under their control, and their attention to the men's welfare. Ratings for these categories ran the gamut from excellent, very good, good, tolerable, indifferent, to bad. Chaplain Plummer consistently scored "good," "very good," or "excellent" on his evaluations. In the report's section for remarks, Plummer's first rater, Major Guy V. Henry, wrote that the chaplain was "a good preacher" and "a good man, anxious ...to do good." On another, the new regimental commander, Colonel James Biddle, wrote that Plummer was "a good man...conscientious in the performance of his duty." Fort Robinson commander, Lieutenant Colonel George Sanford, noted that he had never seen such large [chapel] attendance at a military fort and recognized Plummer's role due to the "efficient manner in which the chaplain carries out his work." He also added that the clergymen was "entitled to high commendation" for his efforts.[50]

The civilians on post also recognized Plummer's achievements. Mrs. Mary Gerrard, an officer's wife and the chapel organist, stated that Plummer was "energetic, faithful & devoted to his duties," and, that he had a "decidedly good" influence on the enlisted men. She also commented that she had never seen a

---

[49]Schubert, Buffalo Soldiers, Braves and the Brass: 128.

[50]Stover, "Chaplain Henry V. Plummer, His Ministry and His Court-martial," 24, 25. Schubert, Buffalo Soldiers, Braves and the Brass: 18, 129.

chaplain with "such large congregations," and credited Plummer for the attendance due to "his own untiring efforts."[51]

But Chaplain Plummer eventually went beyond these measures and began to promote the temperance cause. If Abolitionism was *the* social cause of the antebellum period, temperance was the most significant reform movement in the second half of the nineteenth century. The temperance movement, largely an outgrowth of Protestant evangelicalism, had swept across the United States in three successive waves. The first surge, which occurred, during the antebellum period, had culminated with the Maine Law of 1846 and with subsequent prohibition legislation in thirteen other northern and western states. The second wave began in the 1870s under the leadership of Frances Willard and the Women's Christian Temperance Union (W.C.T.U.). The final push began in the 1890s with the formation of the Anti-Saloon League. The temperance movement had a profound impact on American history, and in the words of church historian Sydney Ahlstrom, "united Protestants as nothing else had or would."[52]

Army chaplains, black and white, were not immune to the religious and cultural influences of their day, and as one historian has written: "the temperance movement...had the greatest influence upon chaplains" -- including Chaplain Plummer.[53] Evangelical chaplains supported prohibition from both a religious and practical viewpoint. Many had witnessed firsthand the harmful effects of alcoholism upon their soldiers. The result was that many clergymen organized temperance societies, held temperance meetings, and convinced troops to sign total abstinence pledges. Cephas Batemen, a white chaplain, prayed for a "'cold water army' from top

---

[51]Stover, Up From Handymen, 89.

[52]Sydney E. Ahlstrom, A Religious History of the American People (New Haven: Yale University Press, 1972), 867-872. For further information on Frances Willard see: May Earhart's Frances Willard: From Prayers to Politics (Chicago: University of Chicago Press, 1944). See also Andrew Sinclair's Prohibition: The Era of Success (Boston: Little, Brown and Co., 1962).

[53]Stover, Up From Handymen 63.

to bottom." Chaplain Edward Vattman encouraged his soldiers to sign a pledge that read: "I promise before Almighty God, and upon my honor to abstain from the use of all intoxicating drink for _____ years from date."[54]

Not all of these efforts were popular with the command.[55] Fort Riley's post chaplain, Delmar Lowell, became quite controversial because of his temperance work. He coordinated his efforts with nearby civilian pastors and the local W.C.T.U. At one rally he called upon the participants to elect only politicians who would support Kansas' prohibition law. Local businessmen complained to the Secretary of War about Lowell's interference in politics. Lowell's commander, Colonel James W. Forsyth, agreed with the businessmen's laments and suggested through command channels that the chaplain be transferred. Others, however, like Fifth District Congressman John Davis and the army's commanding general, John Schofield, supported the clergyman's efforts. Nevertheless, eighteen months later Lowell was transferred to Fort Douglass, Utah.[56]

These temperance chaplains received encouragement from a new outfit called the "Chaplain's Movement" which had been established by Chaplain Orville J. Nave at Fort Omaha, Nebraska in 1887. This group initially worked to increase the number of chaplains in the Regular Army and to petition Congress and the churches to establish a Chaplain's Corps. In May 1891 Chaplain Nave called a Conference of Army Chaplains at Fort Leavenworth, Kansas. Among other results, the chaplains passed three temperance resolutions with the most significant one calling for an end to the army's policy of selling alcoholic beverages on post. Earlier the army decided that in order to curb excessive drinking among enlisted men at off-post saloons, it

---

[54]Stover, Up From Handymen 63, 64. Pro Deo Et Patria, A Brief History of the United States Army Chaplain Corps, USACHCS Manual 3001 (July 1991), 3-14.

[55]Heavy drinking was quite popular among soldiers of this era, even officers. See: Marguerite Merington, ed., The Custer Story: The Life and Letters of General George A. Custer and His Wife Elizabeth (1950; repr. New York: Barnes and Noble Books, 1994), 192, 193.

[56]Stover, Up From Handymen, 64, 65.

would establish alcohol sales on posts. This plan backfired for the result was more rather than less alcoholic consumption. Nave's group wanted these sales ended and a thorough inspection of the entire canteen system conducted. The results of the meeting were printed and distributed to the churches and the elected officials.[57]

Plummer was a participant at Chaplain Nave's conference, and he returned with a renewed enthusiasm for the cause of temperance among soldiers of the Ninth. He began his endeavors with a series of lectures in March 1892 which soon drew up to 125 soldiers. Then he went on to recruit thirty of Fort Robinson's children into a group he established called the "Loyal Temperance Legion" which sang prohibition songs. Next, he began working with like-minded civilians from nearby Crawford, Nebraska. Together, the town's pastor, some Crawford women, Fort Robinson troops, and Plummer turned the chaplain's original small lecture series into a full scale temperance "revival."[58]

From there Plummer moved to attack the alcohol abuse problem directly. He first brought his opposition to alcohol sales in the fort's canteen to Major Guy V. Henry, but without much success. Next, he took the matter up with Lieutenant Colonel George B. Sanford, acting post commander, and Lieutenant Colonel Alfred Smith. All of these officers respected Plummer and gave his complaints a fair hearing, but this was an era in which soldiers often prided themselves in how much alcohol they could consume.[59]

In March 1892, Plummer noted in his monthly report to the Adjutant General's Office that the sale of alcohol on post was "one of the most pernicious and menacing evils that stands in the way of the physical, mental and moral development

---

[57]Stover, "Chaplain Henry V. Plummer, His Ministry and His Court-Martial," 26. Chaplain Nave was a major figure in improving the overall quality of army chaplains in the nineteenth century. He was also the author of Nave's Topical Bible which is still widely used today.

[58]Chaplain Plummer, Monthly Reports to the Adjutant General, July through October 1892, April 1893, Record Group 94, National Archives.

[59]Schubert, Buffalo Soldiers, Braves and the Brass: 129.

110

of the soldier and most seriously affects the well being and discipline of our army."
He then added:

> no one...is benefitted by its existence...[and] many of the most
> promising young men of the service are being made confirmed
> drunkards, mendicants and gluttons by the inducement of this
> system...[They are] being entrapped and enticed by the apparent
> legality...and are on the high way to moral, mental and physical
> ruin.[60]

Plummer concluded that he had seen troops marched from the pay table on pay day directly to the canteen in order to settle their bills. He even noted that while writing this very report, a soldier's wife had pleaded with him to convince her husband to give her some of his pay before he spent it all drinking and gambling as he had done over the past several months. Plummer ended his report with the statement that he in no way blamed the Ninth's command for the problem, stating that they were "doing all in their power to handle satisfactorily and well this matter."[61]

The chaplain's March Monthly Report to the Adjutant General accomplished his intended goal. Word came down from the Department of the Army in Washington to end alcohol sales at Fort Robinson immediately. Colonel Sanford was apparently stunned by the demand and tried to have the order rescinded. Meanwhile, officials at the Department of the Platte requested Plummer document his case and state whether his allegations were merely general or applied specifically to Fort Robinson.[62]

Lieutenant Colonel Sanford forwarded Plummer's response along with his own. The colonel stated that while prohibition was probably the best policy, the truth

---

[60]Chaplain Plummer, Monthly Report to the Adjutant General, March 1892, Record Group 94, National Archives.

[61]Chaplain Plummer, Monthly Report to the Adjutant General, March 1892, Record Group 94, National Archives.

[62]Letters sent to Chaplain Plummer dated 2 and 3 May 1892, Record Group 94, National Archives.

of the matter was that it was not enforceable. He maintained instead that government control of the alcohol sales was the most sensible solution, but that he would do as he was ordered.[63]

It is important to understand that promotions and advancement were hard to obtain in the small, post-Civil War army, so officers took a very dim view of any negative reports concerning them or their post reaching their superiors whether true or not. Therefore, Plummer's popularity with the command was wearing thin by now, yet the clergyman was just beginning his reforming efforts. After filing another verbal complaint, he succeeded in closing the post exchange entirely on Sundays. Then Plummer complained about the distance between the post chapel and the barracks (about on tenth of a mile) which he claimed was hurting his chapel attendance. He also asked that the chapel facility be used exclusively for worship services since "the very idea of divine services in a dance hall destroys much of the impressive solemnity which should characterize divine worship."[64]

The chaplain also lodged a formal objection to his quarters. Despite having rank equal to that of captain, Plummer had been assigned housing on the "lower line" with the enlisted men, their families, and the officers' servants. Plummer needed more room for he was accompanied by his wife, sister, and four of his six children. Further, his particular quarters were in need of repairs and were so damp that the post surgeon, George Adair, ordered the basement filled with lime. The chaplain was told by Colonel Sanford that his facilities were no worse than any other of the officers' quarters. Later, when housing on the "upper line" became available, Plummer requested permission to relocate. Not only was his request turned down, but an order was issued making permanent his present quarters on the "lower line." Plummer

---

[63]Chaplain Plummer File, Record Group 94, National Archives. Stover, Chaplain Henry V. PLUMMER, His Ministry and His Court-Martial," 26, 28.

[64]Chaplain Plummer, Monthly Reports to the Adjutant General, September 1891, January and February 1892, Record Group 94, National Archives. Schubert, Buffalo Soldiers, Braves and the Brass: 129.

complained that this was an insult, especially because the order was read aloud before the entire Ninth Cavalry with great pomp and ceremony.[65]

As bad as relations were now between Plummer and the command, the chaplain continued to press his case as the editor of the *Fort Robinson Weekly Bulletin*, which was a four-page publication complete with local news items, suggestions, and a gossip column entitled "The Owl Notes." He was also the "resident manager" of the Fort Robinson Department of the *Omaha Progress*, a newspaper which contained a special section for African Americans, and which often included news items and letters concerning incidences of racism directed against African Americans in the Omaha area.[66]

On 29 April 1893 a letter appeared in the *Fort Robinson Weekly Bulletin*, which immediately began to stir up trouble in the nearby town of Crawford, as well as on Fort Robinson. The letter told of a recent incident in which a black soldier named Charles Diggs barely escaped, with the aid of friends, a Crawford lynch mob by fleeing to the fort. The letter warned the townspeople that they might "arise some morning to find that the town of Crawford WAS." The writer added that if African Americans were "not protected when we visit Crawford, we will protect ourselves regardless of the consequences." The letter was signed "Yellow Cape."[67]

Soon afterward, a circular was published by the Progress Publishing Company of Omaha, the same company which printed the *Omaha Progress*, and then distributed to the African American troops of Fort Robinson. Both the pamphlet and Yellow Cape's article were similar enough in style and content to lead one to believe that they were authored by the same individual. The circular told the story of the lynching attempt on Charles Diggs, and cited members of the lynched mob by name,

---

[65]Stover, "Chaplain Henry V. Plummer, His Ministry and His Court-Martial," 33. Schubert, On the Trail of the Buffalo Soldiers: 331.

[66]Powell, 29.

[67]Stover, "Chaplain Plummer: His Ministry and His Court-Martial," 29.

one of whom was the local sheriff. The article also urged the soldiers to boycott certain Crawford businesses that discriminated against blacks, citing incidences of black troops being harassed and even pistols whipped. The author ended with the following warning to the citizens of the town:

> You lynch, you torture and you burn Negroes in the south, but we swear by all that is good and holy that you shall not outrage us and our people right here under the shadow of "Old Glory," while we have shot and shell, and if you persist we shall repeat the horrors of San Domingo -- we will reduce your homes and firesides to ashes and send your guilty souls to hell.[68]

Acting post commander, Lieutenant Reuben F. Bernard, believed that Plummer was the author of both the circular and the letter signed Yellow Cape. He wrote a confidential letter to the Commander of the Department of the Platte relaying his suspicions. He told the general that most of the other officers in the command felt the same way, even Lieutenant John Alexander -- the only other black officer in the unit.[69] Supposedly, Alexander stated that Plummer was "a bad man and should be gotten rid of." Bernard pledged to continue gathering evidence until positive proof could be obtained.[70]

The final episode that turned the command against Chaplain Plummer followed quickly on the heels of the newspaper incident. Plummer wrote a letter to the War Department requesting permission to lead a band of fifty to one hundred black enlisted volunteers from the Ninth on a mission to explore and evangelize central Africa. His rationale was that such a mission would accomplish four goals: bring Christianity and American civilization to Africa; offer talented and educated

---

[68] Quoted in Stover, "Chaplain Plummer: His Ministry and His Court-Martial," 30.

[69] John Alexander was born to slave parents in Arkansas in 1864 and later graduated from West Point in 1887. He was assigned to the 9th Cavalry until reassigned as professor of military science at Wilberforce University, Ohio, in January 1894. Alexander had much promise as an officer but died suddenly of a heart attack on 26 March 1894.

[70] Stover, "Chaplain Plummer: His Ministry and His Court-Martial," 31, 32.

114

blacks an unprecedented opportunity; help solve the "so-called Negro problem in the South"; and secure for his people a "slice of the African 'turkey'" before the European nations seized all of the continent.[71]

Plummer was undoubtedly influenced in this by his mentor, A.M.E. Bishop and former army chaplain, Henry M. Turner, who stood in opposition to Booker T. Washington and his accomodationist views. Indeed, Turner openly confronted racism and was not opposed to violent measures in the defense of blacks. In an editorial in the *Voice of Missions,* he urged that "Negroes Get Guns" and defend themselves against white lynch mobs.[72]

Initially, Turner fought for government reparations for blacks due to their years of bondage. Finally giving up this fight, he turned to black emigration and colonization of Africa.[73] The bishop wrote:

> I do not believe that American slavery was a divine institution, but I do believe it was a providential institution and that God intends to make it the primal factor in the civilization and the Christianization of that dark continent, and that any person whomsoever opposes the return of sufficient number of her descendants to begin the grand work, which near future will be consummated, is fighting the God of the universe face to face.[74]

Chaplain Plummer received support for his plan from Turner who wrote to the secretary of war on 28 April 1894 a letter which stated:

> I am sure such a tour would result in infinite good both to that continent and this country in opening the way for many of our young,

---

[71]Chaplain Plummer, Letter to the Adjutant General, 20 April 1894, Record Group 94, National Archives. For more on late nineteenth century imperialism in Africa, see: Thomas Pakenham's book, The Scramble for Africa: The White Man's Conquest of the Dark Continent from 1876 to 1912 (New York: Random House, 1991).

[72]Gayraud S. Wilmore, Black Radicalism and Black Religion (Maryknoll, NY: Orbis Books, 1986), 137.

[73]Wilmore, 137, 138.

[74]Sernett, 264.

educated men and women to the continent and aid in its civilization, and building up great results through commercial relations.[75]

Other supporters included black clergymen from Pennsylvania and twenty-five local Ninth Cavalry veterans, who all signed petitions.[76] Despite these calls, the secretary of war directed the adjutant general to inform Plummer that no army regulation existed which would permit such an exploration.[77]

Plummer's temperance campaign, his attempts to secure quarters with the white officers, his alleged efforts at confronting racism through the printed word, and now his plans for an exploration party to central Africa finally brought the rising tensions between himself and the command to a head. Just three months after his request to explore Africa, Chaplain Plummer found himself facing court-martial charges under Article of War 61, Conduct Unbecoming an Officer and a Gentleman. Three enlisted men, Sergeants Robert Benjamin and David Dillon, and regimental Sergeant Major Jeremiah Jones, claimed they witnessed Plummer inebriated, fraternizing with enlisted men, and purchasing liquor for enlisted men at the Sergeant Major's quarters from 5 to 8 p.m. on 2 June 1894. Then they alleged that Plummer went to the quarters of Sergeant Benjamin where he was wearing the blouse of a sergeant major, used vulgar language, became belligerent, and threatened to "whip" Sergeant Benjamin, all in the presence of Mrs. Benjamin, Sergeant Benjamin's wife.[78]

---

[75]Henry M. Turner, Letter to the Secretary of War, 28 April 1894, Courtesy of the U.S. Army Chaplain Museum.

[76]Schubert, Buffalo Soldiers, Braves and the Brass: 131.

[77]Letter from the Adjutant General to Chaplain Plummer, 22 June 1894, Record Group 94, National Archives.

[78]Transcript, Chaplain H.V. Plummer, 9th Cavalry. Trial by General Court-Martial, at Fort Robinson, Nebraska, p. 3. Courtesy of the U.S. Army Chaplain Museum, Fort Jackson, S.C. Henceforth referred to as Official Court Transcript.

The trial did not begin until late October 1894. In the meantime, Plummer tried to retire from the military claiming old age and an infirmity from his Civil War days. The post commander, Colonel Biddle, eagerly signed off on his request, but the adjutant general refused unless an army doctor verified his condition. The post physician, Doctor Adair, examined the chaplain and reported that he found no disability, which led Biddle to change his recommendation.[79]

Plummer was now forced to prepare a defense. He was ably represented by C. Dana Sayrs, of nearby Chadron, Nebraska. Sayrs was a Civil War veteran and Dawes County, Nebraska judge. Plummer assisted Sayrs by collecting signatures from prominent local white citizens on his behalf. Other people came forward and stated that the chaplain had paid ministerial visits to their homes in times of need, among other good works. Mrs. Mary Gerrard, the chapel organist, confirmed that the chaplain had worked "almost entirely without help or encouragement from the officers." She concluded that she had "never once seen him, even to the smallest degree, show any evidence of being under the influence of alcohol."[80]

The emotional strain of the upcoming trial was such that three days before it began, the chaplain was treated for "nervous prostration" by the post surgeon, yet Plummer found the courage to face his accusers. Two of the prosecution's witnesses, Sergeant Major Jeremiah Jones and Sergeant David R. Dillon, confirmed that the chaplain had a drink with them on 2 June 1894 but nothing else of substance. The most damning testimony came from Sergeant Robert Benjamin and his wife. Benjamin was the man Plummer had put on report for the bakery incident at Fort Riley, Kansas.[81] Benjamin reported that Plummer:

---

[79]Chaplain Plummer to the Adjutant General, 11 September 1894, Record Group 94, National Archives. Schubert, Buffalo Soldiers, Braves and the Brass, 132.

[80]Schubert, Buffalo Soldiers, Braves and the Brass: 132.

[81]Stover, "Chaplain Plummer: His Ministry and His Court-Martial," 36. Official Court Transcript, 3, 4.

"...came over to where I sat on a chair, and tried to take my glass of whiskey away from me, and in doing so, he spilt a great portion of it, and drank the balance. He then asked Dillon for the jug. He poured a glass of whiskey out in Dillon's glass because Dillon drank his while the Chaplain was scuffling with me, and poured a drink in my glass, and we drank together.... The Chaplain then jumped around a little, and was cutting up, and we were all playing.[82]

Benjamin then testified that Chaplain Plummer had been drunk at his house several times before but that this time Plummer threatened to whip him in front of his wife and when warned that Plummer would not appreciate it if he, Benjamin, had said the same thing in front of Plummer's wife, the Chaplain responded, "Damn you, Mrs. Benjamin is nothing. Mrs. Plummer is a lady."[83]

The trial lingered on for eleven days. Finally, on 2 November 1894 a verdict was reached and Plummer was found guilty of two specific incidences of "conduct unbecoming an officer and gentleman" and ordered dismissed from the army. The first charge was that he was drunk in the home of Sergeant Major Jones on the night of 2 June 1894. The second was that he made a spectacle of himself in the home of Sergeant and Mrs. Benjamin later that same evening. This verdict was reached despite that fact that Jones and Dillon's testimony did not support Benjamin's account. Indeed, Dillon testified that he had an unfavorable opinion of Benjamin and had serious doubts as to Benjamin's veracity. [84] Sergeant Major Jones reported that Benjamin had a reputation for being "boisterous and quarrelsome" when drinking and that Benjamin told him, "I am getting even with [Plummer] for reporting me time that time at Fort Riley." [85] Even Trumpeter Louis Fort verified that he heard Benjamin say to the Sergeant Major that he was now getting even with Chaplain

---

[82]Official Court Transcript, 5.

[83]Official Court Transcript, 9,11.

[84]Official Court Transcript, 94-96.

[85]Official Court Transcript, 106, 115.

118

Plummer.[86] Sergeant Benjamin also admitted to witnesses to being angry with Plummer for not loaning him $15.00 on one occasion, and for rebuking two of Benjamin's friends for failing to render Plummer the proper salute. [87] Several witnesses concurred that Benjamin was so drunk earlier that night at the fort's canteen that he vomited on himself and others. [88] Further, the defense presented the testimony of Private John Miller and his wife who stated that they had spoken to Plummer after the alleged incident and found him sober.[89]

Another key witness, Emma Howard, testified that when she asked Mrs. Benjamin about the alleged incidents after the fact, Mrs. Benjamin told her "that the Chaplain was not doing anything, only sitting on the floor playing with [Benjamin's] daughter Clara, and telling her how smart [Clara] was in Sunday School, when her husband came in."[90] This version was supported by Private Charles M. Pettis who said that Mrs. Benjamin:

> "told me that the Chaplain had not done any harm that she knew of except putting on the Sergeant Major's blouse; that he was playing with the little girl, and then she said she was not going to try to do the Chaplain any harm because he had done no harm, and her husband came in at the time and raised a fuss over it."[91]

Plummer testified under oath that he had indeed been present at the Benjamin's house that day but only to try to gain support for an entertainment program created to raise $40.00 to pay off the chapel's new organ. He denied all the

---

[86]Official Court Transcript, 119.

[87]Stover, "Chaplain Henry V Plummer, His Ministry and His Court-Martial,", 38.

[88]Official Court Transcript, 119-126.

[89]Schubert, Buffalo Soldiers, Braves and the Brass: 132, 133. Official Court Transcript, 64, 67, 80, 85, 86, 102, 104.

[90]Official Court Transcript, 127-128.

[91]Official Court Transcript, 128-129.

prosecution's charges except for taking two or three drinks offered him in celebration of Dillon's promotion.[92]

On 9 November 1894, Plummer received a copy of the General Orders confirming the verdict from the adjutant general's office. Plummer acknowledged receipt of the orders but added:

> I have violated no law of the Army, nor of morality. I gave my service, yea laid my life upon the altar of this country in the dark days of her peril. I was dismissed from the service upon false testimony and prejudice. I cannot help to remember, that patriotism and devotion to duty, counts for naught against falsehood and prejudice in the regiment under the present regime.[93]

Bishop Henry M. Turner wrote to President Grover Cleveland on Plummer's behalf stating that "some color prejudice in the demand for his dismissal" was the prime motivating factor behind the court-martial. Turner pleaded with Cleveland to grant Plummer clemency and not dismiss him from the service. African American Congressman J.M. Langston of Virginia and Allan Rutherford of Washington, D.C. also wrote Cleveland on the chaplain's behalf, and even included nine letters, affidavits, and testimonials to add further support for him. Despite these appeals, Cleveland approved the army's decision and the verdict stood.[94]

Plummer left the Ninth Regiment a bitter and broken man. He moved to Kansas, along with his wife and four children, where he pastored churches in Kansas City and Wichita. He applied for and received an invalid pension of $8 per month to help him survive. He became involved in Republican politics and tried to no avail

---

[92]Official Court Transcript, 136. 137-139.

[93]Letter from Chaplain Plummer to the Adjutant General, 9 November 1894, Record Group 94, National Archives.

[94]Stover, "Chaplain Plummer: His Ministry and His Court-Martial," 43.

to use his political connections to reverse his dismissal. He died in Kansas City on 10 February 1905.[95]

Several revelations emerge from a careful examination of the ministry and court-martial of Chaplain Plummer. Plummer admitted in open court to drinking with Jones and Dillon.[96] This made Plummer appear to be a hypocrite because he had long been an advocate of temperance -- a point which the prosecution continually repeated. But on the other hand, Plummer had been ostracized by the white officers from the start as evidenced by his assignment of quarters on the "lower line," and Mrs. Gerrard's testimony.[97] As Plummer stated, "Socially I am a stranger to the [white] officers of my regiment and their families and it has been so for ten years." [98] If the white officers would not socialize with him, to whom else could he turn but his fellow African Americans even though most were enlisted? Further, Plummer stated that he was almost wholly dependent upon donations from the enlisted soldiers in order to conduct his church work and Sabbath school, and to buy religious books and materials since the government furnished none of these items. Therefore, he said that this compelled him "to be friendly as a preacher with the enlisted people."[99] Finally, as the Ninth's chaplain, was it not Plummer's duty to be on friendly terms with all the soldiers of the unit regardless of their rank?

The second charge leveled against him by Benjamin warrants further evaluation. Jones and Dillon both had doubts about Benjamin's character. In fact, Jones, who had known Benjamin for fourteen years, stated that his reputation for truthfulness was "bad." There was also considerable evidence that Benjamin was

---

[95]Powell, 31. Schubert, On the Trail of the Buffalo Soldiers:" 331.

[96]Official Court Transcript, 136.

[97]Official Court Transcript, 140.

[98]Official Court Transcript, 140.

[99]Official Court Transcript, 143.

drunk the night of the 2 June, and that Mrs. Benjamin was pressured by her husband to perjure herself. Most importantly, Benjamin had a longstanding grudge against Plummer dating back to the bakery incident at Fort Riley.[100] Indeed, Jones testified that:

> On Sunday morning after this occurrence Sergeant Benjamin was talking to me about the matter and in conclusion he remarked, well, I am getting even with him now for reporting me that time at Fort Riley.[101]

Benjamin's desire for revenge was also backed up by the testimony of Trumpeter Louis Fort who stated:

> Then [Benjamin] said, "oh well I am getting even with [Plummer] anyhow," for something that had occurred between them sometime, I do not know where or how.[102]

Evidence also shows that Colonel Biddle, who had praised Plummer early on, had developed a negative attitude against Chaplain Plummer probably because of his work with the temperance movement and attempts to lead a party to Africa. He now wrote that he was not satisfied with Chaplain Plummer because his "usefulness as an Officer and Chaplain" had "virtually ceased." Biddle wanted a trial by court-marital and Plummer specially charged under Article of War 61, not 62, because a guilty verdict under 62 would permit Plummer to remain in the regiment, but a guilty plea under 61 would force Plummer out of the army permanently. Biddle even noted of Plummer that "I fear that the high character and purity of the christian [sic]

---

[100]Stover, "Chaplain Plummer, His Ministry and His Court-Martial," 43. Official Court Transcript, 92-97, 104, 121, 124, 128.

[101]Official Court Transcript, 106.

[102]Official Court Transcript, 119.

life cannot be conceded to him as the church would require, or the sentiments of Christianity demand."[103]

Nevertheless, the trial itself seems to have been fair and in accordance with the prevailing rules under *Winthrops Abridgment of Military Law* in use at the time. Further, Plummer's attorney was well qualified and delivered a vigorous defense. Yet two points stand out: first, the military court failed to apply the standard of reasonable doubt to Plummer; and second, the evidence against him was not overwhelming and was probably insufficient to sustain the charge -- especially such a serious charge: Violation of War, Article 61.[104] Plummer was not the first chaplain to be charged with drunkenness yet he seems to have been treated harshly. Chaplain D. Eglington Barr, a white minister assigned to the all-black Twenty-fifth Infantry had been charged with being intoxicated and unable to perform a funeral in 1872. His commander, however, gave him the option to resign or face court-martial; Barr chose to resign.[105]

Finally, there appears to have been a serious degree of racism at work throughout the entire command structure at Fort Robinson. The two black line officers, Lieutenants John Alexander and Charles Young, both experienced the same aloofness that Plummer felt. [106] Further, a black weekly newspaper published during the same time reported:

> There is considerable discrimination going on at Fort Robinson, Neb. There are three white clerks in the commissary department, two in the post exchange, two in the post bakery, two in the post adjutant's office, two in the officers' club and mess room, the post librarian is a

---

[103]Stover, "Chaplain Plummer: His Ministry and His Court-Martial," 38.

[104]Stover, "Chaplain Plummer: His Ministry and His Court-Martial," 36.

[105]Stover, Up From Handyman, 25 (fn 62).

[106]In 1888, Charles Young became the third black to graduate from West Point and the last until Benjamin O. Davis, Jr. graduated in 1936. Young served in the 9th Cavalry from 1889 to 1894 and went on from there to have a brilliant military career that finally ended with his death in 1922.

white soldier, two in charge of the post saw mills, five white men in the post quartermaster's department. All these places are filled by enlisted men of the Eighth Infantry, of which there are only two companies at the post, while there are six cavalry companies, all colored. whew![107]

Henry V. Plummer, the first African American chaplain since the Civil War, was forced to confront the awful tension of "double-consciousness" first mentioned by W.E.B. Du Bois in *The Souls of Black Folk*. As a black man *and* officer in an all-white command, Plummer must have felt a tremendous tension and internal conflict over having to be an official in an organization that supported the oppression of his own people. Such a tension had to have led, as Du Bois claimed, to confusion, a double life, double thoughts, double duties, and double social classes, which gave rise to double words, double ideals, and tempted the mind to pretense or to revolt, to hypocrisy or radicalism.[108] As long as he confined his efforts to just preaching the gospel at Sunday services his efforts were approved by the all-white command of the Ninth Cavalry, but the moment he went beyond that he found himself in serious trouble.

The heart of the problem seems to have been that Plummer was too energetic and aggressive for a black man of the age, and he was not alone. In 1880, Johnson C. Whittaker was one of the first black cadets at West Point. The white cadets totally ostracized him refusing to even speak or look at him. On 6 April 1880, Whittaker was found beaten, cut, and tied up to his bed. He reported that three masked attackers had broken into his room and left him in that condition. West Point officials promptly charged *him* with staging the entire incident! Whittaker's case attracted national attention. He was found guilty twice but eventually the verdict

---

[107]Schubert, <u>Buffalo Soldiers, Braves and the Brass;</u> 133.

[108]Du Bois, 3, 141-145.

was overturned by the secretary of war and president. Yet the strain was so much that Whittaker failed his exams and was forced to leave West Point after all.[109]

The very next year, Henry O. Flipper, the first black to graduate from West Point was accused of "embezzling funds and conduct unbecoming an officer and a gentleman" because he allegedly failed to turn in $4000 in commissary funds to his unit, the Tenth Cavalry. White officers accused of such crimes were confined to quarters. Flipper, on the other hand, was locked in the Fort Davis's stockade until his trial began. He was found innocent of the charges of embezzlement, yet somehow was convicted of the broad and loosely defined charge of "conduct unbecoming and officer and a gentleman." For the rest of his life, Flipper maintained that he was innocent and blamed the entire matter on racial prejudice because he often took horseback rides with one of the few white ladies in the Fort Davis area.[110]

American history in the late nineteenth century witnessed some of the most severe discrimination ever unleashed against blacks. Between 1895 and 1908, every southern state enforced disenfranchisement laws against blacks by means of the grandfather clause, poll taxes, and literacy tests. Between 1889 and 1909, more than 1,700 blacks were lynched.[111] Plummer's efforts at temperance, his newspaper articles opposing racism, and his attempts to start a missionary effort in central Africa were deemed "conduct unbecoming a black man." In short, Chaplain Plummer "forgot his place" and he paid for it by losing his career.

---

[109]Logan and Winston, 651, 652. Coffman, 227,228.

[110]Logan and Winston, 227, 228.

[111]Mary Beth Norton and others, A People and a Nation (Boston: Houghton-Mifflin Company, 1994), 524.

Chaplain George W. Prioleau

George Washington Prioleau was selected to replace Plummer as Chaplain of the Ninth Cavalry in June 1895. Prioleau's army career proved far less stormy than Plummer's. Indeed, Prioleau was able to quietly serve his nation in uniform until his retirement in 1920. He did have unique experience, however, in that he was the only black Regular Army chaplain to spend any length of time in an official capacity in the Jim Crow South. Therefore, his observations were singular in this area.

George Prioleau, the son of L.S. and Susan Prioleau, was born a slave in Charleston, S.C. in 1856. Later, he was educated at Charleston's public schools and in 1875 enrolled at Claflin College in Orangeburg, S.C. During his four years at Claflin he taught at the public school of Lyons Township, Orangeburg County. It was during this period that he joined the A.M.E. Church at St. Matthews, S.C. where his father pastored. While there, he assisted as choir leader, Sunday school teacher, superintendent, class leader, and local preacher.[112]

Upon graduation from Claflin, Prioleau served as pastor of the Double Springs Mission in Laurens County, S.C. In 1880, the Columbia, S.C. Conference of the A.M.E. Church sent him to Wilberforce University in Ohio to further his education. Prioleau completed his Bachelor of Divinity degree from Wilberforce by working as a farm hand in nearby Green and Clark counties, Ohio. He also served the Selma, Ohio A.M.E. Mission.[113]

---

[112]Chaplain George W. Prioleau File, Courtesy of the U.S. Army Chaplain Museum, Fort Jackson, S.C.

[113]Prioleau File.

After graduation Prioleau taught at a public school in Selma, Ohio, and pastored several churches including ones at Hamilton and Troy, Ohio. He married Anna L. Scovell, a graduate of the Wilberforce Class of 1885 and native of New Orleans. During the next several years he served simultaneous positions as both church pastor and professor of Ecclesiastical History and Homiletics at Wilberforce. After Wilberforce added Payne Theological Seminary to the university, Prioleau became the chair of historical and pastoral theology, a post he held from 1890 to 1894. In addition to his teaching duties, he also held several key positions in the A.M.E. church hierarchy such as Presiding Elder and Conference chair of the Springfield District of the Northern Ohio Conference, district delegate to the General Conference in Philadelphia beginning in 1892, secretary of the Northern Ohio Conference (1892-1895), and Associate Editor of the A.M.E. *Lesson Leaf.* [114]

On 25 April 1895, Prioleau was commissioned a chaplain in the U.S. Army by President Grover Cleveland and was forthwith assigned to the Ninth Cavalry. Fort Robinson, Nebraska was a far cry from the elite, upper-middle class circles in which Prioleau had grown accustomed to traveling. Like most nineteenth-century Protestants, he placed great emphasis on right living and high moral standards. What shocked the new chaplain most about the army was the rapid manner in which many of his church-trained troops threw off the religious instruction of their youth and resorted to drunkenness, gambling, and prostitution upon joining the military. He wrote that the army was an "atmosphere pregnated with evil and sin" which "tempted [many] to fall in and content themselves with the new situation."[115]

Prioleau believed that army chaplains had to counter temptation by always taking the high moral road thus setting an example for the men. Prioleau wrote that the...

---

[114]Prioleau File.

[115]George W. Prioleau, "Is the Chaplain's Work in the Army a Necessity?" Theophilus G. Steward, ed., <u>Active Service or Gospel Work Among U.S. Soldiers</u> (New York: U.S. Army Aid Association, 1897), 28.

> Chaplain who falls in with this [immoral] class, and closes his eyes
> to the debased condition of things around him, -- sears his conscience,
> and acts as "Rome" acts, will lose his influence, thwart his high
> purposes, and make void the Gospel of the Lord Jesus Christ. The
> Gospel in the army with such an ambassador is weak, aimless, and
> will be of no avail.[116]

Prioleau added that often the chaplain felt that his work was to no avail given the great odds, yet through God he could succeed. His fear was that some clergymen in uniform would grow weary in this struggle. Chaplains could succeed, however, if they would "carefully study the work before them," "adapt themselves to the circumstances," and "take the Holy Ghost as their teacher and guide." He also added that the cooperation of the command "may greatly advance his work" while the lack of it may greatly retard it.[117]

Chaplain Prioleau remained at Fort Robinson for three years and worked diligently to raise the morale of his troops, run the post school, maintain the post Sunday School, and perform the typical chaplain duties. He also took the opportunity to preach at the Congregational Church in the nearby town of Crawford. Listeners reported that Prioleau's sermon, based on Judges 14:14, was "ably and eloquently" delivered. Later, he received that church's pastor, the Reverend H.V. Rominger, as a guest speaker at Fort Robinson's Chapel. Another black chaplain, William T. Anderson, was once Prioleau's guest while he was en route to Montana to join his unit, the Tenth Cavalry.[118]

By 1890, the Indian wars were over, and the U.S. Army was settling down to the lazy routine of fulfilling its peacetime mission. But during the late 1890s tensions between the U.S. and Spain over Spanish colonial policy in Cuba intensified leading to the Spanish-American War in 1898. Among the war's causes was the new

---

[116]Steward, 27.

[117]Steward, 27.

[118]Schubert, <u>Buffalo Soldiers, Braves and the Brass,</u> 135.

American imperialism that developed during the latter part of the nineteenth century. In contrast to the European method of military domination, American style imperialism involved controlling other countries' economies rather than actual territory. William H. Steward, an early advocate of economic imperialism, worked hard to try to establish this new policy through the purchase of Alaska from Russia, and the Virgin Islands from Denmark. He also pushed for the creation of a transcontinental railroad and telegraph system to link the various markets together.[119]

Several small but powerful minority groups led the way in getting the U.S. involved in overseas expansion and ultimately the Spanish-American War. The first were business people and commercial farmers who were constantly on the lookout for new markets. The second group was Christian missionaries who supported expansion of U.S. trade abroad for they believed that the best way to convert the "heathen" to Christ was by winning them over to Western culture through Western goods. Another group was the navy lobby led by Alfred Thayer Mahan, author of *The Influence of Sea Power on History* (1890). Mahan's call for an enlarged navy to protect expanding trade routes was welcomed by the navy officer corps who saw this as a means for promotion and opportunity.

The final group was an intellectual elite who provided the ideology for the new expansionism. Members included people like Theodore Roosevelt, John Hay, Henry and Brooks Adams, Henry Cabot Lodge, and Elihu Root. Much of their thinking was influenced by Social Darwinism, and Rudyard Kipling's "White Man's Burden." The Reverend Josiah Strong's book, *Our Country,* characterized this Anglo-Saxon superiority complex well when it noted "As America goes, so goes the

---

[119]Seward was a New York Senator and later secretary of state under the Lincoln and Johnson administrations. For more on this new style economic imperialism see William Appleman Williams' The Tragedy of American Diplomacy (New York: Dell Publishing, 1972).

world...The rule of the survival of the fittest applies to nations as well as to the animal kingdom."[120]

The more immediate causes of the Spanish-American War are quite familiar: strong U.S.-Cuban business ties, the harsh treatment the Cubans received at the hands of their Spanish masters, especially General Valeriano Weyler; the Spanish minister de Lome's letter, yellow journalism; jingoism; and the sinking of the U.S.S. *Maine* in Havana harbor, that resulted in the deaths of 260 Americans, including 22 black sailors.[121]

Despite the jingoism and saber rattling that preceded this thinly veiled war of imperialism, the U.S. Army was hardly prepared to fight, even against an impotent nation like Spain. Unlike the U.S. Navy, which had been modernized recently thanks in large part to the creative thinking of men like Captain Alfred Thayer Mahan, the army had been permitted to deteriorate since the end of the Indian War era (1865-1890). Further, most of its efforts had been concentrated against fighting the guerrilla tactics of Native Americans, which left it ill-prepared it for conventional warfare against a European nation. Because of the army's unpreparedness, literally ten times more soldiers would die of disease, unfit food, unhealthy and unsanitary training camps, and other non-combat causes, rather than from Spanish bullets.[122]

These events affected the life of George W. Prioleau and the Ninth Cavalry, for soon the unit was ordered to prepare for deployment to Cuba. One of his last acts at Fort Robinson was a memorial service for those who died on the U.S.S. *Maine*. Over 400 people came and listened to Mrs. Prioleau sing, Mrs. Gerrard play, and

---

[120] See Josiah Strong, Our Country: Its Possible Future and Its Present Crisis, rev. ed. (1891)

[121] William Loren Katz, The Black West, third edition (Seattle, Washington: Open Hand Publishing Company, 1987), 22. See also Ivan Musicant's Empire By Default: The Spanish-American War and Dawn of the American Century (New York: Henry Holt, 1998)

[122] R. Ernest Dupuy and Trevor N. Dupuy, Military Heritage of America (New York: McGraw Hill, 1956), 317. Matloff, 324, 325.

Chaplain Prioleau spoke in memory of the patriotism of the brave dead of that vessel.[123]

Prioleau and the Ninth were sent to Tampa, Florida, which was the largest debarkation site for U.S. forces deploying to Cuba. What they found in Tampa was quite unsettling. The four African American regiments had been stationed on the American frontier since 1866. There they had experienced racism, but it was nothing like the type they encountered in the Jim Crow South.[124] Despite their racial prejudice, frontier people of the American West realized that the Buffalo soldiers were often the only force standing between them and certain death at the hands of hostile Native Americans, bandits, and renegades. In the South, the situation was quite different.

Chaplain Prioleau addressed southern racism in several letters he wrote to the *Cleveland Gazette*. In one piece he protested that blacks were not able to purchase goods at the same counter as whites, and that southerners had made segregationist laws which the local blacks obeyed without question. Then he criticized the hypocrisy of American racism by noting:

> You talk about freedom, liberty, etc. Why sir, the Negro of this country is a freeman and yet a slave. Talk of fighting and freeing poor Cuba and Spain's brutality; of Cubans murdered by the thousands, and starving reconcentradoes. Is American any better than Spain? Has she not subjects in her midst who are murdered daily without trial, judge or jury? Has she not subjects in her own borders whose children are half-fed and half-clothed, because their father's skin is black?

In an angry tone Prioleau continued:

---

[123]Schubert, Buffalo Soldiers, Braves and the Brass, 135.

[124]For more on the Jim Crow laws see: C. Van Woodard's The Strange Career of Jim Crow (New York: Oxford University Press, 1974) and Origins of the New South: 1877-1913 (Baton Rouge: Louisiana University Press, 1974) and Howard N. Rabinowitz's Race Relations in the Urban South, 1865-1890.

Yet the Negro is loyal to his country's flag. O! He is a noble creature, loyal and true. Forgetting that he is ostracized, his race considered as dumb as driven cattle, yet, as loyal and true men, he answers the call to arms and with blinding tears in eyes and sobs he goes forth: he sings "My Country 'Tis of Thee, Sweet Land of Liberty," and though the word "liberty" chokes him, he swallows it and finishes the stanza "of Thee I sing."[125]

Exposure to another country complete with a different culture led many blacks like Prioleau to reexamine their own experiences in the United States. Later in World War II, blacks would note the irony of fighting Nazi and Japanese racism abroad while suffering from white racism at home.

Because the army camp conditions at Tampa were so miserable and unsanitary, much sickness and disease resulted. Prioleau fell victim to malaria just before the Ninth deployed to Cuba and was left behind to recuperate. Once he recovered, the army sent him on a recruiting mission for his unit in order to bolster its numbers. His letters to the *Cleveland Gazette* provided a sort of traveler's journey of his experiences in the Jim Crow South. While in Tuskegee, Alabama he lamented that when...

an officer of the United States Army, a Negro chaplain, goes in their [whites'] midst to enlist men for the service of the government, to protect the honor of the flag of his country, and the chaplain goes on Sunday to M.E. Church (White) to worship God, he is given three propositions to consider, take the extreme back seat, go up in the gallery or go out. But as we were not a back seat or gallery Christian, we preferred going out.

Prioleau complained to the white citizenry that their behavior toward him was "heinous, uncivilized, unchristian, and un-American." Responding to his complaints the day after, the good Christians...

informed [him] that niggers have been lynched in Alabama for saying less than that. We replied that only cowards and assassins would overpower a man at midnight and take him from his bed and lynch

---

[125]The Cleveland Gazette, 13 May 1898.

him, but the night you dirty cowards come to my quarters for that purpose there will be a hot time in Tuskegee that hour; that we were only three who would die but not alone. We stayed there ten days, enlisted 34 men.[126]

Prioleau found that this type of racism was prevalent even in Orangeburg, South Carolina, home of his alma mater, Claflin College. He recognized:

"the prejudice is not so much against the ignorant Negro, the riff-raff, as it is against the intelligent, educated, tax-paying Negro; the Negro who is trying to be a man...My recruiting party was most brutally treated and there was no redress.[127]

Prioleau learned an ugly truth described by Du Bois that even when blacks "played by the rules" established by whites by bettering themselves through hard work and education, whites still treated them with hatred and contempt.

Prioleau never forgot this prejudice even during the emotional postwar outpouring of pride and nationalism which spread through the hearts and minds of most Americans. These celebrations led some within the white community to forget the color barrier -- temporarily. Black and white troops were greeted at train stations with picnics and parades by citizens of all races. The Buffalo soldiers had earned this praise by their bravery during the fighting, as evidenced by the five Medals of Honor and twenty-five Certificates of Merit they received. It is no wonder that pictures of the two black cavalry units charging up San Juan Hill were proudly displayed in many black homes for years later.[128]

Because of the praise awarded black soldiers, many in the African American community predicted that "Negrophobia" would dissipate after the war. Chaplain

---

[126]The Cleveland Gazette, 1 October 1898.

[127]Fowler, 32, 46, 47. Hershel V. Cashin, Under Fire With the Tenth U.S. Cavalry (1899; repr., New York: Arno Press, 1969), 110. William B. Gatewood, ed., "Smoked Yankees" and the Struggle for Empire: Letters From Negro Soldiers, 1898-1902 (Urban: University of Illinois Press, 1971), 74, 75.

[128]Fletcher, 32, 46, 47.

Prioleau found that not to be the case after the Ninth returned from Cuba and began making its way to its new home at Fort Grant, Arizona Territory. In a letter which appeared in the *Cleveland Gazette* on 22 October 1898, the chaplain described the reception the Ninth received, first at Long Island, New York, and then at Kansas City, Missouri. At Long Island, the black soldiers were treated as returning heroes, leading him to write:

> Our reception along the line of the B & O [Railroad]...was all that could make the hearts of soldiers glad, and inspire them with courage and renewed vigor to lay their lives as sacrifices upon the altar of their country.[129]

By the time the Ninth reached Kansas City, the mood had changed dramatically. Both the all-black Ninth and all-white First Cavalry appeared together in that city, but whereas the First was received as conquering heroes praised for their exploits in Cuba, the Ninth was "unkindly and sneeringly received." Prioleau noted of the two units that:

> both were under the same flag, both wore blue, and yet these black boys, heroes of our country, were not allowed to stand at the counters of restaurants and eat a sandwich and drink a cup of coffee, while the white soldiers were welcomed and invited to sit at the tables and eat free of charge. You call this American "prejudice." I call it American "hatred" conceived only in hellish minds.[130]

Prioleau realized that patriotic service and military duty would not erase the color line in the minds of many white Americans.

Prioleau had been born into slavery but had risen to the ranks of the upper-middle class black community and was now one of only a handful of commissioned army officers. He was intelligent, well educated, articulate, and an obviously gifted man and leader. He fit within the army system better than Plummer for two reasons. First, he focused on the more traditional chaplain activities rather than the

---

[129]Gatewood, 83.

[130]Gatewood, 83.

controversial issues that Plummer embraced such as his work in temperance, the editorship of an African American publication, and his attempts to explore central Africa. Second, Prioleau had the advantage of not making so many enemies as Plummer, adversaries who later worked toward his demise. Nevertheless, the feelings of shock and disappointment must have been great for this proud and successful man when he returned to his native South and especially his home state of South Carolina. Had he worked hard and risen up the social ranks only to be reminded now that he was still just a "nigger" in the eyes of most whites? Why should he be held in contempt by people, most of whom did not possess half his intelligence or education? His sense of frustration and hurt must have been particularly acute coming in the midst of a war in which his fellow black soldiers were fighting and dying abroad for the American ideals of freedom and democracy -- something that African Americans did not share fully here at home.

Prioleau ministered during an era in which several powerful themes were shaping U.S. foreign and domestic policy. One of these themes was the Social Darwinist ideas of Herbert Spencer and William Graham Sumner. The other was the new imperialism fostered by Christian missionary advocates like Josiah Strong, writers like Rudyard Kipling, thinkers like Henry and Brooks Adams, and military men like Alfred Thayer Mahan. Social Darwinists believed that only the strongest survived. In their view this meant the Western, and especially Anglo-Saxon, nations. Imperialism was justified by the need to expand markets, spread the so-called superior Western culture, and Christianize the "pagans."

A major consequence of these two themes was that not only were dark-skinned peoples abroad looked down upon, but so, too, were the African Americans at home. Chaplain Prioleau experienced this prejudice firsthand in his work in the Jim Crow South. As a result, he felt the tremendous tension of double-consciousness even more than most. Not only did Prioleau have the dual identity of both an American and a Negro, but he was also an army officer and Negro. How disheartening it must have been for him to have been hated and despised by the very people he was committed to defend.

Despite his frustrations, Chaplain Prioleau continued to believe that the military was one of the best opportunities available to black men of his day and proved it by staying in the military. Prioleau served two tours of duty in the Philippines with the Ninth Cavalry and was later transferred to the Tenth U.S. Cavalry which in 1915 was stationed along the Mexican border. In 1917, he was promoted to major and was transferred to the Twenty-fifth Infantry which was now at Schofield Barracks, Hawaii. His wife died in 1903 and he remarried Ethel G. Stafford of Kansas. They produced four children. He continued fighting for the cause of his people and in 1917 raised $3200 from the men of the Twenty-fifth for the NAACP and black victims of the East St. Louis, Illinois race riot. He retired from the army in 1920 and settled in Los Angeles where he helped to organize an A.M.E. Church. He died in 1927.[131]

---

[131]Logan and Winston, 505.

Chaplain Henry V. Plummer
9th U.S. Cavalry

Chaplain George W. Prioleau
9th U.S. Cavalry 1896-1915
U.S. Army Chaplain Museum Collections, Ft. Jackson, SC

Chaplain William T. Anderson
Regular Army - Black Chaplain - 10th Cavalry
Appointed August 16, 1897
U.S. Army Chaplain Museum Collections, Ft. Jackson, SC

DIVISION MILITARY MEET

Monday, January 13th, 1908

7.30 P. M.

* *

SUPERSTITIONS

A HUMOROUS LECTURE

By Chaplain William T. Anderson

10th U. S. Cavalry

This lecture was very popular at Ft. McKinley and Cavite.

We will not be responsible for ruptured blood-vessels, strained sides, or other injuries caused by this Mirth-Provoking, Side-Splitting Lecture.

* *

ADMISSION FREE!!

All are invited.

If you miss this lecture you will miss a treat.

A. A. PRUDEN, Chaplain 2nd Inf.

CHAPLAIN OF THE MEET.

Flyer for lecture by Chaplain William T. Anderson

Captain Allen Allensworth
Chaplain 24th Regiment U.S. Infantry
U.S. Army Chaplain Museum Collections, Ft. Jackson, SC

Captain T.G. Steward
Chaplain 25th Regiment U.S. Infantry
U.S. Army Chaplain Museum Collections, Ft. Jackson, SC

CHAPTER IV

CHAPLAIN WILLIAM T. ANDERSON,

TENTH UNITED STATES CAVALRY

The second all-black cavalry unit fielded by the army between 1884 and 1901 was the Tenth United States Cavalry. The Tenth Cavalry became the most famous Buffalo soldier regiment for several reasons. First, it gained recognition because of the fame of its first commander, Benjamin H. Grierson, a Civil War hero and friend of Generals U.S. Grant and William T. Sherman. The regiment also achieved national celebrity because of its successful military exploits against the Native Americans, particularly the Apache leaders Victorio and Geronimo and their respective war bands. Finally, the Tenth Cavalry was the first unit to adopt the nickname, "Buffalo soldiers."

This chapter begins with a brief overview of the Tenth Cavalry and Benjamin Grierson in order to provide the background and context for an examination of Chaplain William T. Anderson's role in this unit. Anderson was unique among chaplains because he was a physician as well as clergyman who used his medical skills to save lives during the Spanish-American War and Philippine Insurrection. He also stands out because he served briefly as post commander of Fort Robinson, Nebraska making him the first African American to hold such a position. His example helped to establish an important precedent when later black officers would seek similar commands. Anderson was the only African American chaplain in the Regular Army to serve in Cuba during the Spanish-American War which makes his experience distinctive. Chaplain Anderson's struggle with doubleness was apparently less dramatic than that of Henry Plummer and George Prioleau. Nevertheless, in the end he, too, was confronted with racism which led to his early retirement from the service.

I

Buffalo Soldiers of the Tenth
Regiment of U.S. Cavalry

The same congressional act of 28 July 1866 which established the Ninth Cavalry also created the Tenth. Lieutenant General William T. Sherman, Military Division of the Mississippi commander, issued General Order No. 6 on 9 August 1866 to formally establish the Tenth Cavalry. By September, the unit had 1,092 recruits.[1]

The man selected to command the Tenth was Benjamin H. Grierson. Like Edward Hatch, his friend and counterpart in the Ninth, Grierson did not begin his career as a professional soldier. Instead, he started out as an Illinois bandleader, composer, and music teacher. In 1854 he married and became a merchant in order to better provide for the economic needs of his new family. By 1861 his business was in such serious financial difficulty that Grierson, his wife, and two small children were forced to more in with his parents.[2]

---

[1]Theodore F. Rodenbough and William J. Haskin, The Army of the United States (New York, 1896) quoted in John M. Carroll, ed., The Black Military Experience in the American West (New York: Arno Press, 1969), 77-79.

[2]William H. and Shirley A. Leckie, Unlikely Warriors: General Benjamin H. Grierson and His Family (Norman: University of Oklahoma Press, 1984), xi.

When the Civil War broke out Grierson attempted to enlist in Company I of the Tenth Illinois Infantry only to learn that there were no more vacancies. His political connections in the Republican Party enabled him to secure an appointment as aide-de-camp with the rank of lieutenant without pay to an old friend, Brigadier General Benjamin M. Prentiss.[3]

Grierson's assignment provided him with the opportunity to prove himself in battle during the border clashes that broke out between U.S. and Confederate forces in the upper Mississippi region, and to win the friendship and respect of men like U.S. Grant and William T. Sherman. These contacts helped him to land a position with the Sixth Illinois Cavalry, and also served him well after the Civil War as commander of the Tenth.[4]

Grierson's assignment with the Sixth Illinois Cavalry proved to be a turning point in his new military career. His skill and leadership abilities enabled him to become unit commander in a short period of time, and later brigade commander over both the Sixth and Seventh Illinois Cavalry. As General Grant's primary cavalry leader in the Western theater, Grierson became a northern hero in the 1863 Vicksburg campaign when he conducted a six hundred mile raid into the heart of Confederate-held Mississippi which resulted in more than one thousand rebel casualties, a thousand horses and mules captured, sixty miles of railroad and telegraph lines destroyed, and the diversion of thirty-eight thousand southern troops away from Vicksburg's defenses. Grierson's audacious feat was even more stunning because it came at a cost of only three Union troops killed, seven wounded, five ill left behind, and nine missing. The *New York Herald* and *Memphis Bulletin* wrote glowing reports of Grierson's "great raid through Mississippi," while *Harper's Weekly* and *Leslie's Illustrated* featured his picture on their front page. General Sherman said that his was "the most brilliant expedition of the war." Grant stated the

---

[3]Leckie and Leckie, 48.

[4]Leckie and Leckie, 61.

"Grierson...first set the example of what might be done in the interior of the enemy's country without any base from which to draw supplies."[5] Grierson's demonstration later inspired Grant to launch in a similar manner, his own main assault on Vicksburg.

Before the war ended Grierson was promoted to Brevet Brigadier General. With the conclusion of hostilities after Robert E. Lee's surrender at Appomattox Courthouse, Grierson sought to maintain his brevet and secure a Regular Army commission as a colonel. His efforts were successful, and, with the help of Grant and Sherman, he was also selected to command the newly formed Tenth Regiment of United States Cavalry.[6]

Elijah Guion was the Tenth Cavalry's first chaplain. Guion had been the rector of St. Paul's Protestant Episcopal Church in New Orleans when the Civil War commenced. His openly Unionist loyalties resulted in his Confederate parishioners forcing him to resign, which paved the way for Guion to become a Union Army chaplain to the First New Orleans Volunteers. The positive reputation he earned with this unit, in turn, led to his appointment as chaplain to the Tenth Cavalry.[7]

Fort Leavenworth, Kansas was the first home for the Tenth. There, Colonel Grierson was kept busy trying to secure decent mounts and equipment for his new unit. The colonel complained that most of what he received was of poor quality and in short supply, especially in comparison with what white units obtained. He was also plagued by the influx of new recruits who did not measure up to the army's standards much less his own personal requirements. Only after writing several

---

[5]Leckie and Leckie, 99.

[6]Leckie and Leckie, 139, 143.

[7]Earl F. Stover, Up from Handyman: The United States Army Chaplaincy, 1865-1920 Volume III (Washington, D.C.: Office of the Chief of Chaplains, Department of the Army, 1977), 15.

forceful letters to the recruiting officer did the quality improve. The problem of inferior horses and equipment was never resolved.[8]

But Grierson's obstacles did not end here. The worse predicament came from Leavenworth's post commander, General William Hoffman. Hoffman felt that black troops had no place in the U.S. Army, and the contempt he had for these men extended to the white officers who commanded them. Therefore, Hoffman took every opportunity to harass members of the Tenth by lodging petty complaints against them, and by not permitting black troops to participate in post parades. Hoffman was also responsible for placing the troopers of the Tenth in a low marshy area of the fort which led to a serious outbreak of cholera. Twenty-three soldiers died of this nasty disease in the month of July 1867 alone. Grierson was greatly relieved when he was ordered to move the Tenth to Fort Riley, Kansas.[9]

Before moving to Riley in the autumn of 1867, however, the regiment participated in its first skirmish. The Buffalo soldiers were deployed from Leavenworth in such a manner as to offer protection for workers engaged in constructing the Union Pacific Railroad. In this role, Captain G.A. Armes, commander of Troop I, along with two other officers and thirty-four men were suddenly attacked by 300 Native American warriors near the Saline River. The battle lasted six hours before the soldiers were forced to retreat but not before Captain Armes was wounded, and Sergeant W. Christy was killed. Later in the same month Armes, along with forty troopers and ninety men of the Eighteenth Kansas Volunteers, were attacked by 500 warriors. One trooper was killed and scalped, thirteen were wounded, while the Eighteenth lost fifteen killed and three wounded.

---

[8]Rodenbough and Haskin quoted in Carroll, 79. Leckie, The Buffalo Soldiers, 13. The Seventh Cavalry usually received the newest and best equipment, especially after it was led by George A. Custer, a favorite of General Philip Sheridan who eventually replaced Sherman.

[9]Leckie and Leckie, 147, 148. Rodenbough and Haskin, quoted in Carroll, 79, 80.

In addition, twelve horses were killed and two guides were wounded.[10] The Tenth's baptism by fire had been a bloody one.

The Kansas and Texas plains to which the Tenth was assigned had become a very dangerous place for settlers since the outbreak of the American Civil War. The local Comanches, Kiowa, and Cheyenne tribes were quick to discover and then exploit the vacuum created by the departure of so many U.S. troops shipped out to fight the Confederacy. Further, the downsizing of the post Civil War army meant that there were far too few soldiers brought back after the war to do an adequate job keeping the peace. Indeed, from just 1865 to 1867 alone, 162 whites were murdered, forty-three more captured, and twenty-four wounded. In addition, Native American warriors stole 3,838 head of cattle along with 4,000 horses. The Tenth's task in 1867 was to restore peace and order in this region.[11]

Most of the men of the Tenth were young and many had no prior service experience whatsoever. Therefore, their first few months of duty entailed simply making the transformation from raw recruits to soldiers. Though much was accomplished through drill and strict discipline, the best teacher was actual combat and the troopers of the Tenth did not have long to wait for their "instructor." In October 1867, Private John Randall of Company G, along with two civilians, was attacked by sixty to seventy Cheyenne Indians near the Union Pacific Railroad line. The two civilians were killed outright while Randall was shot once in the hip. Despite his wound he managed to crawl into a hole for safety. The pursuing warriors were relentless in their attack, though, and inflicted eleven lance wounds upon Randall before giving up on trying to force him out of his place of refuge.[12]

---

[10]Rodenbough and Haskin, quoted in Carroll, 80, 81.

[11]Leckie, The Buffalo Soldiers, 19, 20.

[12]Herschel V. Cashin, Under Fire with the Tenth U.S. Cavalry (1899; repr. New York: Arno Press, 1969), 28.

The Cheyenne then moved on to assault the main body of troops to which Randall belonged, which was several miles down the railroad line. The soldiers were led by Sergeant Charles H. Davis who was quick to respond to the Indian challenge. His men grabbed their carbines and opened up with such a withering rate of fire that the Indians' ponies, which had been placed in a nearby ravine, were so startled that they broke free and ran off. This fortuitous turn of events ended the Cheyenne attack, thus ensuring the survival of Davis and his men. Then the sergeant set out to find Randall who was retrieved still alive, but only barely.[13]

Historian William H. Leckie has noted that around 1867 the men of the Tenth Cavalry were given the nickname "Buffalo soldiers." As stated earlier, the reason appears to be due to the similarity between the black soldiers hair and skin and that of the buffalo. Because the buffalo was a sacred animal to the Indians, the men of the Tenth accepted this nickname with pride and even incorporated the buffalo into their regimental crest.[14]

Over the next several years, Colonel Benjamin Grierson and the men of the Tenth continued their occupation duty in Kansas and Texas participating in the Kiowa and Cheyenne campaigns of 1867-1868 and 1874-1875.[15] In addition, they also helped to chase bandits, protect wagons trains and mail routes, as well as offer defense to new settlers moving into the area. When not engaged in combat or out on patrols, the soldiers were kept busy building and repairing the various and sundry posts and forts to which the scattered regiment was assigned.[16]

---

[13]Cashin, 29, 30.

[14]Leckie, The Buffalo Soldiers, 25 26.

[15]For the role of the Tenth in these campaigns see William H. Leckie's The Military Conquest of the Southern Plains (Norman, Oklahoma Press, 1963), Chapters 4, 8 and 9.

[16]Many of these facilities are still used today by the U.S. Army such as Fort Riley and Forts Leavenworth, Kansas; Fort Sill, Oklahoma; and Fort Huachuca, Arizona to name but a few. Others such as Fort Concho and Fort Davis, Texas remain only as historical sites.

143

Records do not show what Colonel Grierson thought of his chaplain, Elijah Guion, but there are several letters that reveal his views toward another chaplain who ministered to the men of the Tenth Cavalry, Norman Badger. A fifty-nine year old Civil War veteran, Badger had served at several previous assignments before becoming post chaplain at Fort Concho, Texas from 1871 to 1876. It was his toughest assignment. Fort Concho had no chapel building which meant that services were held at sundry places such as the hospital ward, post trader's bar room, mess hall, barracks, and even his own cramped quarters. Badger was apparently a hard worker who sought diligently to execute his duties as pastor, post gardener, post treasurer, and manager of the post bakery.[17]

Nevertheless, Colonel Grierson apparently did not care for Badger, or any chaplain for that matter. Badger died after Grierson and the Tenth Cavalry had been at Fort Concho only four months. Upon learning that Chaplain George E. Dunbar would be Badger's replacement, Grierson wrote his wife, noting that Dunbar would be good only "to occupy quarters and eat commissary stores and to attend strictly to everybody's business but his own." He added sarcastically that he hoped the new chaplain would "succeed in saving a great many souls, his own included."[18]

Despite the colonel's prejudicial views, Dunbar seems to have made a favorable impression on Grierson. After hearing the new chaplain preach, the colonel again wrote his wife:

> The Chaplain preached quite a good sermon. He has an easy delivery, and set forth some plain, sensible, conservative, democratic, religious ideas in an effective and agreeable manner. He is to preach tonight again, more especially for the soldiers and colored people. There were a good many soldiers present today. He, the Chaplain, has taken hold of matters as if he was determined to put forth his very best 'endeavor' to make himself useful in every possible proper way and I am rather inclined to think he will be quite successful.

---

[17]Stover, 15-17.

[18]Quoted in Stover, 17.

144

But then Grierson added a warning:

> A new broom is apt to sweep clean for a time, however, and he may
> hereafter get to playing the Old Soldier.[19]

During the Tenth's Indian fighting days, there were two more noteworthy campaigns. The first was the fight against the Apache leader, Victorio, and his band of warriors who broke out of the San Carlos Reservation in Arizona. The Apaches who followed Victorio were never happy with reservation life and missed their native New Mexico deeply. Therefore, on 2 September 1877, Victorio, along with 310 others, made a break for home. For more than two years the Apaches eluded troopers and alternated between doing battle and participating in negotiations.[20]

Skirmishes between the Apaches and soldiers were sudden and ferocious. On 6 September 1879, sixty of Victorio's men wiped out an eight-man guard detail of Buffalo soldiers and stole forty-six horses. Victorio's success enticed other Native Americans from nearby reservations to join him. By 1880, he had his band virtually dominated the Arizona-New Mexico border region by the utilization of stealth, ambush, and the nearby border as a safe haven. Because of the mistreatment he had received at the hands of whites, Victorio became so ruthless that some within his own band considered him a madman. Indeed, he seemed to relish torturing and mutilating white prisoners.[21]

Because of the serious threat to white settlers, Colonel Grierson and the Tenth were deployed from Texas to New Mexico to join Colonel Hatch and the men of the Ninth. Grierson arrived on the scene with a well conceived plan for defeating Victorio. He believed that Hatch had failed to subdue the Apaches because he had divided his men into small units designed to set out in pursuit of the renegades

---

[19]Quoted in Stover, 17.

[20]Utley, 359-361.

[21]Utley, 359-361. Dee Brown, Bury My Heart at Wounded Knee (New York: Washington Square Press, 190), 375.

wherever they struck. The natives knew the land too well for this to be successful, however, thus most patrols ended up either wasting their time or running into well-laid ambushes. Grierson reasoned that the best approach was to set up his own ambushes at the key water holes and wait for the Native Americans to arrive. He also believed that Victorio would try to reenter the United States through Texas and not New Mexico this time.[22]

The colonel received permission to relocate his troops to Texas and implement his plan. In order to ensure success, Grierson elected to participate in the ambush personally and chose as his site a water hole named *Tinaja de las Palmas*. As fate would have it, Victorio and 150 braves came there on 30 July 1880. Grierson, two other officers, twenty-one cavalrymen, and his teenage son Robert manned their well-fortified position and held Victorio off until reinforcements arrived. The Apaches finally broke off their siege and retreated into Mexico.[23]

The next month Victorio and his band tried to enter Texas again. Grierson and two troops of the Tenth dashed sixty-five miles in twenty-one hours to outrun the Apaches and seize the all important Rattlesnake Springs water hole first. After an intense firefight Victorio was once again driven back into Mexico.[24]

Victorio was finally killed in Mexico on 15 October 1880 by Mexican troops. Nevertheless, the work done by the Buffalo Soldiers in leading to his demise was invaluable. As historian Robert Utley had written:

> In truth, as both Generals Ord and Pope acknowledged, the black soldiers who pursued Victorio had endured some of the most punishing ordeals in the history of the Indian wars. The deserts and mountains of southern New Mexico and western Texas quickly broke down conventional troops. Yet despite a condition of almost constant exhaustion, the black soldiers kept at the task, four times prompting

---

[22]Utley, 362, 363. Robert Wooster, The Military and United States Indian Policy, 1865-1903 (New Haven: Yale University Press, 1986), 95, 96, 186, 187.

[23]Utley, 363.

[24]Utley, 363.

146

Victorio to drop into Mexico to rest and refit. Grierson conducted a masterly campaign that turned the land's hostile feature back on the enemy. Victorio at last met his match in Chihuahua, but in Texas and New Mexico he met some worthy foes.[25]

With the demise of Victorio, the effort to pacify Texas was at last completed and the War Department's focus turned westward. In March 1885, the Tenth Cavalry was transferred to the Department of Arizona to deal with a new threat posed by Geronimo and his Chircahua Apaches. For the first time all twelve companies of the regiment, including their thirty-eight officers and 696 enlisted men, marched together as a single unit. Upon their arrival in Arizona, however, the regiment was divided once more and sent to several different locations to include Forts Grant, Thomas, Apache, and Verde, along with Whipple Barracks where Grierson set up his headquarters.[26]

The Apaches had long since become bored with the monotonous routine of reservation life, and sick of being cheated out of their rations by dishonest Indian agents placed in charge of their care. Therefore, Geronimo and more than 150 renegade warriors escaped from the reservation's confines, prompting the transfer of the Tenth to Arizona. Like Victorio before him, Geronimo was a worthy adversary who was also adept at using the Mexican-American border to his advantage. Nevertheless, the Buffalo soldiers were relentless in their pursuit and hounded the Apaches until most of their horses broke down from exhaustion. Geronimo finally surrendered to U.S. forces on 3 September 1886, and he and his men were sent to Fort Marion, Florida as prisoners.[27] Although the Buffalo soldiers had played only a small role in the actual capture of Geronimo, they are credited with contributing to

---

[25]Utley, 364, 365. Brown, 376.

[26]Leckie, 239.

[27]Leckie, 243-245.

the final surrender of the great was chief by helping to wear him down by constant pursuit.

Throughout these events, the Tenth Cavalry's chaplain was there ministering to the needs of his men. Chaplain Francis H. Weaver, the unit's new white chaplain and William T. Anderson's immediate predecessor, noted that "more persons proportionately, attend [worship] service in military than in civil life." He also pointed out that the chaplains were successful "not only in conversion, but in leading men back to renewal of active Christian life." In fact, he claimed that the gospel work in the army compared "more than favorably with like conditions in civil life." Like most army chaplains of the period, Weaver seemed to take great pains to defend the record of the Chaplains, noting that the "influence of godly a Chaplain in the garrison had been referred to even by men who outwardly seemed to have no interest in the Chaplain's work." He was also proud of the fact that many discharged men would later write thanking him for the work he had done.[28]

Chaplain Weaver had much to be proud of when his tenure with the Tenth Cavalry finally came to a close in 1897. He could also rest assured that his replacement, William T. Anderson, was a worthy successor who would keep up the fine efforts that both he and Chaplain Guion had begun.

II

Chaplain William T. Anderson

Chaplain William Thomas Anderson was born into slavery on 20 August 1859 in Seguin, Texas. At the age of three he and his family escaped bondage and

---

[28]Theophilus G. Steward, ed. Active Service: or Religious Work Among U.S. Soldiers (New York: United States Army Aid Association, 1897), 51, 52.

fled to nearby Galveston, Texas. One of his earliest memories was on 19 June 1865 when Union Major General Gordon Ranger arrived in that city and announced to the African American community that they were all freed by virtue of the 1 January 1863 Emancipation Proclamation. For years afterward, blacks in Texas still celebrated their freedom on 19 June rather than 1 January.[29]

Anderson was perhaps the best educated African American chaplain of his era. His family was a motivating force in establishing an A.M.E. church and ecclesiastically run grade school in Galveston after the Civil War ended. As one of the brightest students, Anderson was encouraged by the Texas Conference to attend the A.M.E.'s flagship school, Wilberforce University. Stephen Watson, vice president of the London Exchange Bank of Madison County, Ohio, became Anderson's benefactor while at Wilberforce making sure that he had the money to graduate and to go on to the Theological Seminary of Howard University, and also to earn the Doctor of Medicine degree from the Cleveland University School of Medicine and Surgery in 1888. That school's registrar noted that Anderson was "the first of a very large class." Finally, on 27 June 1896, Wilberforce University granted him the Doctor of Divinity degree.[30]

Anderson was a longtime resident of Cleveland and later Toledo, Ohio. In each city he maintained a private practice as a physician, as well as serving as pastor of St. John's A.M.E. Church in Cleveland, and later at Warren A.M.E. Church in Toledo. He was also involved in working for the Republican Party which helped him later to secure an appointment as a chaplain.[31]

---

[29]Telephone interview with retired Army General John Q. Taylor King, 5 January 1995. General King is a nephew of Chaplain Anderson and remembers him well from the days of his youth.

[30]Chaplain William T. Anderson File, Record Group 94, National Archives. King interview. Logan and Winston, 13.

[31]Chaplain Anderson File, Record Group 94, National Archives. King interview.

In 1897, Anderson began a campaign to fill Chaplain Weaver's vacant slot in the Tenth U.S. Cavalry Regiment. Numerous prominent people wrote letters of recommendation of his behalf, including the Reverend J.E. Rankin, President of Howard University, S.T. Mitchell, President of Wilberforce University, and Booker T. Washington, President of Tuskegee Institute. Washington noted in his letter:

> This is to say that I know Rev. W.T. Anderson, of Cleveland, Ohio, to be a Christian minister of the highest type of character and reliability, and I cheerfully recommend him as a proper person to represent our race as a Chaplain in the United States Army.[32]

Anderson's application was accepted by President William McKinley and on 18 August 1897 he took the oath of office in his hometown of Cleveland. Special Orders No. 230 dated 1 October 1897 ordered him to Fort Assiniboine, Montana, the new home of the Tenth U.S. Cavalry. Anderson settled down in his new position and remained at Assiniboine from November 1897 to June 1898 when he deployed to Cuba during the Spanish-American War.

Soldiers of the Tenth were ready to go to Cuba and do their duty. They believed their cause was just, and one soldier, Sergeant Horace W. Bivins, wrote the following:

> We are not afraid to fight for our country's honor and this cause; for we believe that it is a just one. Tyranny, tyranny is what Spain has kept imposing upon the Cubans for the last century.

Bivins was also confident of the war's outcome and put the upcoming conflict in a theological context noting:

> Spain will lose. Spanish tyranny can no longer be tolerated by the civilized world. Every foot of the island I believe is marked with sad evidences of cruelty. Oh God! at last we have taken up the sword to enforce the divine rights of a people who have long been unjustly

---

[32]Letter from T.A. Baldwin, Lieutenant-Colonel Tenth Cavalry, Brigadier-General Volunteers to the Adjutant dated 6 June 1899, Chaplain Anderson File, Record Group 94, National Archives.

treated. I believe that God will strengthen the hand of those who are fighting for humanity.[33]

Bivins, then, saw himself and other black soldiers as liberators representing the "civilized world."

Chaplain Anderson almost did not accompany Bivins and the rest of the unit to Cuba, however. The Tenth was deployed to Chickamauga on 19 April 1898, and due to a shortage of line officers, Anderson was left behind to serve as post commander, quartermaster, commissary officer, and post exchange officer. For the first time in American history an African American commanded a U.S. miliary post. Anderson handled his duties well and received numerous praise from his superiors, but he complained in a letter dated 13 May 1898 that he felt it was unfair to make him responsible for all of these tasks. He cited the fact that he had less than one year's experience as an officer and chaplain. He requested that he be replaced with a line officer and permitted to join his unit in Cuba.[34]

All of the chaplains who were deployed to Cuba during this war were pioneers in several respects. As historian Earl R. Stover has written:

> For the first time chaplains accompanied American troops into a land not contiguous to the United States. For the first time American chaplains went into a conflict as official noncombatants. Under Articles I and II of the Geneva Conventions of 22 August 1864, to which the Unite States became a signatory in 1882, chaplains employed in ambulance or hospitals were classified with medical personnel...[35]

Chaplain Anderson had an added distinction, however. All four black units -- the Twenty-fourth and Twenty-fifth Infantry, and the Ninth and Tenth Cavalry --

---

[33] Quoted in Hershel V. Cashin and other, Under Fire With the Tenth U.S. Cavalry (1899; reprint New York: Arno Press, 1969), 75, 76.

[34] Chaplain Anderson File, Record Group 94, National Archives.

[35] Stover, Up From Handyman, 111.

deployed to Cuba, but Anderson was the only African American chaplain who was sent to that foreign land.

The conditions Anderson faced once in Cuba were appalling. Indeed, more soldiers died of disease than died of Spanish bullets. The main reason was the total unpreparedness of the army. The entire U.S. Army consisted of only 26,000 officers and men scattered primarily throughout the American West. The last time the army had trained or fought together in a unit larger than a regiment was during the Civil War. The National Guard had over 100,000 men, but they were poorly armed and trained.[36] To make matters worse the army had no mobilization plan, higher staff, or supervisory role over the Guard.[37]

Major General Nelson Miles, Commanding General of the Army, sought to rectify some of these deficiencies by a plan that included gathering together and training a combined force of 80,000 Regulars, Volunteers, and Guardsmen at Chickamauga Park, Georgia. In the meantime, the navy was to blockade Cuba while the Cuban guerrillas waged a war of attrition against the Spanish. Miles's plan was shelved, however, when Secretary of War Russell M. Alger gave in to public demand for immediate action and ordered the army to deploy as soon as possible. The result was that Regular, Volunteers, and Guardsmen found themselves thrown into unsanitary camps in Georgia and Florida where they were flooded with bureaucratic red tape and delays, and experienced a lack of decent food, clothes, shoes, medical facilities and in some cases even arms.[38]

When the survivors finally arrived at the debarkation post of Tampa, they found only one railroad track leading to one pier. The consequence was a backlog of men and supplies and days and weeks of delay and frustration. The slipshod

---

[36]The Regular Army used the smokeless powder firing Krag-Jorgensen rifles while the National Guard units still carried the black powder Springfields.

[37]Matloff, 322, 323.

[38]Matloff, 324, 325.

manner in which units and their equipment were finally shipped out resulted in many troops unable to locate their own supplies once they landed in hostile Cuba.[39]

Major General William R. Shafter, Commander of the U.S. invasion force, ordered his troops into action almost immediately upon their arrival on 22 June 1898. Both the Ninth and Tenth Cavalry were part of Brigadier General Joseph Wheeler's Cavalry Division, as were Theodore Roosevelt's Rough Riders.[40] Their first engagement was the Battle of Las Guasimas. The Tenth was held in reserve initially, but later surged forward and seized the most difficult point away from its Spanish defenders. White officers who had any doubts about the ability of the Buffalo soldiers to fight changed their minds after this engagement.[41]

The Tenth went on to fight in the war's most famous battle, San Juan Hill, which set the stage for the eventual capture of Santiago. If Las Guasimas convinced the American skeptics that the Buffalo soldiers could fight, San Juan Hill earned the African American fighting men the respect of their Spanish foes who dubbed them "Smoked Yankees." All told, their bravery earned black troops five Medals of Honor and more than twenty Certificates of Merit due to their bravery.[42]

By the time Chaplain Anderson arrived in Cuba, on 25 July of 1898, the heaviest fighting was over, yet there was much work left for him to do. The very next day, Anderson used his medical training to treat fourteen members of his

---

[39]Matloff, 328. Marvin Fletcher, The Black Soldier and Officer in the United States Army, 1891-1917 (Columbia: University of Missouri Press, 1917), 32, 33.

[40]Ironically, Wheeler had been a Confederate general in the American Civil War. The Spanish-American War served to help heal old wounds between the North and South. Wheeler's troops were dismounted because they had neither the time nor means to bring their horses with them to Cuba.

[41]Willard B. Gatewood, Jr., "Smoked Yankees" and the Struggle for Empire: Letters from Negro Soldiers, 1898-1902 (Urbana: University of Illinois Press, 1971), 41, 42. Theophilus G. Steward, The Colored Regulars in the United States Army (1904; reprint: New York: Arno Press, 1969), 135, 136, 145, 146.

[42]Edward A. Johnson, History of Negro Soldiers in the Spanish-American War (Raleigh, N.C.: Capital Printing, 1899), 57-69. Fletcher, 46.

regiment who were suffering from fever and dysentery. Sergeant Bivins was one of the men and he credited Chaplain Anderson with saving his life. [43] Eventually Anderson became ill as well. He requested sick leave and was permitted to return home to Cleveland from August to September 1898. Upon his recovery, he received permission to engage in recruiting duty for his unit and was sent to Montauk Point, New York. From there he was shuttled about for the next year or more. He was transferred to Huntsville, Alabama from October 1898 to January 1899, and to Fort McIntosh, Texas from February to May 1899. He was sent back to Cuba but stayed only from May to September 1899. On 27 September 1899 he wrote the Adjutant General the following: "I am unable to stand the climate in Cuba, having contracted rheumatism in the Santiago Campaign last year." The Adjutant granted his request for more sick leave and he was sent home again from September to December of that same year. Finally, once his health returned, he was again transferred back to Manzanillo, Cuba where he remained, despite contracting malaria, until the Tenth was moved to Fort Robinson, Nebraska in April 1902.[44]

While on occupation duty in Cuba with the Tenth, Anderson carried out the normal duties of a chaplain which included Sunday worship services, prayer meetings, and baptisms. The Young Men's Christian Association (YMCA) provided him with tremendous assistance. He also set up a library, and gave a "Steroptican Exhibition" that was "very much enjoyed by the men."[45] But Anderson did more. Utilizing his skill and training as a physician, he began ministering to the physical as well as spiritual needs of his men and the Cuban citizens. Lieutenant Colonel T.A. Baldwin of the Tenth later described Anderson's services:

> He at once applied himself to assisting in the relief of many [Yellow] fever patients then in the regiment by visiting and nursing the sick

---

[43]Logan and Winston, 15.

[44]Chaplain Anderson File, Record Group 94, National Archives.

[45]Chaplain Anderson File, Record Group 94, National Archives.

and cheering them by his Christian example and fortitude even after he was sick and suffering himself and effected much good. While Chaplain Anderson is not an applicant for promotion or brevet, I think that his services should be recognized and I believe that all of the officers of the regiment that served in Cuba will bear me out to that end. I would request that this communication be made a matter of record and that it be forwarded to the War Department to be placed upon file.[46]

Major Charles H. Grierson, General Benjamin Grierson's son, added more praise and said that while Anderson was in Cuba he inspected every house and school personally, and twice a month checked houses in the nearby Cuban villages up to sixty miles away for signs of sickness and disease.[47]

The Spanish-American War provided blacks with an opportunity to demonstrate their professionalism as soldiers. Great pride was taken in the black community over the heroism of their fighting men. Edward A. Johnson's 1899 book, *History of Negro Soldiers in the Spanish-American War*, was a contemporary account filled with stories of individual acts of bravery by black soldiers at such battles as El Caney and San Juan Hill, and served as an example of their pride. It is complete with reprints of praise heaped on black units by important figures of the day such as William McKinley and others.[48] Chaplain Anderson played a key part in documenting the role of the black soldiers in Cuba as well when he joined with Herschel Cashin, a recorder at the U.S. Land Office in Huntsville, Alabama, Charles Alexander, Arthur M. Brown, and Sergeant Horace Bivins in writing a book

---

[46]Cashin, 291, 292.

[47]Chaplain Anderson File, Record Group 94, National Archives.

[48]Edward A. Johnson, History of Negro Soldiers in the Spanish-American War and Other Items of Interest (Raleigh, North Carolina: Capital Printing, 1899), 39, 40, 55-60. Marvin Fletcher, The Black Soldier and Officer in the United States Army, 1891-1917 (Columbia, Missouri: University of Missouri Press, 1974), 46, 47.

documenting the role of the Buffalo soldiers in Cuba entitled, *Under Fire with the Tenth Cavalry.*[49]

Chaplain Anderson and the Tenth Cavalry spent the next five years at Fort Mackintosh, Texas and at Fort Robinson, Nebraska where he continued to work for the welfare and morale of his troops. In 1902 he endeavored to stop alcohol abuse among the troopers by individual counseling sessions. Later that year, he strove to get local druggists in nearby Crawford, Nebraska to stop sales of cocaine and opium to the troopers of the Tenth. Then in 1903, he joined with local Crawford citizens in an effort to curtail gambling.[50]

There was also a lighter side to his ministry. Sports soon became a popular off-duty pastime and Chaplain Anderson offered a blessing at a banquet held to celebrate a football victory after a 1904 game. He also worked hard to get an organ, and during the Christmas season held special services in which he spoke on the origin of Christmas.[51]

In April 1907, Chaplain Anderson and the men of the Tenth were transferred to Fort William McKinley near Manilla in the Philippines. Because of his medical background, he was placed in command of the U.S. Morgue near Manilla. Like all army chaplains, Anderson was also very much involved in education. While in the Philippines, he took over the post school and expanded its curriculum by adding Spanish. But he was also interested in character building, and the creation of self-esteem for young, black soldiers struggling to survive in a white-dominated, racist world. He communicated his views through sermons, counseling sessions, and also

---

[49]Logan and Winston, 15.

[50]Chaplain Anderson File, Record Group 94, National Archives.

[51]Schubert, 108, 109.

through a local chapter of the YMCA which he started that conducted programs of recitations, musical recitals, essays and debates.[52]

All of these efforts met with praise from his superiors. The regimental commander, Colonel Jacob Augur, wrote that Anderson did "good work among the men" and had the best "interest of the men in all his efforts in their behalf." The surgeon, Samuel McPheeters, concurred and noted that the chaplain was "very well though of by the officers."[53] When Congress changed the law permitting chaplains to be promoted past the rank of captain, Anderson was one of the select few who was chosen to become a major and this in August 1907 just a few days after meeting the minimum ten year service requirement.[54]

The Tenth was eventually transferred back to the United States and stationed at Fort Ethan Allen, Vermont. Shortly afterward, Chaplain Anderson retired on 10 January 1910 at age fifty-one. He and his wife, Sada, moved back to Wilberforce and then spent the next several years traveling to Europe and other foreign lands. Photographs taken on these tours were used by Anderson to create a lecture series which he presented to numerous A.M.E. churches across the nation. He also served as secretary to the bishop of the Third A.M.E. District, and as a trustee of Wilberforce University. In September 1916, the Andersons moved to Toledo when he became pastor of the Warren Chapel Church. After World War I broke out, he left the church and offered his services to the U.S. Army's Quartermaster Corps. The war ended a few weeks later, however, and Anderson now retired to Cleveland. Never one to stay inactive, Anderson spent the next year raising money for the legal defense of Dr. Bundy, a black man who was accused of murder during the East St.

---

[52]Schubert, 118, 119. King.

[53]Schubert, 136, 137. Nevertheless, the white officers still attended another church because Anderson was black. As one scholar had noted "eleven o'clock on Sunday morning was probably the most segregated hour in America."

[54]Logan and Winston, 15.

Louis, Illinois riot of 1917. Finally, after a long and successful life, Chaplain Anderson died on 21 August 1934 at the age of eighty-five. Local veterans honored him by naming an area American Legion post after the chaplain. [55]

Anderson's career was distinctive in several ways. In addition to being a chaplain, he was also a physician whose medical training proved quite valuable to the men of the Tenth and to local civilians in both Cuba and the Philippines. His expertise and skills helped to dispel the myth that blacks were intellectually inferior. Anderson also helped to improve the image of the army chaplaincy by utilizing the full range of his training and talents in order to serve his unit and his country. Furthermore, he was singular in that he proved himself capable of commanding a U.S. post and morgue that had both black and white troops. His leadership set a precedent by demonstrating that blacks had the ability to command even white soldiers.

Finally, of all the African American chaplains he was the only one who served in Cuba during the Spanish-American War. Once again his spiritual and medical skills proved invaluable. His initiative and organizational abilities in supervising the activities of the YMCA, and his leadership in classes and sports he helped sponsor greatly benefitted the Buffalo soldiers of the Tenth United States Cavalry.

Chaplain Anderson's struggle with Du Bois' concept of double-consciousness was much less painful than that experienced by Chaplains Henry Plummer and George Prioleau. In fact, Anderson thrived in the army probably because he concentrated his efforts on more traditional ministries and avoided the highly emotional and confrontational issue of racism that Plummer embraced. Second, Anderson never spent any time in the Jim Crow South, thus avoiding the kinds of ugly incidences which beleaguered Prioleau. There can be little doubt, too, that

---

[55]King interview. Logan and Winston, 16.

Chaplain Anderson's medical knowledge helped to increase his usefulness and enhance his status in the unit and whatever local region the Tenth found itself.

Having said all of that, Chaplain Anderson's retirement was not something that he wanted, however. The official reason Anderson retired was due to "tropical fever" which he contracted while on duty in Cuba, but the *Cleveland Gazette* reported, on 7 August 1910, that the real reason was that President William Howard Taft seemed "determined to oust from office every Negro holding a decent position with the federal service." The article continued stating that this was "in accordance with his infamous 'new Southern policy.'"[56]

President Taft appointed several blacks to federal office in Washington, but was careful, in his words, not to "force them upon unwilling communities in the South itself." He wrote that the "greatest hope that the Negro had, because he lives chiefly in the South, is the sympathy of the white man with whom he lives." Considering the fact that over 1,700 blacks were lynched during this era, the "sympathy of the white man" was in short supply. Taft also believed that blacks should avoid seeking university education and focus instead on vocational skills. Taft's negative views toward blacks meant that a well-educated black man like Chaplain Anderson found his welcome in federal service wearing thin. Although very disappointed over his forced retirement, he continued to hold a positive view of the army until the day he died.[57] The sad irony is that whether a black chaplain openly fought racism like Plummer and Prioleau, or kept a low profile like Anderson, the result was still the same.

---

[56]The Cleveland Gazette, 7 August 1910, p.1. 25 August 1910, p. 34. Taft's so-called "new Southern policy to remove blacks from office in the South was first reported in an article in the New York Herald.

[57]Telephone interview with Major General John Q. Taylor King, 10 March 1995. Paolo E. Coletta, The Presidency of William Howard Taft (Lawrence, Kansas: University of Kansas Press, 1973), 30.

CHAPTER V

CHAPLAIN ALLEN ALLENSWORTH,

TWENTY-FOURTH UNITED STATES INFANTRY

Allen Allensworth was the second African American to receive a Regular Army commission as a chaplain. He made his mark on history in three distinctive ways. First, like Plummer, Prioleau, and Anderson, his life was an "up from slavery" story in which he rose from poor bondsman to become an officer and a gentleman in the United States Army. He served as chaplain of the Twenty-fourth U.S. Infantry from 1886 to 1907. Allensworth's promotion to lieutenant colonel in 1906 was especially noteworthy because he was the second chaplain and the very first black to obtain this high rank. Second, he became a prominent leader in promoting education for the troops in order to enhance their military careers, as well as their civilian lives later. His pioneering work in the education field set new standards, was recognized by educators in the civilian community, and was adopted army-wide. Finally, after his retirement from the army, he went on to found Allensworth, California, the first all-black town in that state.

Allensworth's struggle with doubleness seemed to be the least painful among the five black chaplains. His method of combating prejudice was similar to that of Booker T. Washington's accommodationism. Washington's approach, however, came with a high price when it meant acquiescing to racism, the same problem that Chaplain Allensworth of the Twenty-fourth U.S. Infantry faced.

Allen Allensworth was born into slavery in Louisville, Kentucky on 7 April 1842. Both he and his parents, Phyllis and Levi Allensworth, were the property of Mrs. A.P. Starbird of Louisville. Levi died while Allen was still an infant and it was his mother who had the biggest influences on him.[1]

Like most mothers, Phyllis had high hopes for her child and so she named him after the founder of the A.M.E. Church, Richard Allen. She believed that he had to learn to read the Bible if he was ever to become a great man like the Reverend Allen. Laws prevented slaves from learning to read but an opportunity availed itself and the determined Phyllis seized the occasion. While Allen was still quite young, he was given to Mrs. Starbird's son, Thomas, to be the white child's playmate and confidant. This proved to be a significant event, for Allensworth's mother encouraged the boys to play school everyday so that the knowledge Thomas acquired at his real school would be transmitted to her own son covertly. This plan worked for a time and provided young Allensworth with both a strong educational foundation, and a thirst for knowledge.[2]

Eventually, Allensworth and his mother were separated and sold by the Starbirds, but the two remained in the Louisville area. Allensworth continued his education on his own by reading a copy of *Webster's Spelling Book*. As his biographer noted, "After the Bible, no work [other than Webster's] was so popular or more highly praised among slaves as this little volume."[3]

Allensworth's new home was much different from the one provided him by the Starbirds, for he was now a member of a large plantation and was expected to work the fields. This abrupt change proved very difficult for him, especially after

---

[1]Charles Alexander, <u>Battles and Victories of Allen Allensworth </u>(Boston: French and Company, 1914), 7-9.

[2]Alexander, 7-10.

[3]Alexander, 21. William J. Hourihan, "An Officer and a Gentleman: Chaplain Allen Allensworth of the Twenty-fourth Infantry," <u>U.S. Army Chaplain Museum Association Newsletter </u>(July 1989), 1. Copy courtesy of the U.S. Army Chaplain Museum, Fort Jackson, S.C.

suffering under the lash of the plantation's cruel white overseer, Pat Smith. The unhappy youth was determined to run away and, in 1855, at the age of thirteen, he set out for Canada but was caught in a nearby town and returned bound hand and foot to a mule by the notorious slave catcher Bill Quinn.[4] After his second failed escape attempt, he was branded a troublemaker and was sold to a buyer from Memphis, Tennessee, and later to one from New Orleans, Louisiana. During this period he picked up several skills including shoe repair and the mastery of five different musical instruments. He was also trained as a horse jockey and competed throughout the South for the various masters who bought and sold him over the next several years.[5]

The American Civil War finally provided Allensworth with the opportunity he needed to successfully gain his freedom. When federal forces came near his plantation home, he fled his master and joined the Forty-fourth Illinois Volunteer Infantry, part of the Army of the Cumberland. He served in this unit as a civilian nursing aide from September to December 1862. On 3 April 1863 he joined the U.S. Navy and served aboard the U.S.S. *Queen City*, *Pittsburgh*, and *Cincinnati* on the Mississippi River, and the U.S.S. *Tawah* on the Tennessee River. He worked as the captain's steward and clerk and rose to the rank of petty officer first class by the time he was honorably discharged on 4 April 1865.[6]

After the war ended, he was reunited with his mother in Louisville and sent on to work as commissary to the commandant of the U.S. Navy Yard at Mound City, Illinois. Later, in 1867, both he and his brother William established two successful restaurants in St. Louis which they later sold at a profit.[7]

---

[4] Alexander, 131-133.

[5] Hourihan, 2. Alexander, 169.

[6] John Phillip Langellier, "Chaplain Allen Allensworth of the 24th Infantry, 1886-1906," The Smoke Signal XL (Fall 1980), 190.

[7] Hourihan, 2.

With the money he made from the sale of his businesses, Allensworth was afforded the opportunity to continue his formal education. His first school was the Ely Normal School near Louisville, which had been established by the American Missionary Society of New York and the Freedman's Bureau. Allensworth proved to be the institute's star pupil and was recommended by Major Ben P. Runkle of the Freedman's Bureau and Professor Hamilton of Ely to begin teaching at a small school at Christmasville some five miles from Louisville. Later he served as teacher at other nearby schools at Cave City and Hopkinsville.[8]

It was during this same period that he began to grow in his Christian faith which led him to join the Fifth Street Baptist Church in Louisville. From 1868 to 1871 he worked at two callings: Freedman's Bureau teacher and Baptist missionary. Finally, on 9 April 1871 he was ordained as a Baptist minister due to his "piety, splendid character, ministerial gifts...and evidences of a Divine call to preach the gospel."[9]

He was chosen by the First District Baptist Association to serve as a traveling minister throughout southwestern Kentucky, but he quickly felt the inadequacies of this theological training. He enrolled at the Baptist Theological Institute (Roger Williams University) at Nashville, Tennessee in order to rectify these deficiencies, and was aided financially by the Judson Missionary Society of the Second Baptist Church of Cleveland, Ohio. He also served as pastor of a thirteen-member church in nearby Franklin, Kentucky. Before he left this tiny congregation, Allensworth ensured that the church had increased its membership to 160, built a church building, and created a Sunday School.[10]

---

[8]Alexander, 191, 192. Professor Hamilton's first name is unknown.

[9]Alexander, 191.

[10]Alexander, 193.

Later Allensworth was called to serve the troubled First Negro Baptist Church of Elizabeth, Kentucky.[11] He accepted the pastor's position offered him by a telegram announcing that he had been elected unanimously. Upon his arrival he found his election had been opposed by one of the church's two factions. The tensions dividing the church offer a fascinating glimpse into the struggles and evolution of African American Christianity in the 1870s and beyond. Two renowned black scholars of an earlier era, Carter G. Woodson and E. Franklin Frazier, both recognized the tensions that developed within African American Christianity, which ultimately divided many black churches, like the one at Elizabeth, into two opposing camps: conservatives and progressives. Conservatives sought to retain the black folk religion element in worship, while progressives stressed discipline, orderliness, and an educated ministry. Among the causes leading to the dissension were the new freedom, combined with urbanization, industrialization, secularization, and the immigration of African Americans form the South to the North during the latter part of the nineteenth and early twentieth centuries.[12] Both Woodson and Frazier acknowledged the stress placed on the advocates of the rural folk religion as they were forced to encounter a changing and modernizing world. However, Woodson lamented the decline of folk religion while Frazier celebrated its apparent defeat.[13]

------

[11]Allensworth and several other area Baptist ministers had been called into this same church the month before in order to help calm tensions.

[12]William Wells Brown's book, My Southern Home; or, The South and Its People, is excellent source for understanding the struggle between progressives and conservatives and their competing visions for black Christians. Brown was a runaway slave who eventually acquired an education. He was critical of the uneducated southern black ministers who encouraged excessive enthusiasm in the black worship services. Brown also believed that "the only remedy for this great evil lies in an educated ministry, which is being supplied to a limited extent." But unlike Allensworth he was not overly optimistic and concluded that it was "very difficult, however, to induce the uneducated and superstitious masses to receive and support an intelligent Christian clergyman."

[13]See: Carter G. Woodson, The Rural Negro (Washington, D.C.: The Association for the Study of Negro Life and History, Inc., 1930, and E. Franklin Frazier, The Negro Church in America (New York: Schocken Books, 1964). Woodson stated: "The urban church has become a sort of uplift agency; the rural church has remained a mystic shrine. When the rural church assembles in the spirit it is much more of a seance. Persons have come together to wait upon the Lord. He promised to meet

The church dispute at Elizabeth forced Allen Allensworth to get involved in the confrontation between conservatives and progressives. Charles Alexander, Allensworth's contemporary biographer, called the conservative group "Holy-toners." Typically, these people were seeking to preserve many of the older African American folk religion traits carried over from slavery days. They were given to emotional outbursts and ecstatic visions and were dismissed as backward superstitious and ignorant. Alexander argued that...

> Naturally excitable and emotional in his ignorance, the Negro allowed his feelings to take full control of him when stirred by the appeals of the preacher. He was easily worked up into a frenzy over the pictures of heaven and hell so vividly drawn by the eloquent preacher. Faith and knowledge were synonymous terms with these ignorant "Holy-toners."[14]

Alexander held the black preachers responsible for the views and behavior of their parishioners,

> Criticism of the Negro's religious views and moral code of that period [Reconstruction era] should begin with his preachers, for they held the religious type of the race in their hands. The tendency of the preachers is to cling to the customs of the past and belittle whatever dignity and refinement the educated members of the race have acquired and display in their religious worship.[15]

One of Alexander's stunning statements bears recording here. He noted that "Judged by the standards of white men, the work and methods of the Negro preacher at the

---

them there. They have no time for the problems of this life [beyond trying to] extricate themselves from the difficulties which will ever beset them here until that final day." pp. 155, 156. The folk religion element survived and was revived at the turn of the nineteenth and twentieth centuries in one aspect through the Pentecostal movement.

[14] Alexander, 199.

[15] Alexander, 197.

time that Rev. Allensworth took charge of the church at Elizabethtown, were superficial and crude."[16]

Allensworth was a progressive but he evidently thought that the uniqueness of African American Christianity and its folk religion element need not be denied. That faith had helped sustain Allensworth and countless others while serving in bondage. Instead, he believed that the issue before black Christians was how they should adapt themselves and their religious beliefs to the new realities facing them. Fought along both sacred and secular lines, the struggle boiled down to a central question: should they accommodate or resist the dominant culture? Once that was decided, what means should they use? Some black leaders, such as Alexander Crummell, Henry M. Turner, W.E.B. Du Bois, called for resistance; others such as Booker T. Washington sought accommodation.

Allensworth sought the latter route. He recognized and appreciated the distinctive aspects of black folk religion and culture, but his days in the U.S. Navy and later in the classroom taught him organization and discipline, elements which he believed were needed in the black churches. Specifically, his training led him to pursue four goals: (1) to set up the church on the same organizational order as a school; (2) to maintain a conservative fiscal policy thus keeping the infant black churches out of debt, a problem which plagued many congregations at the time; (3) to bring a measure of order and decorum to the worship service; (4) to develop character and morality among his parishioners.[17]

An apparent master at running church business meetings, Allensworth worked toward obtaining these four goals by utilizing persuasion, logic, reason, the bylaw of the church, and the laws of the state. Through the use of these measures he was able to win over his opponents and recast the little church at Elizabethtown into a model he felt could best deal with the challenges presented African Americans in this new

---

[16]Alexander, 189.

[17]Alexander, 199-202, 212.

era of freedom.[18] The lessons he learned here helped him enormously later when he began serving as an army chaplain.

Continuing his work in Kentucky as both a teacher and church pastor, Allensworth's growing popularity afforded him the opportunity to go on a speaking tour of New England. But "a feeling akin to dread overcame him when in the presence of white people," his biographer noted, because "he suffered a sense of inferiority, the result of ancestral oppression. He could not rid himself of the feeling of timidity and nervousness when facing an audience of white people or when conversing with a white man."[19] Therefore, he sought help and enrolled in the National School of Elocution and Oratory in Philadelphia where he learned successfully to overcome his "Southern brogue."[20]

Over the next several years, Allensworth stayed quite busy. On 20 September 1877 he married Josephine Leavell and soon fathered two daughters. He also served as interim pastor of the Joy Street Baptist Church of Boston for four months, and later became pastor of the Union Baptist Church of Cincinnati, Ohio. In 1880 and 1884, he attended the Republican National Convention in Chicago as Kentucky's only black delegate.[21]

In 1882 he became interested in becoming a U.S. Army chaplain after an African American soldier told him that all four black regiments had white chaplains only. His interest heightened two years later when he heard two pieces of information: that Henry V. Plummer had become the first black chaplain since the Civil War; and that the chaplain's position in the Twenty-fourth Infantry Regiment

---

[18]At one point Allensworth even brought a copy of the Kentucky Penal Code with him into the pulpit and warned the "Holy-toners" that he would press charges against them it they disturbed the peace of the church. After a tense standoff, the "Holy-toners" backed down. Alexander, 199-202, 212.

[19]Alexander, 232.

[20]Alexander, 232.

[21]Alexander, 216, 237-241.

was vacant. Thus, Allensworth began a two-year letter writing campaign to secure an appointment as an army chaplain, which included obtaining letters of recommendation from congressmen, senators, businessmen, ministers, and even his former owner, Mrs. A.P. Starbird.[22]

Allensworth's political connections, acquired through years of hard work and campaigning among northerners and southerners, Democrats and Republicans alike, paid off. In 1885 and 1886, two southern senators, Charles P. Jacob and Joseph E. Brown, spoke to President Grover Cleveland on his behalf. Allensworth, a Republican, also spoke for himself, writing a clever letter to the Democratic president. He explained why he was seeking an appointment:

> a number of my Democratic friends, who desire to strengthen your administration among the colored people, particularly in the south, and to show the good feelings which exist and is growing between the two races, have encouraged me to ask for an appointment.[23]

He continued noting that his appointment would show on "behalf of the race, that a Negro can be an officer and a gentlemen."[24]

Allensworth wrote a letter to the Adjutant General of the Army which contains the following fascinating statement:

> I know where the official ends and where the Social life begins and have therefore gaurded [sic] against Social intrusion. As I served as a petty officer in the Navy during the Civil War, I know, to some extent, what the feelings of the officers in the Army and Navy are on this subject, and am prepared to gaurd [sic] against allowing myself in any position to give offense.[25]

---

[22]Hourihan, 2.

[23]Letter from Allen Allensworth to President Grover Cleveland, dated 1 April 1885, Allen Allensworth File, National Archives, Record Group 94.

[24]Letter from Allensworth to President Cleveland, dated 1 April 1885, Record Group 94, National Archives.

[25]Letter from Allensworth to the Adjutant General of the Army, dated 3 March 1886, Record Group 4, National Archives.

To the Honorable J.P. Brown, a U.S. Senator, he wrote:

> I am and have been on pleasant terms with the whites of my
> state...Allow me to further say that my Southern training had taught
> me enough to know how to appreciate the position of those who are
> my superiors: intellectually, socially and financially, and to act
> according to my relation to them, without undue assumptions.[26]

These statements show that Allensworth clearly can be counted as a member of the accommodationist school of Booker T. Washington. He knew all to well the racist views of the dominant white culture, but chose not to confront them directly. Instead, he sought to find a place for himself and for his people within that culture. His accommodationism can be seen in one of his speeches he delivered on the lecture tour entitled, "The Battle of Life and How to Fight It."[27] The address basically outlines a list of historical figures who rose from humble origins to great heights by discipline and hard work. The key to their success was several essential attributes: industry, fidelity, gentleness, fortitude, and in addition, prudence. For Allensworth (and Washington) prudence was key for it was...

> a knowledge of what is to be obtained and avoided, else failure may
> be expected. A wise discrimination as to choice of both ends and
> means, and a power of suiting words and actions with reference to
> controlling circumstances are indispensable to one who engages in
> the battle of life;[28]

Despite the later scholarly controversies over the philosophy of accommodationism, Allensworth's approach was successful. On 1 April 1886 his application was

---

[26]Letter from Allensworth to U.S. Senator J.E. Brown, dated 22 March 1886, Record Group 94, National Archives.

[27]This speech is found in Alexander, 221-230.

[28]Alexander, 226, 227.

accepted and he was commissioned as the second black chaplain since the Civil War.[29]

Allensworth was given two months to conclude his civilian affairs before he was to report to his unit stationed at Fort Supply, Indian Territory (Oklahoma). His church was very proud of him for by now the fame of the Buffalo soldiers had spread east to those in the African American community. Allensworth was proud, too, and hurried to purchase his uniforms.[30] He wore his new outfit in downtown Cincinnati which excited many but confused others. The chaplain's uniform of this period was different from that of line officers and consisted of a "fine black coat, trouser, shoulder straps, [with] shepherd's crook in the center, five braided frogs across the front of the coat, [and] nine black buttons down the front." Some people in Cincinnati thought he was a member of the Salvation Army or some other benevolent society; while one man on a railroad thought he was the train's porter. Ten years later Allensworth would help lead an effort to modify the chaplain's uniform in order to make it more military looking.[31]

After concluding his personal affairs two months later, he made the long trek from Cincinnati to Fort Supply by train. The fort garrisoned only the Headquarters Company of the Twenty-fourth, along with troops from the all-white Fifth Cavalry.[32] The rest of the Twenty-fourth's men were spread over a wide area in order to protect as much territory as possible. The deployment of his regiment, of course, meant that

---

[29]Efficiency Report for Allen Allensworth, Record Group 94, National Archives.

[30]Unlike enlisted soldiers, officers had to purchase their uniforms at their own expense. The same policy holds true today.

[31]Hourihan, 3. Alexander, 254, 255. Stover, Up From Handyman, 203, 204.

[32]The Fifth Cavalry was the unit that William F. "Buffalo Bill" Cody used to scout for some ten years before.

171

he would have to travel much like the circuit riders of old in order to meet with all the troops of the Twenty-fourth.[33]

Allensworth was the third chaplain to serve in the Twenty-fourth Infantry Regiment, following in the footsteps of John W. Schultz and James C. Laverty. Schultz began his military career as chaplain for the old Thirty-eighth Infantry Regiment (Colored), and continued in this role when the Twenty-fourth Infantry Regiment was created. He went with the Twenty-fourth to the Texas frontier where he established a school for the men and ministered to their spiritual needs until he was forced to resign in 1875. He was followed by Chaplain James C. Laverty who continued the education work started by Schultz, drawing upon his own background in both secular as well as religious education. Chaplain Allensworth was destined to make vast improvements on the education programs of Schultz and Laverty.[34]

Allensworth found Fort Supply to be a pleasant place but very lonely and isolated. Situated in the middle of the Indian Territory, it was surrounded by Cheyenne, Arapaho, and Kiowa Indians, and off limits to American traders and settlers. Fortunately, however, the fort was in good repair, especially when compared to other posts of the era.[35]

He arrived at Fort Supply alone, because before departing from Ohio, he made the decision to leave his wife and daughters behind for the first two months. It was probably the wisest choice, for he had many adjustments to make and numerous new things to learn concerning army life on the frontier. African American troops in the Union army had numbered 123,156 three months after the

---

[33]Langellier, 194. For more on the circuit rider nature of the army chaplain's work see: "Roughing It" by Chaplain Charles C. Pierce found in Active Service or Religious Work Among U.S. Soldiers, pages 71 through 77, edited by Chaplain T.G. Steward.

[34]Schultz was forced to resign due to indiscretions with an enlisted man's wife. Arlen L. Fowler, The Black Infantry in the West (Westport, Connecticut: Greenwood Publishing Corporation, 1971), 93, 105, 109. Earl F. Stover, Up From Handyman: The United States Army Chaplaincy, 1865-1920 (Washington, D.C.: Office of the Chief of Chaplains, Department of the Army, 1977), 12, 55.

[35]Langellier, 194.

Civil War ended. The largest percentage of these men were in the 130 all-black infantry regiments. When Congress reorganized the postwar army, this number was reduced to five. The last of the congressional acts dealing with the postwar reorganization, the Act of 3 March 1869, consolidated the five all-black units into two: the Twenty-fourth and Twenty-fifth Infantry Regiments. Colonel Ronald S. MacKenzie was the Twenty-fourth's first commander; Major Henry C. Merriam served as the second in command.[36] The Twenty-fourth Infantry Regiment had been deployed to Texas from 1869 to 1880, and then to Oklahoma. In typical fashion, troops of the regiment were scattered among several posts where they quickly assumed their duties.[37]

Soldiers who ended up in the Twenty-fourth began their military careers at one of three recruit depots: David's Island and Jefferson Barracks, Missouri, and Columbus Barracks, Ohio. There they learned to be soldiers by personal instruction and through study of their army issue *Soldier's Handbook*. This pocket-size, leather-bound volume contained most everything a troop in the United States Army was supposed to know. After three months at the recruit depot, the men were shipped out to their respective regiments.[38]

Once assigned to his units, the infantryman's task was quite different from that of his mounted comrade in the cavalry. While the cavalry was sent out on patrol, the infantry was usually left behind to guard the post and to perform 'fatigue,' "a military euphemism for hard manual labor."[39] Troops complained that they joined

---

[36]Rodenbough and Haskin quoted in John M. Carroll, ed. The Black Military Experience in the American West (New York: Liveright, 1971), 91, 92. Billington, 3-5. William Loren Katz lists LTC William R. Shafter as the unit's first commander. See: The Black West, page 216.

[37]Rodenbough and Haskin quoted in Carroll, 92.

[38]Fletcher, 78.

[39]Utley, 83. Robert Wooster, The Military and United States Indian Policy (New Haven: Yale University Press, 1988), 30. For a brief but colorful description of the infantryman by Frederic Remington see Harold McCracken, ed., Frederic Remington's Own West (New York: The Dial Press, 1960), 19.

the military to fight, not work as serfs. In 1878, one group of soldiers protested to Congress stating:

> We first enlisted with the usual ideas of the life of a soldier;...but we find in service that we are obliged to perform all kinds of labor, such as all the operations of building quarters, stables, storehouses, bridges, roads, and telegraph lines; involving logging, lumbering, quarrying, adobe and brick making, lime-burning, mason-work, plastering, carpentering, painting, &c. We are also put at teaming, repairing wagons, harness, &c., blacksmithing, and sometimes woodchopping and hay making. This in addition to guard duty, care of horses and equipment, cooking, baking, police of quarters and stables, moving stores, &c., as well as drilling, and frequently to the exclusion of the latter.[40]

Even some officers complained that turning the men into jack-of-all trades was not the best use of the soldiers. General John Pope, for instance, lamented that his posts were "garrisoned by enlisted laborers rather than soldiers." Such officers tried to get the War Department to hire civilian workers so that soldiers would be free to perform their military tasks, but Congressional budget restraints meant that such relief was seldom acquired.[41]

The posts that infantrymen protected were a miserable lot and reflected Congress' miserly mood. Southwestern forts were infested with centipedes, scorpions, tarantulas, and snakes; dust frequently blew through the log roofs and adobe walls. One trooper noted that Fort Grant, Arizona was "the place where everything that grows pricks and everything that breathes bites." Forts of the Northern Plains had their own unique problems too. Most were overrun with rats, mice, and insects; in winter, drifting snow found its way into every building.[42]

---

[40]Quoted in Utley, 83, 84.

[41]Utley, 84. Black troops do not appear to have had to endure more fatigue work than their white counterparts. See Fletcher, 82.

[42]David Nevin, The Old West: The Soldiers (New York: Time-Life Books, 1973), 58. Arlen L. Fowler, The Black Infantry in the West, 1869-1891 (Westport, Connecticut: Greenwood Publishing Corporation, 1971), 20, 21.

Officers like Chaplain Allensworth had their own private quarters which usually included two to four separate rooms; the enlisted men were crammed into open bay barracks lined with row upon row of bunks. A few candles provided a pauper's amount of light; one pot-bellied cast iron stove created a little warmth. One contemporary, Major George Forsyth, described these enlisted accommodations as "too small, poorly constructed, illy ventilated, frequently overcrowded, generally cold in winter, hot in summer."[43]

Toilet facilities consisted of outhouses, and bathhouses were almost nonexistent. The War Department required that the men bathe once a week, but as one officer noted: "The regulations say the men must be made to bathe frequently; the doctors say it should be done; the men want to do it; the company officers wish them to do so; the Quartermasters' Department says it is important. Yet we have no bathhouses."[44]

The complaints of one young lieutenant's wife's summed up garrison life in general for the typical infantryman when she noted: "This country itself is bad enough and the location of the post is most unfortunate, but to compel officers and men to live in these old huts of decaying, moldy wood, which are reeking with malaria and alive with bugs, and perhaps snakes, is wicked."[45] A regimental chaplain at Fort Davis, Texas concurred and added that run down desolate posts "tend to superinduce a restive spirit, and creates a cheerless atmosphere -- which render temptations to intemperance very strong."[46]

Chaplain Allensworth's new "congregation" was quite a bit different from the Baptist parishioners he had known back home. Because of the harsh conditions and

---

[43]Nevin, 57, 58.

[44]Nevin, 57, 58.

[45]Nevin, 58.

[46]Fowler, 22.

the rough type of men who enlisted in the service in the first place, discipline was frequent and meted out in hard and heavy doses usually by the noncommissioned officers (NCOs). They were a tough bunch very much up to the challenge posed by the unruly men under their charge; and First Sergeants were the toughest NCOs of all. These men virtually ran the companies and served as a link between the officers and the troops. Most were like First Sergeant McMakin of the 17th Infantry, a Civil War veteran described by one soldier as "mean as hell."[47]

Infantry officers had to be tough, too. One officer physically threw out two troublemakers from a squad room and then made the pair march about the post wearing a barrel accompanied by a heavy log strapped across their shoulders. Other officers and NCOs resorted to bucking and gagging rowdy men, or tying them up spread eagle, confining them in a sweat box, dunking them in a stream, loading them down with bricks and them marching them to the point of exhaustion, or hanging them up by their thumbs or wrists. Lucky ones were simply court-martialed with the most common charges being desertion, drunkenness, insubordination, disobedience, and neglect of duty.[48] Despite the harsh conditions, however, the records bear out that black troops deserted far less frequently than white troops, and kept up their morale and discipline better than their white counterparts during difficult challenges like long winter marches.[49] Perhaps one reason was that they had fewer options than whites.

As tough as these hurdles were, the infantry had an additional problem. Despite the fine record established by the men of the Twenty-fourth and other infantry units, many leading military authorities like General Sherman believed that cavalry was the only arm capable of dealing effectively with the highly mobile

---

[47]Nevin, 64.

[48]Utley, 84.

[49]Nevin, 25.

Native Americans. This meant that the infantry was viewed as having only a minor, supporting role in the Indian wars.

Other experts had different opinions, however. For instance, infantry officers brought attention to the fact that cavalry horses quickly deteriorated after extended rigorous duty even when they were fortunate enough to receive full grain allowances.[50] Colonel William B. Hazen of the Sixth Infantry defended his branch by noting:

> After the fourth day's march of a mixed command, the horse does not march faster than the foot soldier, and after the seventh day, the foot soldier begins to outmarch the horses, and from that time on the foot soldier has to end his march earlier and earlier each day, to enable the cavalry to reach the camp the same day at all.[51]

Others pointed out that, because cavalry almost always fought dismounted, they were now merely mounted infantry and not very effective infantry at that. The reason was twofold, the critics maintained: first, the cavalry's shorter barreled carbines lacked the range of the infantry's longer barreled Springfields; and second, one trooper was always needed to hold the reins of his buddies' horses during a firefight, thus cutting down on available firepower.[52]

Infantry officers felt a bit vindicated in 1882 when the Quartermaster General of the army wrote that "Unless cavalry operate in a country well supplied with forage a large amount of wagon carriages must be furnished for forage, and in such cases cavalry is of little value except to guard its own train, and to do that in the presence of an enterprising enemy it will need the addition of infantry."[53]

------

[50]Few campaigns permitted the full grain allowances needed for what contemporaries called "American" horses. This term was used to contrast these beasts with the Native American ponies that could survive on a much more skimpy diet of prairie grass.

[51]Quoted in Utley, 49.

[52]Wooster, 33.

[53]Quoted in Utley, 49.

General Nelson Miles demonstrated in battles against Sitting Bull, Crazy Horse, and Chief Joseph that the infantry was not obsolete and was needed to act in coordination with cavalry forces, especially in mountainous terrain.[54] General Crook believed it took four mounted troopers to equal one mounted Sioux warrior because one in four of the troopers had to hold the reins for the rest. But, he considered one foot soldier armed with a Springfield rifle worth six mounted Sioux.[55]

The following report offered one of the best testimonies to the infantry, however. In 1889, troops of the Twenty-fourth, along with a detachment from the Ninth Cavalry, were ambushed by bandits in the Arizona outback while serving as payroll guard. The men of the Twenty-fourth fought so well that the paymaster later reported:

> Sergeant Brown, though shot through the abdomen did not quit the field until again wounded, this time though the arm.
> Private Burge, who was to my immediate right, received a bad wound in the hand, but gallantly held his post, resting his rifle on his fore-arm and continuing to fire with much coolness, until shot through the thigh and twice through the hat.[56]

The paymaster concluded noting:

> I was a soldier in [General U.S.] Grant's old regiment, and during the entire [Civil] war it was justly proud of its record in sixteen battles and of the reflected glory of its old Colonel, the "Great Commander," but I never witnessed better courage or better fighting than shown by these colored soldiers, on May 11, 1889, as the bullet marks on the robber positions to-day abundantly attest.[57]

---

[54]Utley 289. Wooster, 36, 181.

[55]Oliver Knight, Following the Indian Wars (Norman: University of Oklahoma Press, 1960), 249.

[56]Quoted in Katz, 217.

[57]Quoted in Katz, 217.

Though they have not received the glory lavished upon their cavalry counterparts, the foot soldiers of the Twenty-fourth were every bit as proud of the job they did and proved that they could fight well.

Tough, crude, unruly, and brave, the men of the Twenty-fourth Infantry presented quite a challenge to their new chaplain, but Allensworth was determined to work hard and make a good impression. He was well received by the regiment's commander, Colonel Zenas Bliss, and most of the other officers of the Twenty-fourth. However, the white troops of the Fifth Cavalry, which were co-located with the Twenty-fourth at Fort Supply, were not overly enthusiastic about his arrival, with some declaring that they would never salute a black officer. Allensworth was well within his rights to bring these disrespectful men up on charges, but instead he chose to preach a humorous sermon based on Hamon's refusing to salute Mordecai in the Biblical Book of Esther. His approach worked and the men of the Fifth never failed to salute him again.[58] Later when junior white officers refused to render him a salute, he chose to ignore the insult too. In time, many of these same officers were won over and approached the chaplain in an apologetic manner after witnessing his sincerity, honesty, and earnestness in performing his duty.[59]

After two years in Oklahoma, the Twenty-fourth was moved to New Mexico. The headquarters and three companies were located at Fort Bayard, while the rest of the regiment was sent to Camp San Carlos, and Forts Grant and Thomas, and Huachuca, Arizona. Most of these units were later consolidated at Fort Huachuca.[60]

The change of climate and conditions from Oklahoma to the desert country of the American Southwest was dramatic. The forts were in need of repair which meant much backbreaking labor, and, with temperatures that often soared up to 118

---

[58] Alexander, 258, 259, 263, 265.

[59] Alexander, 329.

[60] Langellier, 195.

degrees Fahrenheit, the task was not easy. Added to the repair work were additional duties such as road marches and signal exercises. One such march covered 474 miles in 29 days; and a signal practice was engaged at a distance of 406 miles.[61] The fact that many soldiers of this era turned to alcohol and prostitutes as a means of relief from such conditions was at least understandable. It does bear recording, however, that an 1889 report from the Secretary of War noted that the black units were "neat, orderly, and obedient," "seldom brought before court-martial and rarely desert."[62]

Chaplain Allensworth deserves his due in helping to maintain high morale among the soldiers. He set out to achieve his goals in several ways. First and foremost he was their pastor. Army regulations specified only that he conduct a religious service each Sunday; the form was left to each chaplain's discretion. No chapel existed and so his services were held in a schoolroom. No hymn books, Bibles or other religious material were available, either.[63] Nevertheless, through hard work, prayer, and resourceful creativity, his religious services were quite popular with the officers and men. He wrote that "on the Sabbath our garrison is as quiet as if governed by a code of Connecticut Blue-laws."[64]

As an army chaplain, Allensworth, a Baptist minister, had to minister to all troops regardless of their religious preference. The pluralistic spirit was not common among religious groups of the nineteenth century, which competed for souls and believed that they alone had a monopoly on truth. Thus, it took a unique individual to minister to persons of all faith groups as an army chaplain. When a white civilian employee of the post came to Allensworth to have his child baptized, an inquiry revealed that the man was Roman Catholic. When asked if he wanted his baby

---

[61]Fowler, 81, 82. Fletcher, 81-81.

[62]Fowler, 87. Langellier, 195.

[63]Alexander, 260, 261.

[64]Report to the AGO from Allensworth dated 4 June 1892, Allensworth File, Record Group 94, National Archives.

baptized in the Church of Rome the man replied in the affirmative. Allensworth went into the nearby town and brought the local priest back with him in order to ensure that the infant was baptized properly. Later that same month, a Methodist soldier requested his child be christened, too, and so Allensworth arranged to have the local Methodist minister perform the ceremony. By being sensitive to the diverse religious needs of his men, Allensworth did much to keep the spirit and morale high.[65]

On another occasion he acted as a public defender for a soldier accused of burglary. The young trooper was caught by a guard coming out of an officer's house late one night. When questioned, he admitted his guilt, but Allensworth did not believe him. Upon further inquiry, he got the man to admit that he had actually been visiting the maid that night and had tripped when trying to leave which alarmed the officer's wife, thus leading her to call the guard. Allensworth successfully convinced the jury that the trooper came to tryst, not to rob, and the young soldier was acquitted.[66]

He also provided lectures, which were very popular among the men. Some were on the same themes he had delivered to audiences on his New England lecture tour, namely: industry, fortitude, fidelity, gentleness, and prudence.[67] In an article in the *New York Age*, he expressed another theme that he shared with Booker T. Washington.[68] Allensworth wrote that the main problems suffered by the black race were due to poor leadership within the black community. He lamented that whenever such men, "fat indolents and dangerous libertines" he called them, were rebuked, those doing the criticizing were themselves attacked as being "stuck up and trying to

---

[65]Alexander, 273.

[66]Fletcher, 105.

[67]Report to the AGO from Allensworth, dated 4 June 192, Allensworth File, Record Group 94, National Archives.

[68]The entire article is reprinted in Alexander, 265-267.

get away from the race." In Bookerite fashion, Allensworth believed that true leaders should set a good example so that African Americans could "pull themselves up by their own bootstraps." As he noted, "We must improve our social status, we must have social distinctions; we must draw a line between the refined and unrefined."[69] If African Americans distinguished among themselves, the Bookerites hoped that whites would make the same distinctions when judging blacks. The problem was that most whites looked at all blacks in a derogatory way.

The soldiers were not the only ones elated with the hard work of this black officer. After an eight-day inspection tour of Fort Bayard, Major A.R. Chafee of the Inspector General's Office noted in his report that Chaplain Allensworth "is credited with being very energetic and greatly interested in his duties."[70] His *alma mater*, Roger Williams University, was delighted as well and in 1887 conferred upon him an honorary Master of Arts degree for being a "Christian gentleman and a man of scholastic habits."[71]

But what impressed people the most were Allensworth's endeavors in the field of education. While at Fort Supply, he basically just continued the educational work begun by his predecessors, Chaplains Schultz and Laverty; but at Fort Bayard he began his own program. The army now required enlisted troops to attend classes which meant that he had 118 new students to absorb. Allensworth went to work and established a well-organized school which utilized the brightest soldiers as teachers.[72] He also created a graded course of study for both soldiers and their children entitled, *Outline of Course of Study, and the Rules Governing Post Schools of Fort Bayard,*

---

[69]Alexander, 256, 257.

[70]From an extract from the reports of the Inspector General's Officer. Allensworth File, Record Group 94, National Archives.

[71]Stover, Up From Handyman, 55.

[72]Powell, 25.

N.M. This pamphlet described in detail his program and each course of study for every grade level by day, time, and subject matter.[73]

Allensworth was also an innovator. Not just content with traditional teaching methods, he purchased a stereopticon, which was a special slide or movie projector, which greatly enhanced his lectures through the use of visual aides. When he had no more space in his chapel/schoolroom, he requested that an old gun storage shed be converted into an additional classroom. When the army could not provide him the textbooks, slates, pencils, etc., he needed for his students, he obtained donations from civilians or procured them from money out of his own pocket. He even had soldiers with exceptional teaching abilities from other posts transferred to his own for temporary teaching duty with his men. He also went beyond the basic reading, writing, and arithmetic courses required by the army and promoted the teaching of vocational skills, such as telegraphy, printing, baking, clerkship, and cooking.[74] Like Booker T. Washington, Allensworth believed that such skills were needed by his fellow blacks if they were to succeed as freedmen.

Word of his efforts soon spread and was met with enthusiasm from both inside and outside the army. A letter in the *Army-Navy Journal* stated that if all officers did as much as Allensworth in the field of education that "there could be no question anywhere of starting up a school for lack of paraphernalia or suitable teachers."[75] After an 18 March 1892 inspection, Major A. R. Chaffee noted that "Chaplain Allensworth is justly entitled to praise for his earnestness and seemingly good work in his school."[76] Brigadier General Cook, Commander of the Department

---

[73] Allensworth File, Record Group 94, National Archives.

[74] Sergeant Major Rudi Williams, "Chaplain Allensworth and his all-Black colony," Monmouth Messenger (3 February 1989), p.7. Billington, 162, 163.

[75] Army-Navy Journal, 30 November 1889, p. 278 quoted in Stover, Up From Handyman, p.55.

[76] Extract from the reports of inspections by the Inspector General, Allensworth File, Record Group 94, National Archives.

of Arizona, was so impressed that he wrote to the Department of the Army that Allensworth's program should be adopted army-wide. Thanks in large part to his efforts, the army passed new regulations in 1889 that promoted more efforts in education for troops.[77]

In 1891, the National Education Association invited him to speak at its convention in Toronto, Canada. In his address entitled, "History and Progress of Education in the U.S. Army," he stated:

> In the earlier history of the army it was considered sufficient for a soldier to be able to march and handle his gun. This view has been changed and it is now a recognized fact that to be a good soldier a man must be a good citizen, therefore the government aims at giving its soldiers a fair...education...It does this not only with a view of utilizing their increased knowledge in its defense, but with a further view of returning him to civil life a more intelligent citizen and well disciplined for the business of life.[78]

That the army possessed an ulterior motive was somewhat of an overstatement on Allensworth's part. However, because of his efforts the army adopted, in time, his vision.

Allensworth's talk was a success with the members of the National Education and the press. A reporter for *The Toronto Globe* wrote that the chaplain was "a fluent speaker as well as a graceful writer." Because of this triumph, he was invited to the World Columbian Exposition in Chicago in 1893 to superintend an exhibit on religious organizations.[79]

In 1896, due in part to his efforts, Allensworth and the men of the Twenty-fourth were transferred to Fort Douglas, Utah. Like all the black regiments, the Twenty-fourth had always been deliberately stationed at the roughest, most remote

---

[77]Foner, 64. Hourihan, 3.

[78]Allensworth File, Record Group 94, National Archives. Allensworth traveled to this convention at his own expense.

[79]Powell, 26.

posts far from white civilization. Many of the Twenty-fourth's officers and men asked the chaplain to use his political connections to get the unit assigned to a better location. Allensworth was somewhat reluctant to exploit his Washington, D.C. ties, but when a soldier left the unit rather than reenlist because of the bad posts the chaplain wrote an article to the *New York Age* describing in detail the reasons the soldier departed. Allensworth then forwarded the article, accompanied by a letter he wrote to Congressman John M. Langston, requesting the latter's assistance. The congressman spoke with General Nelson Miles who promised that all the black regiments' "interests should, while he was in command, be duly and impartially considered and promoted." When the next yearly unit changes were made, Miles ordered the Twenty-fourth to replace to Sixteenth Infantry at Fort Douglas.[80]

While the officers and men of the Twenty-fourth cheered the transfer, the good citizens of nearby Salt Lake were up in arms at the prospect of black troops coming to their state. An article in *The Salt Lake Tribune* warned that drunken colored soldiers would try to force themselves into train cars with white ladies and gentlemen. The article stated that black troops were afforded their rights, but to force them on the white citizens of Salt Lake would produce "a strong revulsion in the minds of the best people in the city."[81] Ironically, in the same year, 1896, the Supreme Court case of *Plessy v. Ferguson* firmly established the Jim Crow principle of "separate but equal" in railroad cars and other public accommodations.

Following his typical pattern, Allensworth declined confronting this racism directly and instead wrote his Washington, D.C. friends that he would use all of his influence to ensure that the troops were on their best behavior. He then personally addressed each soldier in the regiment known for heavy drinking and implored him to conduct himself in an orderly manner. Once the unit reached Utah, the chaplain followed up his words with a great deal of personal attention to the men. He even

---

[80] Alexander, 289-291.

[81] Alexander, 292.

stayed in Salt Lake a few days each month around payday to make certain that any soldier caught drinking was immediately returned to the fort. Allensworth also visited the head of the Mormon church in order to promote better relations. The chaplain's efforts were successful and one year later the editor of *The Salt Lake Tribune* wrote an article praising Allensworth and the men of the Twenty-fourth.[82]

His educational work, both academic and vocational, continued among the 120 soldiers enrolled in his new school at Fort Douglas. The chaplain could no doubt take pride in the fact that the graduates of this clerkship class were forthwith assigned to positions in the offices of the commanding officer, adjutant, quartermaster, and commissary officer. The *Army-Navy Journal* noted that, because of its success, Allensworth's school should be duplicated at other posts.[83]

When news reached Fort Douglas that war with Spain had been declared in April 1898, Allensworth and his men of the Twenty-fourth made preparations for deployment to Cuba. But the chaplain's fate was to remain behind in the United States like all the other black chaplains except for William T. Anderson. Allensworth took the opportunity to address the men before they departed, though, while mounted upon his horse. Unlike many in the African American community who raised serious questions over whether or not blacks should participate in America's war of imperialism, Allensworth offered his full support, with an oratorical flourish:

> Soldiers and Comrades: Fate has turned the war dogs loose and you have been called to the front to avenge an insult to your country's flag. Before leaving this lovely home, leaving family and friends behind, I will way to you, 'Quit yourselves like men and fight.' Keep in mind that the eyes of the world will be upon you and expect great things of you. You have the opportunity to answer favorable the

---

[82]Alexander, 292-294. Many Mormons felt that the deployment of black troops to Douglas was punishment by the federal government because of their reluctance to give up polygamy in order to achieve statehood. Mormons of this era did not believe that blacks would be permitted to enter heaven.

[83]Stover, Up From Handyman, 57.

question, 'Will the Negro fight.' Quit yourselves like men and fight. - Remember the Maine![84]

The men of the Twenty-fourth would not disappoint their chaplain.

While the men of the Twenty-fourth were supporting Teddy Roosevelt and his "Rough Riders" up San Juan Hill, Allensworth, on the other hand, was being ordered to recruiting duty. He served in Louisville, Nashville, and Tuskegee and was responsible for recruiting 465 new soldiers for the ranks of the Twenty-fourth, thus raising the total number to 1,272.[85]

The brief war was soon over and the men returned to Utah for an even briefer rest. The very next year, the regiment was ordered to the Philippines to put down the insurrection led by Emilio Aguinaldo, a former U.S. ally. Because the United States had granted Cuba its independence after the successful conclusion of the Spanish-American War, Aguinaldo and many other Filipinos assumed that the Philippines would be given its freedom, too. Instead, the United States annexed the Philippines in the Treaty of Paris of 1899, and ordered Aguinaldo and his supporters out of Manila. American racial slurs and a paternalistic attitude only served to heighten tensions. When fighting between U.S. forces and the Filipino rebels broke out, it was particularly brutal: U.S. soldiers burned villages, destroyed food supplies, tortured prisoners, and placed Filipino civilians in reconcentration camps.[86] Ultimately, five thousand Americans and more than two hundred thousand Filipinos died as a result of the fighting.[87]

---

[84]Alexander, 319.

[85]Langellier, 201.

[86]Ironically, such brutal tactics against the Cuban rebels by the Spanish general, Valeriano Weyler, had been a major factor in the U.S. decision to launch the Spanish-American War.

[87]Mary Beth Norton, et al. A People and a Nation: A History of the United States, 4th edition (Boston: Houghton Mifflin Company, 1994), 674. Eric Foner and John A. Garraty, ed., The Reader's Companion to American History (Boston: Houghton Mifflin Company, 1991), 836.

Allensworth was deployed to the Philippines along with his unit. Racism in the U.S. Army was rampant in the Philippines and was directed against both blacks and Filipinos, but Chaplain Allensworth did not "consider himself charged with the settlement of political or social questions" and instead concentrated on "well, smaller things."[88] He quickly went to work conducting worship services, delivering mail to hospital patients, encouraging churches to write soldiers with no families, and establishing another school for the men. He also helped to create the first Christian Endeavor Society in the Philippines. But many soldiers remembered him best for the entertaining lectures he gave at the Y.M.C.A. The *Manila Times* reported that one well attended lecture, "Gems from the Life of Napoleon" was quite "interesting and amusing," especially because of the way the chaplain utilized aspects of Napoleon's life as a model for American soldiers. Other lectures were humorous such as "Humbugs" and "The Rise and Fall of the Kiss."[89]

While in the Philippines, Allensworth injured his knee twice and was stricken with repeated attacks of aphasia which eventually required his return to the United States. He was assigned to Camp Reynolds (later Fort McDowell), California where he was joined by his wife and daughter. He remained in California until the Twenty-fourth returned from the Philippines in August 1902.[90]

The rest of Chaplain Allensworth's days in the army were spent at Forts Harrison, Missoula, and Assinniboine, Montana. In 1904 Congress passed an act that permitted chaplains to be promoted to the rank of major for the first time. Fifty-seven clergymen were on duty that year, but only four were deemed "exceptionally efficient" and advanced to that rank; Allensworth was one of the four promoted. In

---

[88] Allensworth File, Record Group 94, National Archives. Chaplain T.G. Steward of the Twenty-fifth Infantry would take a much more confrontational approach.

[89] Stover, 127.

[90] Langellier, 201, 202. The insurrection was broken with the capture of Aguinaldo in 1901, although fighting continued sporadically for months thereafter. Several hundred thousand Filipinos were killed.

1905, Congress passed another act which allowed chaplains to advance to lieutenant colonel. On 7 April 1906 Allensworth was one of only two chaplains selected for promotion. As a lieutenant colonel, he was the highest ranking black officer in the history of the United States Army. A black newspaper, the *Cleveland Gazette*, stated that his final promotion was the "highest honor ever given to an Afro-American."[91]

Allensworth retired from the army in 1907. He was now 64 years old and could have been content to sit back and enjoy his retirement in ease, but he had other plans and embarked on a quest 1908 to create an all-black community in the San Joaquin Valley, thirty miles north of Bakersfield, California. The town, soon named Allensworth, started out with a purchase of twenty acres and grew to eighty acres in a few short years complete with a school, post office, library, and train station. Allensworth's dream was that this community would be a refuge where African Americans could improve themselves and develop skills free from white prejudice. The town prospered until tragedy struck in 1914. That year Allensworth was killed by a motorcycle in Los Angeles. That unfortunate event, coupled with a chronic lack of water, eventually spelled doom for the town. Today it is a state park.[92]

Allen Allensworth lived a truly remarkable life. He had risen from slavery to become an officer and gentleman in the United States Army and was the first black to reach the rank of lieutenant colonel. His work in the field of education became an army-wide model and was recognized by his civilian peers. His all-black community, Allensworth, was the first of its kind in the state of California. In achieving these goals, he faced much prejudice and discrimination and yet never wavered in his quest to improve the lives of his black troops.

---

[91]Allensworth held the distinction of obtaining the highest rank for an African American until Charles Young was promoted to full colonel during World War I. Louis Carter became the first black chaplain to become a full colonel in 1936, and Chaplain Matthew Zimmerman was promoted to Brigadier General and made the Army's Chief of Chaplains in 1989. Hourihan, 4.

[92]Newsletter from the Colonel Allensworth States Historic Park.

A religious progressive, he strove to modify African American Christianity so that the faith could deal with the new challenges facing black churches in the era of ecclesiastical freedom. Allensworth held fast to the black folk tradition which was the heart of African American Christianity, but he made certain that his congregation could deal effectively with church budgets, taxes, and other responsibilities facing the freedman's churches.

Allensworth also attempted to deal with double-consciousness by utilizing the accommodationist approach of Booker T. Washington. By working hard to improve his educational deficiencies and overcome his "Southern Brogue," he believed that whites would be persuaded to judge him differently than the ignorant, uneducated blacks. He then implemented his Bookerite philosophy by turning the army into a first-class training school for black soldiers where they learned basic skills and the industrial arts. His all-black community in California was created for the same purpose.

Unlike Plummer and Prioleau, Allensworth did not confront racial insults directly, opting instead to "turn the other cheek." Such a reaction ran the risk of being subservient to whites, but his goal was reconciliation, not conquest. Today, his methods might be criticized for being too subservient to whites, but, like Booker T. Washington, Allensworth believed that a gradual, accommodationist approach offered the best opportunity for success. The accommodationist approach was controversial and remains so even to the present, but as a member of the armed forced he had little choice as Chaplain Plummer learned. As Allensworth's biographer noted:

> ...it was his ambition to prove to the world that a Negro could be an officer and a gentleman; and further, to educate the Negro soldier up to the point where he could prove himself a man and a soldier, and to educate the Caucasian down to a point of recognizing that a negro possesses sufficient manly virtues to comply with all of the conditions required by the Army regulations and military custom.[93]

---

[93] Alexander, 321.

Indeed, Allensworth was a model as preacher, soldier, and citizen to both blacks and whites.

CHAPTER VI

CHAPLAIN THEOPHILUS G. STEWARD,

TWENTY-FIFTH UNITED STATES INFANTRY

Theophilus Gould Steward, of the Twenty-fifth United States Infantry, was the third African American chaplain commissioned in the period from 1884 to 1901. His background differed significantly from those of the other Buffalo soldier chaplains in several particulars. First, he was the only northerner, the only one freeborn, and the only one who was the product of a long line of racially mixed marriages. He was also intriguing because his approach to racism was very different from that of Chaplain Allensworth, which makes for an interesting comparison. While Allensworth belonged to the Bookerite school, Steward, although an assimilationist, too, was much more confrontational in his reaction to prejudice, thus dealing with his own doubleness in a very different manner. Finally, he was by far the most prolific and serious writer of the five, which facilitates access to, and an understanding of, his views. Indeed, while most chaplains were primarily men of action, Steward was first and foremost a thinker.

Theophilus Gould Steward, the fourth of six children, was born 23 April 1843 in Gouldtown, New Jersey to James and Rebecca Gould Steward. James' family had immigrated to the United States from Haiti in 1824. He was orphaned at an early age and was subsequently reared by Rebecca's uncle, Elijah Gould. Rebecca was a descendant of the founder of Gouldtown, a black man named Benjamin Gould. In 1683, Gould had married Elizabeth Adams, the white granddaughter of English Lord John Fenwick, much to the horror of her family. Later descendants married whites,

Native Americans, or mulattos. Thus, most of the residents of Gouldtown were racially mixed, including Theophilus Gould Steward. Gouldtown soon developed a reputation as being inhabited by "high yellow" people who kept to themselves.[1]

Being racially mixed had a profound impact on Steward to the point that it formed, in the words of one writer, the "core of his intellectual and spiritual life." It also defined his sense of "doubleness." Steward and his family were so light skinned that they could have passed as whites, but instead, they identified themselves as African Americans. The long-held practice of racial intermarriages in Gouldtown was a tradition based on mutual love and consent as opposed to the forced situations in the slave quarters of the American South. Later, Steward would be intensely proud of his family heritage and thought that no one should be discriminated against on the basis of race. He would grow up to believe strongly in racial pluralism and the integration of African Americans into American society. He would even argue for the integration of public schools when such calls were not popular with either blacks or whites. Because of the fairness of their skin, however, the entire family was always caught between both the black and white worlds, discriminated against by each.[2]

Steward was taught discipline and hard work by his father who compelled the boy to labor long hours in the family garden. His mother taught him to be a critical thinker and to challenge orthodoxy. Rebecca Gould Steward was an unusual woman for her day. Although having little formal education, she was a prolific reader who studied Milton, Shakespeare, Greek philosophers, and especially the Bible. She had a critical mind which she used to challenge orthodox religion through analytical

---

[1]T.G. Steward, Gouldtown: A Very Remarkable Settlement of Ancient Date (Philadelphia: J.B. Lippincott Company, 1913), 50, 95. Theophilus Gould Steward, Memoirs of Mrs. Rebecca Steward (Philadelphia: Publication Department of the A.M.E. Church, 1877), 18.

[2]Albert George Miller, "Theophilus Gould Steward, 1843-1924: Striving for an African-American Theology and Civil Society in the Nadir Period" (Ph.D. diss., Princeton University, 1994), 14, 16-20, 91.

194

papers on theology, a trait she passed on to Theophilus. Later one minister stated that, "her writing will give her a rank in the future that scarcely one minister...in a thousand will get."[3]

The emphasis on learning and religion in the Steward household made a great impact on young Theophilus. In 1860, he joined the A.M.E. church and was soon called into the ministry. He later gave two different versions of how this transpired. In his first of two autobiographies, *My First Four Years in the Itinerary* (published in 1876), he wrote that he was called to preach in a vision but hesitated for nine months "until the necessity was laid upon me, and I felt the salvation of my own soul depending upon complying. I felt truly the words, 'woe is me if I preach not the Gospel.'" In his 1921 autobiography, *Fifty Years in the Gospel Ministry*, he wrote that a reading of Baxter's *Saint's Rest* and the influence of the Reverend Joseph H. Smith convinced him to enter the ministry. In either case, he was licensed to exhort in April 1862 and received his preaching license on September 26, 1863.[4]

Steward wanted to go South to begin his ministry but was advised against it until the war ended. In 1864, he received his first assignment which was the Macedonia A.M.E. Church in South Camden, New Jersey. For one year, he served this church, taught at a local normal school, and bided his time.[5]

In 1865, the war finally ended and with it the prewar prosperity of the southern states. Many cities were reduced to rubble, railroad lines were destroyed, farms were left unattended. While the slaves were now free, they were also left without work, food or homes. Many northern white Christians responded to the needs of the freedman by volunteering through the Freedman's Bureau, American Missionary Association, and other like-minded groups. Yankee missionaries quickly

---

[3] William Seraile, <u>Voice of Dissent: Theophilus Gould Steward (1843-1934) and Black America</u> (Brooklyn, N.Y.: Carlson Publishing, 1991), 4.

[4] Seraile, 6. 7.

[5] Miller, 4, 5.

became frustrated, however, with African American Christian practices such as shouting, which one denounced as "heathenish habits." One such missionary was appalled by the "unchristian" behavior demonstrated by an African American woman at a black funeral when she "clapped her hands, threw them over her head screaming 'glory to God'...[while] dancing up and down in front of the pulpit."[6]

Partly as a result of such missionary disdain, the A.M.E. Church quickly "gained ascendancy over its white-dominated rivals, both northern and southern, in the competition for the allegiance of black Methodists."[7] Indeed, 42,000 black Methodists had worshiped in biracial churches in South Carolina before the war; only 600 remained ten years later. As one scholar has noted, "throughout the South, approximately 240,000 blacks would leave to join the A.M.E. church."[8]

Steward joined Bishop Daniel Payne on a missionary journey to the Reconstruction South as part of the A.M.E.'s effort to reach out to the freedmen. Conditions were extremely difficult and lack of food was a real problem in this war-torn land. Steward even became ill at one point because of the deprivations, but he persevered. Ordained a deacon and elder by Payne on 15 May 1865 in Charleston, South Carolina, he was commissioned to serve at missions in Georgetown, Beaufort, Summerville, and Marion. In 1866, he was appointed pastor of Morris Brown Church and also taught school in Charleston.[9]

---

[6]Eric Foner, Reconstruction: America' Unfinished Revolution: 1863-1877 (New York: Harper and Row, 1988), 91.

[7]Eventually, though, the A.M.E..Church was overshadowed by the black Baptist churches because many Southern blacks resisted the more sedate worship style and heavier emphasis on an educated ministry stressed by the A.M.E. The decentralized nature of Baptist polity with it greater freedom than the episcopal system of the A.M.E was another attractive feature of the Baptist denomination. See: Foner, 92.

[8]Seraile, 11.

[9]Steward, Fifty Years in the Gospel Ministry: From 1864 to 1914 (Philadelphia: A.M.E. Book Concern, n.d.), 166, 167, 279, 280. Seraile, 14-17. Discrimination continued even in the Freedman's Bureau and American Missionary Association which both paid black and female teachers on average ten dollars less than their white counterparts.

Steward met Elizabeth Gadson while in Charleston and the two were soon married. The union produced eight sons: three died early, but the rest went on to graduate from college, including two who completed degrees at Harvard. One son, Frank, served as a captain in the Forty-ninth Volunteer Regiment during the Spanish-American War.[10]

The next several years were busy ones for Steward. He was assigned to the Georgia Conference in 1867 and assumed the duties of pastor of the A.M.E. church in the town of Lumpkin. Wanting churches of their own, free from white paternalism, the freedman created many new church structures or purchased and renovated abandoned white facilities. Thus, Steward helped build the Lumpkin church literally from the ground up. The next year he succeeded Henry McNeal Turner as pastor of the church in Marion, after Turner entered Reconstruction politics. Steward worked in politics as well by helping to write the Georgia Republican Platform in 1868 and leading a successful protest by Americus, Georgia freedmen against compulsory work contracts. He found time to serve as cashier at the Freedman's Bank in Marion and speculate in cotton at the same time. He also wrote numerous articles in *The Christian Recorder*, the A.M.E.'s weekly magazine.[11]

Steward was transferred to Delaware in 1872 and remained there for the next couple of years save for a brief stint as a missionary to Haiti. His experience in Haiti was unpleasant due to his ignorance of Haitian culture, his homesickness, and poor health. Steward was sent next to Philadelphia to serve at the Zion Mission A.M.E. Church. During his stay in that city he took the opportunity to further his formal

---

[10]Steward, Fifty Years, 166, 167, 279, 280.

[11]Miller, 6. For more on the efforts of the freedmen to establish their own independent churches see the Autobiography of Bishop Isaac Lane, LL.D. with a Short History of the A.M.E. Church in American and of Methodism (Nashville: Publishing House of the A.M.E. Church South, 1916) and My Southern Home: or, The South and Its People (Boston: A.G. Brown and Company, 1880). Logan and Winston, 570.

education by attending the Episcopal Divinity School, from which he graduated with honors in 1883.[12]

Over the next several years, he pastored numerous churches in Philadelphia, Baltimore, and even the prestigious Metropolitan A.M.E. Church in Washington, D.C. He also found time to write several scholarly books and articles, some of which brought him into conflict with the conservative elements of his denomination.

Two of the most controversial were his *Genesis Re-Read* and *The Divine Attributes*, which placed Steward in the more liberal camp theologically.[13] By the late nineteenth century the writings of James Hutton in the *Theory of Earth*, Sir Charles Lyell's *Principles of Geology*, and especially Charles Darwin's *Origin of the Species* and *The Descent of Man* had advanced new scientific thinking on the origins of the world and humanity. These ideas clashed with the Genesis Creation account and caused much consternation among Christian thinkers. Along with this, and in many respects going hand in hand, came the development of the so-called "high criticism" of the Bible. Advocates in this camp found inconsistencies and contradictions in the Bible and theorized that the holy writ was actually a very human product made up of numerous sources from diverse points of view all woven together by editors with their own particular themes in mind. Christian scholars now became divided into two camps: conservatives who held fast and firm to the older view; and liberals who sought to reconcile these new scientific and scholarly findings with Christianity.[14] Most ministers in the A.M.E. Church were conservative; Steward was

---

[12]Miller, 7. Seraile, 51, 52.

[13]T.G. Steward, Genesis Re-Read: or the Latest Conclusions of Physical Science Viewed in Their Relation to the Mosaic Record. To which is Annexed an Important Chapter on the Direct Evidences of Christianity by the Bishop J.P. Campbell, D.D., LL.D. (Philadelphia: A.M.E. Book Rooms, 1885). The Divine Attributes: Being An Examination of What is Said of God with Relation to Nature and Sentiment, and Rational Creatures, with Special Treatment of Omnipresence, with Analysis and Notes (Philadelphia; Christian Recorder Print, 1884).

[14]Charles Hodge of Princeton retorted in his What is Darwinism? that Darwinism was atheism because the theory of natural selection contradicted the omnipotence and omniscience of God as sovereign. Many in the A.M.E. Church like Daniel Payne and Benjamin Tanner agreed. For more

not. In *Genesis Re-Read*, he challenged traditional theology which stated that the biblical book of Genesis was a divinely inspired work dictated to Moses. He clearly sided with the new higher criticism school which countered that Moses penned it utilizing ancient sources.[15] Steward wrote:

> Moses compiled two traditions or blended two documents, - the one Elohistic (from Elohim) the other Yahvistic (from Jehovah). This would indicate two shades of early religion, a Yahvistic and an Elohistic, and of these, the Elohistic would appear earlier.[16]

He went on to acknowledge the mythical nature of the Genesis creation account, adding that because Moses had not been present at the beginning, and had received his information secondhand from God either "directly or indirectly," then part of it could be wrong. However, he believed that not all of Genesis was inaccurate, indeed, much was correct.[17]

On the other hand, while Steward respected the new science, he did not accept it without critical evaluation either. In the end, he believed that evolution was simply God's way of doing business, and that the supremacy of the Bible was not shaken but strengthened by the new sciences:

> How will we account for that given condition upon which evolution begins? Whence came those first elements and how came they possessed of those exact possibilities which are evolved...? Evolution cannot tell, and we may reassert with increased boldness that for all evolution has yet shown, Moses may have yet spoken the exact truth

---

on this subject see George M. Marsden, Fundamentalism and American Culture: The Shaping of Twentieth-Century Evangelicalism: 1870-1925 (New York: Oxford University Press, 1980).

[15] Julius Wellhausen, though not the first, is the best known nineteenth century advocate of the four source construction of the Torah generally referred to as the "Documentary Hypothesis." See: Julius Wellhausen, Prolegomena to the History of Israel. Trans. by J.S. Black and A. Menzies (Edinburgh: A & C Black, 1885). A few modern books of further interest on this study include: C.R. North, "Pentateuchal Criticism," in H.H. Rowley, ed., The Old Testament and Modern Study (Oxford: The Clarendon Press, 1951), Martin Noth, A History of Pentateuchal Transitions. Trans. by B.W. Anderson (Englewood Cliffs, N.J.: Prentice-Hall, Inc., 1972).

[16] Steward, Genesis Re-Read, 171.

[17] Steward, Genesis Re-Read, 56, 89. Miller, 76.

when he said, "In the beginning God created the heavens and the earth." Evolutionists say we do not know how the universe began; Genesis gives a direct statement of this beginning and there is nothing in evolution to interrupt out confidence into his statement.[18]

Thus, he saw no conflict between the creation account in Genesis and the theory of evolution.

Divine Attributes was written to serve as a textbook on theology and it, too, proved controversial. In it, Steward proposed a triadic theory for the existence of God. The first part of the triad was "traditional," meaning the original revelation of God to the biblical people which had faded over time. The second was "constitutional or that the idea of God was inherent to all human beings. The third, the "sensational," was the concept that nature's laws and experiences complemented the first two and supported the God-idea. These concepts poised no problems for the conservative wing of the A.M.E. Church, but Steward went further and added that God had created within all people an inherent ability to discern between good and evil free from God's assistance or guidance. Thus, in the words of one writer, "Steward's proposal came close to suggesting that humanity was ultimately independent of God."[19] Powerful A.M.E. leaders Daniel Payne and Benjamin Tanner were quick to notice his proposal and were just as quick to criticize him in the pages of *The Christian Recorder*.[20]

Steward's writings were not the only point of controversy he had with the A.M.E. establishment. He clashed with numerous leaders over the adoption of a prescribed liturgy that had been developed by J.C. Embry. This standardized liturgy included a reading of the Ten Commandments and Apostles' Creed each Sunday. Steward believed that such formalism was an "attempt to convert the church into the

---

[18]Steward, Genesis Re-Read, 96.

[19]Miller, 59. Steward, The Divine Attributes, 5, 6, 60.

[20]Miller, 60.

cathedral type" which would "result in confusion." He called for a return to freer, simpler liturgy, noting:

> ...We are getting to depend upon the externals of worship. We hear and feel the breeze, but do not see it. Early Methodism was simple, earnest and spiritual. There must be the power as well as the form of godliness in our worship. There are other churches who can furnish the formalist what his soul desires - a dead and formal worship. It is better to have the fugue tunes than a graveyard stillness, though we plead for neither.[21]

Steward's controversies did not end here, however. He also collided with the powerful Bishop Henry McNeal Turner. He had opposed Turner's nomination as bishop in 1880, due, in part, to unproven accusations of adultery leveled against Turner while the two were working in Reconstruction Georgia. Now he and Turner clashed over whether bishops should be permitted to vote at the General Conference. Steward believed that such voting privileges gave the bishops too much power; Bishop Turner did not. When Steward and his allies eventually won their point, the hostility between the two men continued.[22]

In 1881, Steward was awarded the Doctor of Divinity degree by Wilberforce University and almost won the presidency of the school in 1884. But his unorthodox writings, his critical articles denouncing the new liturgy, and his controversies with Bishop Turner, all worked to make him numerous enemies within the A.M.E. Church. By 1888, he had lost much of his visibility on the national church level. Therefore, he saw the opportunity to enter the army chaplaincy as a welcomed occasion and eagerly began work to achieve this appointment.[23]

Like all black aristocrats of this era, Steward was dependent upon powerful benefactors for assistance in helping him to resist the tide of racism and accomplish

---

[21]Quoted in Miller, 82, 83.

[22]Miller, 84-87.

[23]Miller, 87, 88. Logan and Winston, 570.

career goals that fell within the realm of the white world. Therefore, he called not only upon the aid of black U.S. Senator Blanch Kelso Bruce, but also on such whites as John Wannamaker, the faculty of the West Philadelphia Divinity School of the Protestant Episcopal Church, and others to write letters of recommendation for him. He also received an endorsement from Frederick Douglass and the A.M.E. ministers of the Baltimore area as well. Finally, on 25 July 1891, he was commissioned as the third African American chaplain since the end of the Civil War.[24]

Steward joined his unit, the Twenty-fifth United States Infantry Regiment, at Fort Missoula, Montana on 21 August 1891. He was alone since his wife and children remained behind temporarily. The Twenty-fifth Infantry Regiment had been created along with the Twenty-fourth by the Congressional Act of 3 March 1869. It was made up of the officers and men of the old Thirty-ninth and Fortieth regiments which were now consolidated. By late April 1869, the Twenty-fifth had its full complement of personnel which meant it totaled 1,045 soldiers. The Twenty-fifth was initially appointed occupation duty in Louisiana.[25]

D. Eglinton Barr was the Twenty-fifth Infantry's first chaplain. Barr, a white man, was an Episcopal priest who had been appointed rector of St. John's Church in Baton Rouge, Louisiana by Bishop Leonidas Polk in 1860. When the Civil War broke out, Polk joined the Confederate cause, while Barr stayed with the Union. Later, Barr became a chaplain in the 81st U.S.C.T. and was captured at one point by the Confederates. As chaplain of the Twenty-fifth after the war, Barr worked hard to educate the men of his unit even conducting classes at night in his quarters for

---

[24]Seraile, 11.

[25]Rodenbough and Haskin quoted in John M. Carroll, ed., The Black Military Experience in the West (New York: Liveright, 1971), 95, 96.

those who had duty during the day. This dedicated minister was missed after he resigned in 1872.[26]

George Mullins, another white man and a Disciples of Christ pastor, was Chaplain Barr's replacement. Mullins was not happy at being assigned to the all-black unit and seriously considered resigning. He thought that white soldiers were superior to blacks and that the latter were "generally of that abject servile disposition which does just what is absolutely necessary, and nothing more."[27] Mullins went on to become a significant innovator in the field of education in the army, but the negative attitude he displayed toward African Americans meant that his replacement, Chaplain Steward, had his work cut out for him.

In May 1870, the Twenty-fifth had been redeployed to Texas where it remained until 1880. Like all infantry units of the period, the men of the Twenty-fifth spent less time than their cavalry comrades fighting and more time guarding posts, and building and repairing forts, roads, bridges, and telegraph lines -- duties that actually worked to increase ministerial opportunities for the regimental chaplain. Sometimes the soldiers were assigned escort duty which they performed mounted. Other times they were assigned the task of guarding the stagecoach lines' remount stations on the Texas frontier.[28]

The usually boring duty at remount stations was occasionally interrupted with some excitement such as the incident at Central Station, Texas near Fort Stockton. Sergeant Benjamin Stow of the Twenty-fifth and three other soldiers were attacked by a party of Native Americans bent on stealing the station's horses. However, the ensuing firefight claimed no casualties, he reported:

---

[26]Earl F. Stover, Up From Handyman: The United States Army Chaplaincy, 1865-1920 (Washington, D.C.: Office of the Chief of Chaplains Department of the Army, 1977), 13-15.

[27]Stover, 49.

[28]Arlen Fowler, The Black Infantry in the West, 1869-1891 (Westport, Connecticut: Greenwood Publishing, 1971), 23, 24.

After firing ten minutes, they went off and then came back, we drove them off again, when they were joined by the party from the hill and all went off towards the Pecos River. There were fifteen in the party attacking the station...I know of no loss on either side.[29]

Infantrymen of the Twenty-fifth did not mind guarding the remount stations except for the fact that the drivers would not permit off-duty black troops to ride when carrying white passengers. This discriminatory policy meant that the soldiers were compelled to walk back to their respective forts. It was a sad commentary that these men were deemed competent to guard the stage coaches, and yet were not good enough to ride in them when occupied by whites. White Lieutenant William R. Shafter complained to the El Paso Mail Lines about this discrimination, and the fact that neither food nor shelter was provided for these isolated army guards. Sometimes the men themselves, fought back, as in the case of a sergeant of the Twenty-fifth who placed an abusive El Muerto station master under arrest. When the sergeant reported what he had done to his commander, the white officer backed the soldier's actions fully.[30]

The men of the Twenty-fifth participated in several skirmishes with bandits and on two border raids into Mexico with the Tenth Cavalry in pursuit of the Apache leader, Victorio. As a noted historian has written, the Twenty-fifth Infantry:

> took part in most of the historic military expeditions on the Texas frontier from 1870 to 1880, yet seldom is their contribution noted by historians. Nor did they at the time receive official recognition for their service. One exception was the 1874 annual report of General Augur, commander of the Department of Texas, wherein he called attention to the good morale and spirit of the black regiments and their officers. In fact, it seems that the black infantry regiments had an esprit de corps that was often missing in the white regiments.[31]

---

[29] Quoted in Fowler, 25, 26.

[30] Fowler, 24-27, 36, 37. Rodenbough and Haskin quoted in Carroll, 97.

[31] Fowler, 33.

The regiment was transferred again in April 1880, this time to South Dakota where it remained until 1888 when it was sent to Montana. As usual, the pleas of the officers and men for fairness in giving them their turn at a "civilized" duty station like Little Rock, Arkansas, or New Orleans were rejected due to fears that white inhabitants would not tolerate the presence of black soldiers so close by. The move to the northern plains was in itself somewhat controversial because of a prevailing notion at the time that blacks could not function in cold climates due to their tropical heritage. The Quartermaster General of the Army was one who voiced such concerns, stating that the men would suffer terribly and die.[32]

The men of the regiment did not die in the cold northern plains, but rather proved that they could serve effectively anywhere the army sent them. In time, most of the nearby civilian residents came to accept them because of the protection they furnished from the occasional attacks by vagabond reservation Indians and also because of the good will provided by the Twenty-fifth's excellent musical band which local townspeople came to appreciate.[33]

The rough and tumble outback world of the Twenty-fifth was much different from the polite society to which Theophilus Steward had grown accustomed, but the long hours he had spent as a youth toiling in the family garden paid off and the new chaplain readily took to the rigors of frontier army life. He wrote, "I became possessed of the army spirit and identified myself with its discipline and training as well as its outdoor life." He actively sought to identify with the troops of the Twenty-fifth by riding horses, driving mules, hunting, fishing, gardening, and hiking. The men respected his efforts, which helped to dispel their early suspicion that he was an effete easterner.[34]

---

[32]Rodenbough and Haskin quoted in Carroll, 97. Fowler, 48, 49.

[33]Rodenbough and Haskin quoted in Carroll, 97. Fowler, 48, 49, 63, 65.

[34]Seraile, 112, 113.

The officers of the Twenty-fifth quickly came to respect Steward, too. The commander, Colonel George L. Andrews, wrote that the new chaplain was "well educated, gentlemanly, refined and respected by all. He assumed his duties with zeal and prosecuted them with intelligence and the results will be satisfactory." Unlike the treatment Chaplain Plummer received in the Ninth, Andrews and his wife treated Steward as a complete equal and even invited him to live in their home until his quarters were ready. Mrs. Andrews took the chaplain into the nearby town to introduce him to the local merchants. Allen Allensworth was impressed with Steward and wrote the *Christian Recorder*, "your church needed just such a man to represent it in the army [for]...you have but little idea how much good for the race and cause of Christ, he can and is doing where he is, as chaplain."[35]

Like all chaplains of the era, Steward's duties were diverse: post treasure, librarian, teacher, and of course, pastor. He was required to submit a monthly report to the Adjutant General's office. Most were like the one he filed on 31 January 1892, in which he reported a rough average of twenty-eight students present for his 2:30 p.m. Sunday School class, and sixty-eight present for the 7:30 p.m. worship service. He also led a Thursday night Temperance Meeting in which 157 were present, and found time to make nine visits to soldiers in the infirmary, one visit to the guardhouse, one to a local church, and one to a nearby Native American Reservation.[36] The rest of that year followed the same pattern, but Steward also went on to help to establish a Literary Society, work with the local civilian pastor at the pastor's request, and preach for some former members of the Twenty-fifth, along with

---

[35]Chaplain T.G. Steward File, Record Group 94, National Archives. Seraile, 113. Stover, Up From Handyman, 91.

[36]Steward File, Report to the Adjutant General's Office dated 31 January 1892, Record Group 94, National Archives.

their families, who had settled nearby. Sometimes he held joint services with local civilian ministers, the Reverends A.D. Raleigh and Clark.[37]

Steward's only major complaint that first year was low chapel attendance. The regiment's commander Colonel Andrews, always attended and his wife was a very active member. His retirement and subsequent departure from Fort Missoula led Steward to note, "both are very greatly missed in out Sunday evening services."[38] In fact, all the officers and their families usually participated in the worship services, but many of the troops did not. He blamed this lack of participation on the enlisted men's youth. The procurement of religious books by the soldiers themselves, and a heartfelt reading from *The Story of the Gospel* by Steward's seven year old son, Walter, helped to increase the numbers substantially.[39] But in the summer months "baseball fever" gave the chaplain serious competition, causing attendance to drop from a high of ninety-seven down to forty-one.[40] Therefore, like all chaplains Steward ended up providing most of his ministry on an informal basis through personal conduct, for example, speaking with the men one-on-one at the rifle range, guardhouse, mess hall, and across his garden's fence.

Steward was also responsible for the fort's school. He was a scholar and a teacher and had always been a strong advocate of education as a way of improving the status of his race. Through education he believed that African Americans could build a culture that would be equal to and earn the respect of the rest of the world. To achieve this goal, he was convinced that African Americans need to throw off the

---

[37]Steward File, Report to the AGO dated September and November 1892, Record Group 94, National Archives.

[38]Steward File, Report to the AGO dated April 1892, Record Group 94, National Archives.

[39]Seraile, 117.

[40]Steward File, Reports to the AGO dated April and August 1892, Record Group 94, National Archives.

ignorance and superstitions of the past and move forward by continuing their educational quest. Steward wrote:

> For the colored race the era of Mumbo Jumbo, of fetishism, and Voodooism has passed away, and the African has now asserted with the true logic of a true premise, the rights to an equal recognition among the Caucasian races. He has accomplished it at last, not by any pitiful bending of the knee and supplication for the inherent rights of his race, but had for the last decades been silently and industrially working...In all things that go to show scholarship, ready oratory, words to the point, clothing the most practical and progressive theories in language, which for beauty of expression and vigorous, scintillating oratory, it would be difficult to find anything superior throughout the land.[41]

Indeed, he emphasized the educational progress already made by African Americans. With an obvious comparison in mind between Booker T. Washington and Steward, the Reverend R.C. Ransom wrote in the introduction of Steward's book *Fifty Years of Gospel Ministry* that: "Here we have an American of African decent who is not struggling, 'Up From Slavery,' but a Christian scholar who met the freedman on the very threshold of their emancipation, and who had since with singleness of devotion been guiding them and their descendants in the paths of knowledge, character and virtue."[42] Steward, who had first applied his vision to the freedman of the Reconstruction South, was now successfully teaching it to the soldiers of the Twenty-fifth Infantry Regiment.

He was very impressed with the work Allen Allensworth had done in restructuring the army education system and noted that "any soldier has a better opportunity to secure education than...thousands of young men in New York, much better than I enjoyed in my youth."[43] Steward's new found appreciation for the army

---

[41]Steward, Fifty Years of Gospel Ministry, 216, 217.

[42]Steward, Fifty Years of Gospel Ministry, xvii. Miller, 90.

[43]Seraile, 115, 116.

education system led him to write an article in *The Independent* one year after his chaplaincy began, defending the military and denying allegations that it was nothing but a "school for vice," a place "that drunkenness, licentiousness, gambling, and profanity have almost universal sway."[44] He believed that military discipline instilled personal discipline on the men and wrote:

> Military training, and the schools that are established at the post, as well as the special religious work of the chaplains, all bear directly against the prominent vices, as well as in favor of a general harmonious development of mind and body in a soldierly direction. Faithfulness, truthfulness, and a sense of responsibility and carefulness form the basis of soldier character; and these qualities are not against good morals. The soldier is trained to be firm and strong in body, to be careful in receiving an order, to be faithful and exact in executing it. Duty, duty, duty, is the ever-recurring watchword. Hence it is my opinion that the Army...is by no means a school of vice. In a special and limited sense it may be said to train men to virtue.[45]

His soldiers, he anticipated, would soon show beneficial effects of army "schooling."

Convinced that the army was the best place for young black men to learn virtue, Steward expected that when they left the army to return to the civilian world, they would instill their same moral values on the larger African American society, thus successfully uplifting the community where other institutions had failed. Indeed, he lamented that, despite the best efforts of the black church, press, and schools, African Americans had been losing ground to illiteracy, vice, and immortality. The army, on the other hand, was the best bulwark to stand strong and firm against these ills.[46]

In an article he wrote for *The Colored American*, Steward's own particular educational philosophy emerged more completely. The work, entitled "Washington

---

[44]T.G. Steward, "The Morals of the Army," The Independent, 11 February 1892, p. 7.

[45]Steward, "The Morals of the Army," p.7.

[46]Miller, 142.

and Crummell," discussed the strengths and weaknesses of the two major proponents of education and racial uplift of the day: Booker T. Washington and Alexander Crummell.[47] Steward observed that Washington's approach sought to build the African American community "from the bottom up" through an emphasis on practical kills (e.g., farming, business, etc.). Allensworth had stressed much the same. Crummell, on the other hand, focused on the mind rather than the hands and sought to uplift the race through education which concentrated on the classics, art, and culture, much liked W.E.B. Dubois advocated later. In time, Steward believed that African Americans would evolve past Washington's vision, but for now, in contrast to Crummel and Du Bois, Steward believed that both approaches were necessary and complemented each other. "For the evolution of the race," he wrote, "we need the teaching and inspiring example of both Washington and Crummell, the injunction of deep philosophy with daring enterprise, and more." [48]

But Steward went further and asserted that something else was lacking, something not addressed by either Washington or Crummell. The missing element was "the development of moral fiber and force," what Steward believed was the "glue [needed] to make a cohesive unit in the black community." Believing this moral fiber and force was exactly what the United States armed forced provided, he wrote: "nothing will do for the Negro race in this land what the rifle will do for him. War will win-now [sic] out his chaff; war will steady his nerves; toughen his fibre, assure him his limitations, harden his virtue, and lay the foundation for his character." If fifty thousand more blacks would join the army for twenty-five years, the "the race would be carried forward many centuries," because the military taught poor blacks

---

[47]Washington is more well known, but Crummell was an important black leader in his own right. Born in 1819 in New York, he was an Episcopal clergyman who advocated black pride, black liberation, and ultimately black emigration to Liberia. He later went to England and earned a degree from Cambridge University. During this time he matured as a scholar and developed a philosophy similar to Du Bois' Talented Tenth." He died in 1898. Wilmore, 113-116.

[48]Steward, "Washington and Crummell," p.6. Miller, 143, 144.

"respect for law, order, and authority," something that the "church cannot teach;...the press can only point too;...the school but fairly inculcates; [but] the army teaches and enforces." Steward asserted that soldiers became a part of a closely interlocked machine:

> There is no greater civilizing agency for the Negro, whether we look upon the conservative [Washington] or advancing side [Crummell], than the army; and it is through this instrumentality amid the strife and blood soon to engulph [sic] more or less the civilized world, that I look for the American Negro to emerge from his present lot."[49]

From the military experience, men were tempered into a stronger metal.

Despite his optimism about the benefits of army life, Steward found the next several years at Fort Missoula very taxing. In 1893, he sought permission to attend the Chicago World's Fair and to participate in the World's Parliament of Religion. His commander approved his request, but when it was forwarded to the Adjutant General, it was denied.[50] In June of the same year, his oldest son, James, died. In November, his wife passed away after a prolonged illness.[51] Elizabeth Steward was sorely missed by the soldiers of the Twenty-fifth, for she had gained their love and respect by her many kind words and deeds. Later, Steward wrote that "the year 1893 must stand in my history as the year of deep and harrowing grief."[52]

---

[49]Steward, "Washington and Crummell." See also T.G. Steward, The Army as Trained Force and The Birth of the Republic Addresses (Cincinnati: By the Author, 1904?). Miller, 146-148. Because of Steward's own acceptance in the military he seems to have overlooked the persistent racism that still existed in the armed forces, such as black units not being allowed to serve near heavily white populated areas and the difficult time blacks had in obtaining and keeping officer commissions. The court-martial cases of Henry O. Flipper and Chaplain Plummer were but two examples.

[50]Letter from Steward to the AGO dated 25 January 1983. Letter from the AGO to Steward dated 6 February 1893, Record Group 94, National Archives. The Adjutant General stated that the army only issued orders for soldiers engaged in official army business.

[51]Steward File, report to the AGO dated 30 November 1893, Record Group 94, National Archives.

[52]Seraile, 118.

The year 1894 did not start out much better with his own poor health forcing him to cancel two Sunday school services. He complained that few men were willing to make an open profession of faith for Christ though many were trying to lead upright lives. When asked about their lack of religious commitment the men stated, "I cannot lead a Christian life in the army," or, "It's no use playing the hypocrite."[53] Later that year, he was successful in convincing three local saloon keepers to keep their establishments closed during the hours of his Sunday evening worship service, which improved his attendance dramatically.[54]

Steward and the Twenty-fifth were also called out to help put down the Pullman strike of 1894. The dispute followed on the heels of the economic Panic of 1893, and started when George M. Pullman fired one-third of his Pullman Palace Car factory workers and reduced the wages of those remaining by thirty percent. Eugene V. Debs, president of the American Railway Union, ordered workers to walk off the job after Pullman officials refused to negotiate. The strike began in Chicago initially, but quickly spread west threatening to disrupt the nation's economy even further. Despite the protests of Illinois Governor John Peter Altgeld, President Grover Cleveland believed that the deployment of federal troops was necessary to uphold the orders of the federal courts, keep the mail moving, and generally enforce U.S. laws. The Twenty-fifth Infantry was dispatched to guard a section of the Northern Pacific Railroad, particularly the tunnels and bridges which were extremely vulnerable targets. Steward conducted worship services just as he had back in garrison. After the strike ended, he complimented the "valuable and heroic" soldiers for doing their duty, and praised them saying that the "whole nation reaped the

---

[53]Steward File, report to the AGO dated June and August 1894, Record Group 94, National Archives.

[54]Steward File, report to the AGO dated January 1894, Record Group 94, National Archives.

benefit" of their valiant efforts.[55] His comments reflected his philosophy of military life as a civilizing force in opposition to strikes and anarchy.

In October 1896, he married Dr. Susan McKinney while on a six week leave of absence in Brooklyn, New York. McKinney, the widow of the Reverend William McKinney, was the first black female physician in the state of New York and the third in the nation. She was also a dedicated advocate of women's rights, temperance, and church mission societies."[56]

With his new wife by his side, Steward's spirits soared and he was soon back to writing and preaching with full vigor. He edited a remarkable book entitled *Active Service: Or Religious Work Among U.S. Soldiers*, that contained contributions by several different Regular Army chaplains.[57] They discussed issues as diverse as the purpose of the chaplaincy down to the practical matter of how to minister to men in uniform. This was one of the first books of its kind and provides modern scholars with a wonderful window into the minds of chaplains and soldiers of this era.

Steward's confidence and remarkable preaching abilities were very useful in breaking down racial barriers. His skill was appreciated by the local whites who welcomed him whenever he spoke at their churches. He preached at the Missoula Baptist church for two Sundays in a row, and was even voted to speak at the Missoula Presbyterian church for an entire month while that church was looking for a new pastor. A local journalist wrote that he wished the Twenty-fifth would remain

---

[55]Quoted in Stover, 85. Maurice Matloff, ed., American Military History (Washington, D.C.: Office of the Chief of Military History, United States Army, 1969), 286. Eric Foner and John A. Garraty, eds., The Reader's Companion to American History (Boston: Houghton Mifflin Company, 1991), 889.

[56]Seraile, 120.

[57]T.G. Steward, ed., Active Service: Or Religious Work Among U.S. Soldiers (New York: United States Aid Association, no date given).

213

at Fort Missoula just so he could hear Steward speak. Amazingly, many of these same people were former Confederates.[58]

Nevertheless, in the 1890s, racism soared throughout the United States, fueled by the sense of superiority that many whites claimed over blacks. Steward always felt that he was as good as any white man, and in fact, better than most. Through his writings he sought opportunities to defend his race against these unwarranted attacks. In an essay entitled "The Colored American as a Soldier," he cited evidence from the surgeon general's 1892 report that in the military whites had a higher death rate than blacks. He also denounced claims that blacks could not serve in extreme cold weather climates with documentation proving that African American troops could and did regularly withstand temperatures of twenty to thirty degrees below zero.[59] He cited a quote from Brigadier General Wesley Merritt, formerly of the Ninth Cavalry, which read that "the day will come when there will be no more colored soldiers in the army...but [rather] the special defenders of the flag shall be simply Americans - all."[60] When denied the right to dine with visiting white Chaplain J. Newton Ritner at Missoula's Florence Hotel, Steward wrote scathing letters of protest to the local newspaper. The manager of the hotel, fearing a military boycott, wrote an apology to the chaplain.[61]

By now, Steward had spent nearly eight years with the Twenty-fifth at Fort Missoula. World events soon dictated that the nation needed the unit to deploy to Cuba in order to fight in the Spanish-American War. Unlike Allen Allensworth who embraced the war with apparent relish, Steward had some serious misgivings

---

[58]Seraile, 122.

[59]Many people inside and out of the army felt it was a grave mistake to send the Twenty-fifth to the cold climate of Montana. Gary A. Donaldson, The History of African-Americans in the Military (Malabar, Florida: Krieger Publishing Company, 1991), 59.

[60]T.G. Steward, "The Colored American as a Soldier," The United States Service 11 (April 1894): 323-327. Seraile, 123.

[61]Seraile, 123, 124.

214

concerning America's motives. Indeed, many blacks, faced with increased racism and oppression here at home, were somewhat leery over this Republican-led U.S. war of imperialism. As one historian had noted, "The [Republican] party which had freed the slaves was now waging war on behalf of its 'little brown brothers,' while immersing itself in the Anglo-Saxon supremacy that had brought England to the height of jingoism, xenophobia, repression, and racism on a world-wide scale."[62]

White Americans' belief in Anglo-Saxon supremacy was reinforced by Josiah Strong's 1885 book *Our Country*. The Congregationalist minister had combined the views of Charles Darwin, Herbert Spencer, William Graham Sumner and Horace Bushnell to support his claim that the Anglo-Saxon race (which he defined as any European group which spoke English and embraced Protestantism) was superior, and that the American white Protestant population was the most advanced of all Anglo-Saxon people. Their task was to assimilate inferior people into Anglo-Saxon culture through evangelism, thus helping to usher in the post-millennial age of Christ's return.[63]

Steward had already challenged Strong's thesis in a book he wrote in 1888, entitled *The End of the World*. The Anglo-Saxon race would self-destruct, he maintained, which would provide the opportunity for the world's people of color to rise up and make a more just world led by the Lord. God, in turn, would then punish whites for misusing Christianity to enslave Africans and exterminate Native Americans.[64] Ten years later Steward would write that the popular battle cries, "Remember the Maine!," "Avenge the Maine!," and "To hell with Spain!" were tantamount to the taunts of a lynch mob. President William McKinley was right to oppose the Spanish "not in the spirit of revenge, but in the interest of humanity and

---

[62]Donaldson, 69.

[63]Josiah Strong, Our Country, 2nd ed., (New York: The Baker and Taylor Co., 1891, repr; Cambridge, MA: The Belknap Press of Harvard University Press, 1964). Miller, 202-206.

[64]Miller, 201. Seraile, 90.

upon principles sanctioned even by our holy religion." For Steward the war was fought to help save the "starving reconcentrados" and the "noble Christian patriots" from an "inhuman warfare with their mother country." Victory would establish a "stable government in harmony with the ideas of liberty and justice."[65] Meanwhile, he did the best he could to support the men of the Twenty-fifth, despite the rampant jingoism, by making ready for the unit's upcoming deployment to Cuba.

The regiment's first stop on their way to Cuba was the hastily drawn up training center at Chickamauga National Park, Georgia. The reception they received in the Jim Crow South came as shock to the battle-hardened fighters of the West. Steward, never one to take a racist insult lying down, fought back with the pen, writing articles for *The Independent* and the Cleveland *Gazette*. He believed that combat in Cuba would prove that blacks were not cowards and could fight as well as whites.[66]

As the regiment made ready in Chickamauga, Steward found the opportunity to conduct a joint chapel service with Chaplain George W. Prioleau of the Ninth Cavalry. One sermon utilized Isaiah 40 as its text in which the biblical prophet said "comfort ye; comfort ye my people, saith your God." Many of the men were afraid of dying and his words helped to calm them, even those who had earlier professed to be nonbelievers.[67]

Finally, the Twenty-fifth was shipped out to Cuba, but like all the black chaplains except William T. Anderson, Steward was sent on recruiting duty instead. He was not happy at being left behind and expressed his sentiment in a letter to the

---

[65]Theophilus Steward, The Colored Regulars of the United States Army (1899; repr.: New York: Arno Press, 1969), 91, 92, 103. Stover, Up From Handyman, 109.

[66]Steward, The Colored Regulars, 105, 326, 327. Stover, Up From Handyman, 100. Seraile, 130, 131.

[67]Seraile, 130.

War Department from his recruiting station in Dayton, Ohio.[68] The army responded to his request by sending him to Montauk, Long Island, not Cuba. His brief stay on Long Island did, though, provide him with the opportunity to serve as featured speaker at a Brooklyn peace jubilee which was sponsored by the Montauk Soldiers Relief Association in September, 1898.[69]

Steward's optimistic calls for African American officers to lead the legions of young black troops he was recruiting stood in stark contrast to the view taken by Chaplain Prioleau. Both men saw the military as a place to save souls and educate men, but unlike Steward, Prioleau had little faith that fairness would prevail. Steward put his beliefs to the test when he sought an officer's commission for his son, Frank, in the Forty-ninth United States Volunteers. In the end, Frank was commissioned, not due to racial equality, but rather because of the efforts of Steward's influential friends.[70]

With the conclusion of the war and the return of the Twenty-fifth to its new home at Fort Logan, Colorado, Steward sought and received permission from the Department of the Army to write a book detailing the role of the African American soldiers in the Spanish-American War. The project faced a serious threat, however, when the regiment's new commander, Colonel A.S. Burt, worked to have Steward transferred to a remote post in New Mexico or Arizona. Unlike the previous commander, Colonel Andrews, Burt was not impressed with Steward and wanted Chaplain J.B. McCleery brought in as Steward's replacement. Burt had blocked Steward's attempts to become chaplain for West Point earlier.[71] "Chaplain Steward

---

[68]Letter from Steward to the AGO dated 5 July 1898, Record Group 94, National Archives.

[69]Special Orders No. 190 dated 13 August 1898, Steward File, Record Group 94, National Archives. Logan and Winston, 570.

[70]Seraile, 133, 134.

[71]Steward wanted to become West Point's chaplain primarily so that he could be near his son, Frank, who was studying at Harvard.

is of no value whatsoever beyond his Chaplain's functions," wrote Burt, "and there are many posts in Arizona and New Mexico garrisoned by colored soldiers who have no opportunities of receiving religion attention, particularly from a Chaplain of their own color."[72]

Steward called upon all the friends he had in an effort to prevent his transfer. Letters on his behalf flooded President McKinley and the secretary of war. Many were from A.M.E. ministers, but probably the decisive letter was from one of the nation's most well-respected officers, General Nelson Miles, who wrote:

> It has been the custom, with hardly an exception, for the chaplain of a regiment to be retained on duty at the headquarters of his own regiment; and it would, in my opinion, establish a bad precedent, and work a great hardship to Chaplain Steward, to send him to Fort Apache.[73]

The letters paid off and Steward was instead ordered to Wilberforce University where he was able to complete *The Colored Regulars in the United States Army*.[74] The book highlighted the exploits of the black warriors from earliest times, through the American Revolution and Civil War, culminating with the Spanish-American War. Through this work, Steward sought to demonstrate the bold and gallant contribution blacks had made in securing American independence and democracy. The book was printed by a black press, and was well received in the African American community in particular, for it demonstrated that blacks played a major role in the war.[75]

Steward was not able to bask in the glow of his literary success for long, however, for the Twenty-fifth again received orders to deploy, this time to the

---

[72]Letter from Colonel A.S. Burt to the AGO dated 13 February 1899. Steward File, Record Group 94, National Archives.

[73]Letter from General Nelson Miles to the Secretary of War dated 8 March 1899. Steward File, Record Group 94, National Archives.

[74]Special Orders No. 63 dated 17 March 1899. Steward File, Record Group 94, National Archives.

[75]Seraile, 136.

Philippines. President McKinley's decision not to grant the Philippines independence led many Filipinos to the conclusion that their Spanish tyrants had simply been replaced with American ones, thus sparking the so-called Philippine Insurrection. Many white Americans raised concerns over whether the blacks would fight against the Filipinos. One War Department official doubted that "if brought face to face with their colored Filipino cousins [black soldiers] could be made to fire on them." Indeed, many in the African American community identified with the Filipinos, not because of skin color, but because both groups had suffered oppression.[76]

Once in the Philippines, white soldiers wasted little time in imposing Jim Crow practices from home on both Filipinos and African Americans. Filipinos were called "niggers" and were treated with contempt by white officers, which trickled down to the men under their command. Black soldiers were not permitted to patronize "whites only" restaurants and barbershops, and were subjected to listening to abusive songs like "All coons look alike to me" and "I don't like a nigger nohow." Even black officers were not spared this abuse. White enlisted men often did not render black officers the proper military courtesy. White officers treated them like enlisted men while on duty and ignored them totally while off duty. Such abuse worked to drive the Filipinos and blacks closer together, which further galled the whites.[77]

While in the Philippines, Steward was kept busy ministering to both soldiers and civilians, and serving as superintendent of the schools in his province. His fluency in Spanish enabled him to reach out to the Filipinos. The absence of Roman Catholic priests meant that many parishioners flocked to his services for want of religious instruction. He soon felt more comfortable with the Filipino people who accepted him completely, unlike the American whites. Ironically, Steward, an

---

[76]Donaldson, 75.

[77]Foner, 92. William Gatewood, "Smoked Yankees" and the Struggle for Empire: Letters from Negro Soldiers, 1898-1902 (Urbana: University of Illinois Press, 1971), 241-244.

opponent of African American emigration to Africa, would later encourage his fellow blacks to seek job opportunities in the Philippines, a place he described as a "veritable Eldorado for the American Negro."[78]

As school superintendent, Steward worked to organize forty-three schools, train teachers, obtain books, and end the practice of rote memorization. He also worked to remodel the entire system along the American educational plan. His recommendation that English be the primary language taught and utilized in these schools was approved by General Order No. 41, issued on 20 March 1900. Later, when the new American Civil Governor William Howard Taft arrived, the chaplain helped to arrange the importation of one thousand American teachers, one of whom was his son, Gustavus Aldolpus. Thus, Gustavus continued the work started by his father once Steward departed.[79]

Chaplain Steward experienced white racism both indirectly and directly. He complained that when black volunteer regiments were disbanded after the end of the Spanish-American War, black volunteer officers, who had been chosen from the best of the black regular army regiments, lost their commissions and were returned to their original units at their old enlisted rank. Steward wrote that their commissions "were too short lived, and too circumscribed to be much more than a lively tantalization, to be remembered with disgust to those who had worn them."[80]

He also faced racism directly, but unlike Chaplain Allensworth, Steward never overlooked it. When an enlisted medic refused to salute him, Steward reported the incident to the hospital's commander. When three enlisted personnel insulted him along a busy street, he lectured the troops and then reported them to

---

[78]Letter to the AGO dated 16 December 1902, Record Group 94, National Archives. Steward enclosed a newspaper article from the Philadelphia Public Ledger which asserted that since the natives would not work and the whites could not stand the heat that blacks would fit in perfectly. Seraile, 138, 144.

[79]Seraile, 139-142.

[80]Foner, 88. Gatewood, 303.

their commander. While en route back to the United States after the end of the fighting in the Philippines, both Steward and his son, also an officer, were told by the dining room steward that they would have to sit at a side table. Steward complained to the regimental commander who promptly invited him to sit at his table, and told his son to sit with the other junior officers.[81]

Steward's time in the Philippines broadened his perspective on racism so that he now viewed it as an international problem. He saw firsthand the ugly treatment of the Filipino people by many American soldiers, which troubled him immensely. Ironically, however, Steward never saw a tension in his own role as an army officer and thus a contributor to this racism. But his expanded duties as a chaplain and as educator in the Philippines allowed him the cast his role in a positive light.

He believed fully in American democracy, thinking that it was one of the greatest achievements of human civilization. But the U.S. role in the Philippines led him to link racism with imperialism and offer a critique of the new style imperialism that was emerging as U.S. policy. His experiences abroad strengthened his belief that the end of Euro-American world dominance was near and that the world's people of color would ascend to a place of equality with their former white masters. His view of the rise and fall of the history of world civilizations was not linear like that of William Henry Steward or Josiah Strong, but rather cyclical "starting with the rise of the [Ancient] East, that is Egypt and Asia, flowing through the West and flowing its way back to the East, in this case, Africa and African-America."[82]

Steward and the men of the Twenty-fifth departed Manila for the return trip home on 7 July 1902. The chaplain spent the next several years of his military service stationed at Fort Niobrara, Nebraska. Having been abandoned for several years, the fort was in much need of repair. Steward busied himself with his duties which included teaching, preaching and organizing a local Y.M.C.A. chapter. His

---

[81]Steward, Fifty Years in the Gospel Ministry, 341, 342. Stover, 128. Gatewood, 262-264.

[82]Miller, 220.

wife, Susan, who continued practicing medicine, also added much to the worship service by serving as organist and music director.[83]

Steward hoped to take advantage of the Congressional act of 21 April 1904, which permitted chaplains to advance to the grade of major providing they had ten years of service. Having held the rank of captain since he first entered the army back in 1891, the chaplain felt that he was a worthy candidate for promotion. His commander agreed and endorsed his work as having "been very satisfactory and has produced good results." He added that Steward was "energetic, painstaking and possesses the confidence of the officers and men of the command."[84] The chaplain was shocked when his application was denied, with the judge advocate general noting "that there was nothing of record" to show that he was "worthy of special distinction for exceptional efficiency." Steward's son Frank, then a Pittsburgh attorney, personally called on President Theodore Roosevelt, also a Harvard alumnus, for assistance in reversing the judge advocate's decision, but to no avail.[85]

In 1906, the regiment was sent to Texas, much to the regret of the men. Texas was a hostile place for blacks during this time and numerous racial episodes occurred between the men of the Twenty-fifth and the local populace. The worst incident ignited in Brownsville when two soldiers on leave in town passed by a white female talking with a Mr. Tate, a customs official. One soldier accidentally brushed the woman's dress, which resulted in that trooper being knocked to the ground by Tate's pistol butt and his life threatened. Later that evening, more trouble broke out, causing the death of a bartender and the wounding of the Brownsville police chief. Claiming that they no longer felt safe, local white citizens threatened to shoot any

---

[83]Seraile, 147, 148.

[84]The handwritten name is too difficult to make out. Letter from Steward's commander to the AGO. Steward File, Record Group 94, National Archives.

[85]President Roosevelt dated 1 July 1904. Steward File, Record Group 94, National Archives. Seraile, 150-152.

soldier leaving Fort Brown, and demanded that the black troops of the Twenty-fifth be replaced with white ones. The army complied and moved the Twenty-fifth to Fort Reno, Oklahoma.[86]

Army investigators dispatched to the scene found that the soldiers refused to testify, which led them to conclude the men were covering up for their guilty friends. The army then arrested twelve of the soldiers and confined them at Fort Sam Houston near San Antonio. After visiting with the prisoners on 30 August 1906, Steward noted that the men were in "excellent health and spirits" and felt "entirely confident as to the issue." Steward knew the men personally, trusted in their "good reputation," and felt that they were simply the "victims of Texas hate" and that "they [were] not likely to be found guilty."[87]

Booker T. Washington, whom President Roosevelt had invited to dine at the White House in 1901, was now special advisor on racial matters. He felt differently than Steward and sent the chaplain a confidential letter on 10 November, requesting information and promising to keep his name out of it. Sixteen days later, Roosevelt dishonorably discharged 167 men of the Twenty-fifth without a trial. Sixteen of these soldiers were winners of the Congressional Medal of Honor, while thirteen had been cited for bravery in the Spanish-American War. Ironically, some of these men were the very same ones who had saved the life of Roosevelt and his Rough Riders in their famous charge up San Juan Hill.[88]

Strangely enough, Steward never commented on the Brownsville affair publicly. Later in his 1921 autobiography, he refused to condemn the president, even while noting that neither he nor any of the other officers of the Twenty-fifth believed

---

[86] John D. Weaver, The Brownsville Incident (New York: W.W. Norton, 1973), 16, 20. Seraile, 152, 153.

[87] Weaver, 16, 17. Stover, 167.

[88] Weaver, 16, 17. Robert W. Mullen, Blacks in America's Wars: The Shift in Attitudes from the Revolutionary War to Vietnam (New York: Monad, 1973), 41, 42. Seraile, 152-153. The army finally reversed the earlier decision in 1972 and granted the men honorable discharges.

the men to be guilty.[89] As a soldier, Steward chose to do his duty to the very end. He resented it when people called him an "ex-chaplain," noting with pride that even in civilian life he continued to report his address to the Adjutant General each year; and he received his army retirement pay every month.[90] Steward always held fast to his belief that the army, though not perfect, was the best place for African Americans to receive a better opportunity. When pressed, he admitted that some racist incidences had occurred in the volunteer units, but he always maintained that nowhere did "black men and white men mingle so freely and so fraternally as in the United States Army." "The Negro soldier had a friend in almost every [white] officer that had ever served with black troops," added Steward. "The Negro is a friend winner."[91]

By now, the sixty-four year old Steward's health was failing. He suffered from various ailments, the most serious being acute neurasthenia.[92] On 12 January 1907, he wrote that adjutant general from Fort McIntosh, Texas, requesting a medical retirement.[93] His retirement was approved via Special Order No. 90, dated 17 April 1907.[94]

Steward spent his remaining years, until his death in 1925, as professor of history, logic, and French at Wilberforce University. In 1911, he went to London with his wife to hear her present a paper entitled "Colored Women in America" at an

---

[89]Seraile, 153.

[90]Seraile, 157.

[91]Miller, 260.

[92]Efficiency Report of T.G. Steward from 1 July 1905 to 30 June 1902. Steward File, Record Group 94, National Archives.

[93]Letter to the AGO from Steward dated 12 January 1907, Steward File, Record Group 94, National Archives.

[94]Special Orders No. 90 dated 17 April 1907. Steward File, Record Group 94, National Archives.

interracial congress. Always a prolific writer, he kept up with his publications. One of his works, *The Haitian Revolution of 1791 to 1804 or Sidelights on the French Revolution* (1914), was used as a textbook at the school. Other works included *Gouldtown, A Very Remarkable Settlement of Ancient Date* (1913), and *Fifty Years in the Gospel Ministry* (1921). He also continued to work to erase the color line that separated people. As a biographer has noted, "He believed that people of diverse backgrounds, languages, customs, and philosophies would get along if they had something in common. This commonality he believed would be achieved through the acceptance of Americanization..."[95]

Theophilus Gould Steward was unique for several reasons when compared to the other Buffalo soldier chaplains. He was the only northerner, the only one born a freeman, and the only one who was the child of a racially mixed family. He developed a critical and highly analytical mind that he used to challenge orthodox religion. Steward proved that he was a man of action as well as a first-rate thinker and scholar. His numerous writings are an invaluable source in aiding modern scholars understand both chaplains and black soldiers of the Buffalo soldier era. His thoughtful analysis and penetrating writings brought depth and meaning to the ministry provided by army chaplains.

Steward taught his men the basic arts of reading and writing, but he also believed that blacks should progress to higher levels much as Du Bois advocated. Indeed, Steward was a perfect example of Du Bois' "Talented Tenth" blazing a trail for other African Americans to follow. He added another key component to Du Bois' work, though, and that was the need for a moral force to build character and round out black student's education, and prepare them for participation in a democratic society. He believed African American Christianity served the purpose of creating this moral force.

---

[95]Seraile, 170. Logan and Winston, 570.

Although he was quick to respond to individual acts of racism in a much more aggressive manner than many of his black counterparts, Steward's only major blindspot was his unwillingness to see the inherent racism that existed within the army itself. His tour of duty in the Philippines helped him to broaden his view of racism as an international problem and to link it with imperialism. Perhaps his greatest struggle with doubleness was that he was a member of the same military that was enforcing these racist and imperialist policies abroad.

Conclusion

The story of the Buffalo soldier chaplains began, appropriately enough, with the formation of their religious heritage, African American Christianity. The oppressed slaves created this particular religious expression by merging elements from their African Heritage, slave experience, and evangelical Protestantism. The end product was something that possessed the same external forms of their master's evangelical faith, but which was inherently much different thanks to a strong and persistent black folk religion element. Both worshiped Jesus on Sunday morning all across the South, but unlike whites, blacks "shouted" during worship services, sang a new type of song called the spiritual, believed in spirit possession, and were generally much more vocal, lively, and enthusiastic than even those whites caught up in the Second Great Awakening. Black funerals were different, too, for African Americans broke up the possessions of the dead and placed them on top of the grave in order to help release the spirit of the deceased, just as they had in Africa. Therefore, the heart and soul of African American Christianity was black folk religion which gave it its uniqueness and vitality.

African American Christianity helped slaves to deal with everyday life under a cruel system. American slavery was one of the most brutal forms of bondage ever devised for, unlike slavery of the past, it was degrading, based on race, and permanent. Slavery severely damaged the African religious and cultural heritage of the slaves, but African American Christianity helped blacks survive by developing a new coherent world-view in which they felt worthy of love, respect, and dignity, thanks to the saving grace of Jesus Christ. The religion of the slaves, then, stressed the Biblical message of suffering, resistance, and liberation from oppression through preaching on such texts as the Hebrew's exodus from Egyptian slavery, Amos' call for justice, and Jesus' identification with the downtrodden. It was this message of hope, salvation, and ultimately liberation from actual bondage and later from prejudice, racism and discrimination, all proclaimed in the midst of misery and suffering. That was the message preached by the Civil War era black chaplains, and their successors, the Buffalo soldier chaplains.

Blacks first joined the Union army in 1863 after the issuance of the Emancipation Proclamation, and soon, nearly 180,000 were serving in 166 all-black regiments. The fourteen African American chaplains who served in the Civil War beginning in 1863 were the forerunners of the Buffalo soldier chaplains. Many of the first chaplains who entered service after the firing on Fort Sumter, however, were rogues and rascals. Their incompetent behavior resulted in numerous complaints by disgusted soldiers and the handful of good clergymen. These protests finally motivated Congress to revamp the entire system so that by 1863 the chaplain's branch was a sound and thoroughly professional outfit. It was this improved chaplaincy that African Americans chaplains entered. The two-year delay from the start of the war to their official entry into the army proved fortuitous, for it meant that the black chaplains were spared the days of lackluster clergymen in uniform and entered a totally professional organization. The higher educational and ecclesiastical standards of the revised chaplaincy meant that fewer black clergymen qualified, yet those who did were some of the best leaders in the African American community. The example of the fourteen black chaplains of Civil War is important for it set a precedent for the later Buffalo soldier chaplains.

All fourteen of the black chaplains resigned at the end of the Civil War, and for the next fifteen years black clergymen concentrated their efforts on helping the freedmen during Reconstruction. By 1884, the African American community was ready to look beyond the South to the possibilities presented by the opening of the American West. Some young black men had already taken advantage of theses opportunities by joining the army. These were the Buffalo soldiers who had earned a respectable reputation for themselves in the Ninth and Tenth Cavalry, and Twenty-fourth and Twenty-fifth Infantry.

The five black chaplains who ministered to the men of the Buffalo soldier regiments were different men with diverse backgrounds, abilities, styles, and experiences. Four of the five were southerners born into slavery; Theophilus Steward was the only exception. Three of the five were A.M.E. pastors; Plummer and Allensworth were Baptists. All of the men were highly successful civilian pastors who had played a major role in helping the freedman recover in the Reconstruction South. All five were active supporters of the Republican party which helped them obtain their commissions. Each one dealt with Du Bois' concept of double-consciousness and the problem of racism both from army sources as well as civilian; each faced it in his own unique way. Although the five chaplains' lives were not linked directed because they were stationed at posts far from each other, Steward complimented Allensworth's work and held joint chapel services with Prioleau.

Henry V. Plummer, the first Buffalo soldier chaplain, began his ministry in the Ninth Cavalry with high hopes and expectations. Of all the Buffalo soldier chaplains, Plummer's encounter with Du Bois' concept of double-consciousness was the most painful. All of his efforts, temperance, the quest for decent quarters, his writings, the emigration dreams, and so on, were issues that other chaplains addressed but none were rebuked as was he. First, his active support of the temperance movement and his refusal to accept second-class treatment, such as in the assignment of his quarters, angered the command. He also disturbed his superiors by his interest in the black emigration movement whose goal was to remove blacks back to Africa in order to resist European colonizers. Alienated by the white officers of his regiment, Plummer turned to the black enlisted men for companionship. This act of fraternization, coupled with his alleged consumption of alcohol, led to his subsequent court-martial and dismissal from the army.

Plummer's real crime, however, was that he was too outspoken for a black man in the Jim Crow era. After all, he was not the first and certainly not the only chaplain involved in the temperance movement. In fact, temperance was the biggest reform cause among all chaplains of the late nineteenth century. The efforts to curb alcohol abuse might not have been popular with the command of Plummer's regiment, but even they had to admit that there was a serious drinking problem among soldiers of the unit. Indeed, the vast majority of disciplinary problems stemmed from alcohol abuse.

Plummer's objections to being assigned inferior quarters were not out of line, either. Better living facilities were one of the few "perks" awarded officers on military bases. But Plummer was not even permitted housing with the other officers; instead, he was forced to reside on the "lower line" with the enlisted men and the officers' servants. This insult was made worse by the fact that his quarters were damp, moldy, and in serious need of repairs. Evidently, though, Plummer's protest did not sit well with command and added one more mark against him in their eyes because he refused the second-class accommodations.[1]

As for his writings in the *Fort Robinson Weekly Bulletin* and *Omaha Progress*, it was never proven that he was the author known as "Yellow Cape." Whomever, "Yellow Cape" was, he was obviously disturbed by the racism prevalent in the town of Crawford, racism so bad that one soldier, Charles Diggs, was nearly lynched. Threats were made in the newspaper articles, true, but not threatening anything worse than had been perpetrated against the Buffalo soldiers of the Ninth Cavalry. The tragedy was that the law would not protect the black soldiers, the same soldiers sent to defend the very lives of the people of Crawford. Yet, when the soldiers tried to defend themselves from lynch mobs, they were denounced as criminals.

---

[1]Plummer was not the only African American to fight inferior accommodations during the latter part of the nineteenth century. Ida B. Wells Barnett (1862-1931), a black newspaper editor, fought against segregated railroad facilities in which blacks were confined to second class sections.

Chaplain Plummer's call for black emigration was another point that put him at odds with the officers of his unit. Admittedly such a goal was unusual for a chaplain, but it was not a violation of any army regulations. Plummer's quest was one shared by many black leaders of his day such as Henry McNeal Turner, and later, Marcus Garvey.

These incidences, as bad as they seemed to the command, were not enough to bring Plummer up on any specific charges. That problem was finally resolved when he was caught taking a drink with some enlisted men while off-duty. Plummer's having a drink was not unlawful in and of itself, though it was hypocritical after his temperance efforts. Nor was Plummer the first chaplain to ever take a drink; indeed, one had been found too inebriated to perform a funeral. The difference was that the chaplain, a white man, was allowed to resign while Plummer was court-martialed. Apparently there was a double standard that applied to blacks.

As for the charge of fraternization, if the white officers would have nothing to do with Plummer socially, then to whom else could he turn? Was it not also the chaplain's duty to be on friendly terms with the men of this unit, for how else could he minister to them? Line officers had to keep a proper distance between themselves and the rank and file, but chaplains were unique in the fact that they were supposed to have free access to soldiers of all ranks. Evidently this did not apply to Chaplain Plummer.

Plummer' experience in uniform was not a pleasant one, but fortunately it did not prevent other black clergymen from becoming chaplains. George W. Prioleau, Plummer's replacement in the Ninth, had a much better experience. Nevertheless, his letters to the *Cleveland Gazette* offer a sad commentary on race relations during the late nineteenth century. He, too, faced racism particularly while on recruiting duty in the Jim Crow South during the Spanish-American War. He felt first-hand the heartbreak and anguish that all black troops eventually came to know, that, despite the fact they voluntarily put their life on the line to protect this country, many whites still considered them nothing but "niggers." He realized that even successful blacks were discriminated against, a fact that deeply angered a man like W.E.B. Du Bois. In fact, Prioleau discovered while in Orangeburg, South Carolina, home of his college *alma mater*, that many blacks hated him more than most whites precisely because he was educated. The irony was that whites often claimed they hated blacks because of the latter's ignorance, but Prioleau found that no matter how far the black person progressed, he or she would always be treated as a second class citizen by many whites.

Chaplain William T. Anderson of the Tenth Cavalry had much in common with Plummer and Prioleau. He, too, was a southern born freedman and member of the A.M.E. Church. But unlike the chaplains of the Ninth Cavalry, Anderson was less vocal, though no less sensitive, to racism. He concentrated his efforts on trying to save the bodies as well as souls of his men through the use of both his medical and ministerial skills. His experiences as the first black commander of an army post, and the only Buffalo soldier chaplain in Cuba during the Spanish-American War, made him unique. Anderson's abilities as a physician probably helped to spare him from severe abuse during his tenure as chaplain for the Tenth. Nevertheless, he found out in the end that even his more passive demeanor and medical knowledge were not enough to help him escape doubleness. It is not entirely clear from the available evidence whether or not Chaplain Anderson was singled out specifically for early retirement by President Taft in keeping with his "new Southern policy." Nonetheless, enough people in the black community certainly thought so and so did Chaplain Anderson. But even though he was deeply hurt he, too, like all the Buffalo soldier chaplains, kept his faith in the army as the best place for a young black man to acquire the skills needed to make it in America. The sad point is, like Prioleau, his life demonstrates another painful fact of doubleness, that even if one played the game by the rules, still, one could lose.

Allen Allensworth of the Twenty-fourth Infantry rose higher in rank than any of the other Buffalo soldier chaplains of his day by his promotion to lieutenant colonel. He made remarkable achievements in the field of education which were

232

recognized by the civilian community and adopted by the army. After the end of a long and successful military career, he went on to found Allensworth, California, the first all-black community in that state which was created to be a safe place for blacks to grow and develop without having to face the tensions of "doubleness."

Allensworth sought to resolve his dilemma over "doubleness" by validating the Bookerite philosophy. Like Washington, he believed that by his own actions he could persuade whites to distinguish between educated and refined blacks, on the one hand, and ignorant and crude blacks, on the other. He believed that blacks could ultimately compete with whites, but first they had to acquire the skills and training needed. He put this philosophy into practice by turning the army into a first-class training school where young illiterate farm hands were taught to read and write, and then progressed to learn printing, baking, cooking, and other practical skills. This was the same goal he had in mind for his town, Allensworth. It was to be a place of refuge from racism where blacks could improve themselves and then go out into the rest of the world.

In the field of religion, he held fast and firm to the black folk tradition that had made African American Christianity singular, but he was a progressive who wanted to update the faith in order to deal with the new age of black ecclesiastical freedom. The "Invisible Institution" had worked well on the old plantations of the antebellum South when blacks had no churches of their own and thus did not have to concern themselves with church budgets, property taxes, missionary work, and the establishment of colleges. The age of freedom required new talents, and abilities, especially discipline, the same qualities Allensworth had seen employed successfully while in the Union navy during the Civil War.

Allen Allensworth dealt with the tension of racism and double-consciousness better than any other black chaplain; but at what cost? The letters he wrote to congressmen and military officials in his pursuit of a chaplain's position sound as if he were obsequious. Allensworth stated that as a former slave and Union Navy steward, he knew how to keep his place when around white people, and that he

233

would never attempt to breach the race barrier when it came to the social arena. Was Allensworth an "Uncle Tom," or was there more to this man? Perhaps the incidents with the junior officers and enlisted men who refused to salute him offer a clue. He refrained from rebuking the men or placing them on report though he was well within his rights to do so. Certainly most other officers would have. Instead, he chose to "turn the other cheek" and preach a humorous sermon on the subject of saluting which won the men over. Allensworth's goal was reconciliation, not conquest. He had real concern for his opponents and sought to win them over through Christ-like acts of redemptive suffering and *agape* love, much like Martin Luther King, Jr. later on demonstrated.[2]

Theophilus G. Steward of the Twenty-fifth Infantry was different from the other Buffalo soldier chaplains in several ways. He was the only one who was freeborn, from the North, and the product of a racially mixed family. Of all the chaplains, his thoughts and opinions are the most accessible because he was such an extensive writer.[3] Unlike many intellectuals, though, he was able to identify with the common person and proved it to his soldiers by working side by side with them.

Like Washington, Steward believed that young black males needed to learn the basic fundamentals of education; and like Allensworth, he believed that could be achieved through the army. Like W.E.B. Du Bois, Steward believed that these men could eventually rise above vocational careers and achieve success as a member of the "Talented Tenth," as he had. But Steward added another key component to his education vision: the need for religion as a moral force. He thought that moral virtues were important because they helped prepare blacks for participation in a

---

[2]*Agape* is a Greek word that describes an unconditional love, the same type God has for humanity.

[3]Steward was the only Buffalo soldier chaplain to write an autobiography.

democratic nation and to build a black civil society.[4] This emphasis, implied in the ministries of all chaplains, was clearly elaborated by Steward.

Unlike Allensworth, Steward, the northern radical, refused to "turn the other cheek," and so he confronted racism directly, especially through the use of his pen. Steward wanted more than mere survival for the black race, he wanted all out victory and was clearly in the black liberationist camp.

Steward was plagued by double-consciousness in another way, too. He believed that American democracy was one of the greatest achievements of humanity. Yet he condemned American racism and imperialism because of his vision of African American self-determination and his quest to see blacks build a cultured society. His tour in the Philippines broadened his view of racism by convincing him that it was an international problem. This led him to connect racism and imperialism and call on the U.S. to temper its policies toward Haiti, Cuba, Puerto Rico, and the Philippines. If Steward's membership in the same armed forces that the imperialists used to support racism and conquest caused him more anxiety and conflict with his own doubleness, he never mentioned it.[5]

The Buffalo soldier chaplains helped the troops of their command move from mere survival to achieve liberation. Liberation involved freedom from ignorance, persecution, ungodliness, and low self-esteem. The strategies they employed varied, but the goal of liberation remained the same and the means to that goal was African American Christianity. Some like Plummer, Prioleau, and Steward sought the route of protest and resistance; others like Anderson and Allensworth attempted accommodation. Their fight was not easy for the problem of "doubleness" haunted each and every one of them. Nevertheless, the Buffalo soldier chaplains refused to surrender or to retreat to a foreign land. Instead, they held steadfast, setting an

---

[4] Albert George Miller, "Theophilus Gould Steward, 1843-1924: Striving for an African American Theology and Civil Society in the Nadir Period," (Ph.D. diss, Princeton University, 1994), 281.

[5] Miller, 281.

example of pride and dignity for the army, the African American community, and all of American as well.

BIBLIOGRAPHY

Primary Sources

Adams, Virginia M., ed. On the Altar of Freedom: A Black Soldier's Civil War Letters from the Front. Corporal James Henry Gooding. New York: Warner Books, 1991.

Alexander, Charles. Battles and Victories of Allen Allensworth. Boston: French and Company, 1914.

Andrews, William L., ed. From Fugitive Slave to Free Man: The Autobiographies of William Wells Brown. 1848 and 1880; reprint, New York: Mentor Books, 1993.

Ball, Charles, Fifty Years in Chains. 1837; reprint, New York: Dover Publications, 1970.

Berlin, Ira., ed. The Black Military Experience. Series II, Freedom: A Documentary History of Emancipation, 1861-1867. Cambridge: Cambridge University Press, 1982.

Blacket, R.J.M., ed. Thomas Morris Chester, Black Civil War Correspondent: His Dispatches From the Virginia Front. Baton Rouge: Louisiana University Press, 1989.

Bleser, Carol, ed. Secret and Sacred: The Diaries of James Henry Hammond, a Southern Slaveholder. New York: Oxford University Press, 1988.

Bontempts, Arna, ed. Great Slave Narratives. Boston: Beacon Press, 1969.

Brown, William Wells. The Negro in the American Rebellion. Boston: Lee Shepard, 1867.

237

Carroll, John M., ed. The Black Military Experience in the American West. New York: Liveright, 1971.

Cashin, Hershel V. Under Fire With the Tenth U.S. Cavalry. 1899; reprint, New York: Arno Press, 1969.

Douglass, Frederick. My Bondage and My Freedom. 1855; reprint, New York.

_____. Narrative of Frederick Douglass, An American Slave. Boston: Anti-Slavery Office, 1845.

Duncan, Russell, ed. Blue-Eyed Child of Fortune: The Civil War Letters of Colonel Robert Gould Shaw. Athens, GA: University of Georgia Press, 1992.

Emiliio, Luis F. A Brave Black Regiment. 1894; reprint, New York: Bantam Books, 1991.

Fickling, Susan Markey. Slave-Conversion in South Carolina, 1830-1860. Columbia: University of South Carolina Press, 1924.

Gatewood, William B., ed. "Smoked Yankees" and the Struggle for Empire: Letters From Negro Soldiers, 1898-1902. Urbana: University of Illinois Press, 1971.

Gaustad, Edwin S., ed. A Documentary History of Religion in America to the Civil War. Grand Rapids, Michigan: William B. Eerdmans' Publishing Company, 1983.

Gray, John Chipman and John Codman Ropes. War Letters, 1862-1865. Cambridge, MA: The Riverside Press, 1927.

Guernsey, Alfred H. and Henry M. Alden, eds. Harper's Pictorial History of the Civil War. 1866; reprint, Fairfax Press, 1988.

Higginson, Thomas Wentworth. Army Life in a Black Regiment. 1869; reprint, New York: W.W. Norton, 1984.

Johnson, Clifton H., ed. God Struck Me Dead: Voices of Ex-slaves. 1969; reprint, Cleveland, Ohio: The Pilgrim Press, 1993.

Johnson, Edward. History of Negro Soldiers in the Spanish-American War. Raleigh, N.C.: Capital Printing, 1899.

Katz, William Loren, ed. Five Slave Narratives: A Compendium. New York: Arno Press, 1968.

King, Wilma. A Northern Woman in the Plantation South: Letters of Tryphena Blanch Holder Fox, 1856-1876. Columbia: University of South Carolina Press, 1993.

McCracken, Harold, ed. Frederick Remington's Own West. New York: The Dial Press, 1960.

Merington, Marguerite, ed. The Custer Story: The Life and Letters of General George A. Custer and His Wife Elizabeth. 1950; reprint, New York: Barnes and Noble Book, 1994.

Outler, Albert C., ed. John Wesley. New York: Oxford University Press, 1964.

Revised United States Army Regulations of 1861. Washington, D.C.: Government Printing Office, 1863.

Rosenblatt, Emil and Ruth, eds. Hard Marching Every Day: The Civil War Letters of Private Wilber Fisk, 1861-1865. Kansas: University of Kansas Press, 1992.

Rosengarten, Theodore. Tombee: Portrait of a Cotton planter with The Journal of Thomas B. Chaplain (1822-1890). New York: William Morrow and Company, 1986.

Smith, H. Shelton, Robert T. Handy and Lefferts A. Loetscher. American Christianity: An Historical Interpretation with Representative Documents. New York: Charles Scribner's Sons, 1963.

Spener, Philip Jacob. Pia Desideria. 1675; reprint, Philadelphia: Fortress Press, 1982.

Steward, Theophilus G., ed. Active Service or Gospel Work Among U.S. Soldiers. New York: U.S. Army Aid Association, 1897.

_____. Gouldtown: A Very Remarkable Settlement of Ancient Date. Philadelphia: J.B. Lippincott Company, 1913.

_____. Memoirs of Mrs. Rebecca Steward. Philadelphia: Publication Department of the A.M.E. Church, 1877.

_____. Genesis Re-Read. Philadelphia: A.M.E. Book Rooms, 1885.

_____. Divine Attributes. Philadelphia: Christian Recorder Print, 1884.

_____. Fifty Years in the Gospel Ministry: From 1864 to 1914. Philadelphia: A.M.E. Book Concern, n.d.

_____. The Colored Regulars in the United States Army. 1899; reprint, New York: Arno Press, 1969.

Trumbull, Henry Clay. War Memories of a Chaplain. Philadelphia: J.D. Wattles and Company, 1898.

War of the Rebellion: A Compilation of the Official Records of the Union and Confederate Armies. 130 vol. Washington, D.C.: Government Printing Office, 1880-1901.

Wilson, George Washington. A History of the Negro Troops in the War of the Rebellion, 1861- 1865. 1888; reprint, New York: Bergman, 1961.

Wilson, Joseph T. The Black Phalanx: A History of the Negro Troops in the War of the Rebellion, 1861-1865. New York: 1888.

_____. A History of Negro Soldiers of the United States in the Wars of 1775-1812, 1861-1865. Hartford, CT: American, 1890.

Wish, Harvey, ed. Slavery in the South: First-Hand Accounts of the Antebellum American Southland from Northern and Southern Writers, Negroes, and Foreign Observers. New York: Farrar, Strass and Giroux, 1964.

Yetman, Norman R. Life Under the "Peculiar Institution": Selections from the Slave Narration Collection. New York: Holt, Rhinehart and Winston, 1970.

Articles

Prioleau, George W. The Cleveland Gazette (13 May 1898).

_____. The Cleveland Gazette (1 October 1898).

Steward, Theophilus Gould. "Camp Life at Chickamauga." The Independent (12 May 1898): 614.

_____. "Colonel George L. Andrews." Harpers Weekly (7 May 1892): 437.

_____. "The Colored American As A Soldier." The United Service 25 (January-June 1894): 323-327.

_____. "The Gospel in the Army." The Independent (20 February 1896): 249.

_____. "The Morals of the Army." The Independent (11 February 1892): 195.

_____. "Washington and Crummell." The Colored American (29 October 1898): 6.

Archival Material

Military File of William T. Anderson. Washington, D.C.: Record Group 94, National Archives.

Military File of Henry V. Plummer. Washington, D.C.: Record Group 94, National Archives.

Military File of Henry V. Plummer. Fort Jackson, S.C.: U.S. Army Museum.

Trial by General Court-Martial of Chaplain Henry V. Plummer. 1-21 June 1893, United States Army Museum, Fort Jackson, S.C..

Military File of George W. Prioleau. Fort Jackson, S.C.: United States Army Museum.

Military File of Theophilus G. Steward. Washington, D.C.: Record Group 94, National Archives.

Secondary Sources

Ahlstrom, Sydney E. A Religious History of the American People. New Haven: Yale University Press, 1972.

Angell, Stephen Ward. Bishop Henry McNeal Turner and Afro-American Religion in the South. Knoxville: University of Tennessee Press, 1992.

Bailey, Thomas A. and David M. Kennedy. The American Pageant: A History of the Republic. Boston: D.C. Heath, 1991.

Bauer, Jerald C., ed. The Westminster Dictionary of Church History. Philadelphia: Westminster Press, 1981.

Bennett, Lerone, Jr. Before the Mayflower: A History of Black America. 1962; reprint, New York: Penguin Books, 1986.

Billington, Monroe Lee. New Mexico's Buffalo Soldiers, 1866-1900. Niwot, CO: University of Colorado Press, 1991.

Blassingame, John W. The Slave Community: Plantation Life in the Antebellum South. New York: Oxford University Press, 1972.

Brown, Dee. Bury My Heart at Wounded Knee. New York: Washington Square Press, 1970.

Coffman, Edward M. The Old Army: A Portrait of the American Army in Peacetime, 1784-1898. New York: Oxford University Press, 1986.

Coletta, Paolo E. The Presidency of William Howard Taft. Lawrence, KS: University of Kansas, 1973.

Cone, James H. God of the Oppressed. New York: The Seabury Press, 1975.

Cornish, Dudley Taylor. The Sable Arm: Black Troops in the Union Army, 1861-1865. Lawrence, Kansas: University of Kansas Press, 1987.

Davidson, James W. and others. Nation of Nations: A Narrative History of the American Republic. New York: W.W. Norton and Company, 1994.

Donaldson, Gary A. The History of African-Americans in the Military. Malabar, Florida: Krieger Publishing Company, 1991.

242

Du Bois, W.E.B. The Soul of Black Folk. 1903; reprint, New York: Bantam
    Books, 1989.

_____. The Suppression of the African Slave Trade to the United States, 1638-
    1870. 1898; reprint, New York: Russell and Russell, 1965.

Dayton, Donald W. Discovering an Evangelical Heritage. New York: Harper and
    Row, 1976.

Dupuy, R. Ernest and Trevor N. Dupuy. The Encyclopedia of Military History.
    New York: Harper and Row, 1986.

_____. Military Heritage of America. New York: McGraw Hill, 1956.

Elkins, Stanley M. Slavery: A Problem in American Institutional and Intellectual
    Life. Chicago: University of Chicago Press, 1959.

Essig, James D. The Bonds of Wickedness: American Evangelicals Against
    Slavery, 1770-1808. Philadelphia: Temple University Press, 1982.

Faust, Patricia L. ed. Historical Times Illustrated Encyclopedia of the Civil War.
    New York: Harper and Row, 1986.

Fletcher, Marvin. The Black Soldier and Officer in the United States Army,
    1891- 1917. Columbia, MO: University of Missouri Press, 1974.

Foner, Eric. Reconstruction: America' Unfinished Revolution: 1863-1877. New
    York: Harper and Row, 1988.

Foner, Eric and John A. Garraty, eds. The Reader's Companion to American
    History. Boston: Houghton Mifflin Company, 1991.

Foner, Jack D. Blacks and the Military in American History. New York: Praeger
    Publishers, 1974.

Fox-Genovese, Elizabeth. Within the Plantation Household: Black and White
    Women of the Old South. Chapel Hill: University of North Carolina
    Press, 1988.

Fowler, Arlen L. The Black Infantry in the West, 1869-1891. Westport, CT:
    Greenwood Publishing Corporation, 1971.

Frazier, E. Franklin. The Negro Church in America. New York: Schocken Books, 1963.

Genovese, Eugene. Roll, Jordon, Roll: The World the Slaves Made. New York: Vintage Books, 1976.

_____. The Slaveholders' Dilemma: Freedom and Progress in Southern Conservative Thought, 1820-1860. Columbia: University of South Carolina Press, 1991.

Gossett, Thomas F. Race: The History of an Idea in America. New York: Schocken Books, 1965.

Herskovits, Melville J. The Myth of the Negro Past. Boston: Beacon Press, 1958.

Honeywell, Roy J. Chaplains of the United States Army. Washington, D.C.: Office of the Chief of Chaplains, Department of the Army, 1958.

Hudson, Winthrop S. Religion in America. 4th ed. New York: MacMillan Publishing Company, 1987.

Hutton, Paul Andrew. Phi Sheridan and His Army. Lincoln: University of Nebraska Press, 1985.

Katz, William Loren. The Black West. Seattle, WA: Open Hand Publishing Company, 1987.

King, Noel Q. African Cosmos: An Introduction to Religion in Africa. Belmont, CA: Wadsworth Publishing Company, 1986.

Knight, Oliver. Following the Indian Wars. Norman, OK: University of Oklahoma Press, 1960.

Leckie, William. The Military Conquest of the West. Normans, OK: University of Oklahoma Press, 1963.

_____. The Buffalo Soldiers: A Narrative of the Negro Cavalry in the West. Norman, OK: University of Oklahoma Press, 1967.

_____. The Military Conquest of the Southern Plains. Norman, OK: University of Oklahoma Press, 1963.

Leckie, William H. and Shirley A. Leckie. Unlikely Warrior: General Benjamin H. Grierson and His Family. Norman, OK: University of Oklahoma Press, 1984.

Leder, Lawrence H. America - 1603-1789: Prelude to a Nation. Minneapolis: Burgess Publishing Company, 1978.

Levine, Lawrence W. Black Culture and Black Consciousness: Afro-American Folk Thought from Slavery to Freedom. New York: Oxford University Press, 1977.

Lincoln, C. Eric., ed. The Black Experience in Religion. New York: Anchor Books, 1974.

Litwack, Leon F. North of Slavery: The Negro in the Free States, 1790-1860.Chicago: University of Chicago Press, 1961.

Logan, Rayford W. and Michael R. Winston. Dictionary of American Negro Biography. New York: W.W. Norton and Company, 1982.

Matloff, Maurice, ed. American Military History. Washington, D.C.: U.S. Printing Office, 1969.

Millet, Allan R. and Peter Maslowski. For the Common Defense: A Military History of the United States of America. New York: The Free Press, 1984.

Mitchell, Reid. Civil War Soldiers: Their Expectations and Their Experiences. New York: Simon and Schuster, 1988.

McPherson, James. The Negro's Civil War. New York: Pantheon Books, 1965.

Moore, Winfred B. and Joseph F. Tripp. Looking South: Chapters in the Story of an American Region. New York: Greenwood Press, 1989.

Mullen, Robert. Blacks in America's Wars: The Shift in Attitudes from the Revolutionary War to Vietnam. New York: Monad Press, 1973.

Nevin, David. The Old West: The Soldier. New York: Time-Life Books, 1973.

Noll, Mark A. and others. Eerdmans' Handbook to Christianity in America. Grand Rapids, Michigan: William B. Eerdmans Publishing, 1983.

Norton, Herman A. Struggling for Recognition: The United States Army Chaplaincy, 1791-1865. Washington, D.C.: Department of the Army, 1977.

Norton, Mary Beth and others. A People and a Nation: A History of the United States. 4th ed. Boston: Houghton Mifflin Company, 1994.

Phillips, U.B. American Negro Slavery. 1918; reprint, Baton Rouge: Louisiana State University Press, 1966.

Puckett, Newbell N. Folk Beliefs of the Southern Negro. Chapel Hill: University of North Carolina Press, 1926.

Raboteau, Albert J. Slave Religion: The "Invisible Institution" in the Antebellum South. New York: Oxford University Press, 1978.

Rawick, George P., ed. The American Slave: A Composite Autobiography. New York: Greenwood Press, 1977.

Richardson, Alan and John Bowden, eds. The Westminster Dictionary of Christian Theology. Philadelphia: Westminster Press, 1983.

Robertson, James I., Jr. Soldiers Blue and Gray. Columbia: University of South Carolina Press, 1988.

Seraile, William. Voice of Dissent: Theophilus Gould Steward (1843-1924) and Black America. Brooklyn, N.Y.: Carlson Publishing, 1991.

Sernett, Milton C. Black Religion and American Evangelicalism: White Protestants, Plantation Missions, and the Flower of Negro Christianity, 1787-1865. Metuchen, N.J.: The Scarecrow Press, 1975.

Schubert, Frank N. Buffalo Soldiers, Braves and the Brass: The Story of Fort Robinson, Nebraska. Shippensburg, PA: White Mane Publishing, 1993.

_____. On the Trail of the Buffalo Soldiers: Biographies of African Americans in the U.S. Army, 1866-1917. Wilmington, DE: Scholarly Resources, 1995.

_____. Black Valor: Buffalo Soldiers and the Medal of Honor, 1870-1898. Wilmington, DE: Scholarly Resources, 1997.

Shattuck, Gardiner H., Jr. A Shield and a Hiding Place: The Religion Life of the Civil War Armies. Macon Georgia: Mercer University Press, 1987.

Smelser, Marshall. American Colonial and Revolutionary History. New York: Barnes and Noble, 1962.

Stampp, Kenneth M. The Peculiar Institution: Slavery in the Antebellum South. 1956; reprint, New York: Alfred A. Knopf, 1972.

Stover, Earl F. Up From Handyman: The United States Army Chaplaincy, 1865-1920. Washington, D.C.: Office of the Chief of Chaplains, Department of the Army, 1977.

Utley, Robert M. Frontier Regulars: The United States Army and the Indian, 1866-1891. New York: Macmillan Publishing Company, 1973.

Weatherfor, W.D. The Negro from Africa to America. New York: George H. Doran Company, 1924.

Weaver, John D. The Brownsville Incident. New York: W.W. Norton, 1973.

Weinstein, Allen and Frank Otto Gatell, eds. American Negro Slavery. New York: Oxford University Press, 1973.

Wesley, Charles and Patricia Romeo. African-Americans in the Civil War: From Slavery to Citizenship. Cornell Heights, PA: Publishing Agency, 1978.

Wiley, Bell Irvin. The Life of Billy Yank: The Common Soldier of the Union. Indianapolis: The Bobbs-Merrill Company, 1951.

Wilmore, Gayraud S. Black Religion and Black Radicalism: An Interpretation of the Religious History of Afro-American People. Maryknoll, N.Y.: Orbis Books, 1986.

Wilson, Charles Reagan. Baptized in Blood: The Religion of the Lost Cause, 1865-1920. Athens: University of Georgia Press, 1980.

Woodson, Carter G. The Rural Negro. Washington, D.C.: The Association for the Study of NegroHistory and Life, Inc., 1930.

_____. The History of the Negro Church. Washington, D.C.: Associated Publishers, 1945.

Wood, Peter. Black Majority: Negroes in Colonial South Carolina from 1670 through the Stono Rebellion. New York: W.W. Norton and Company, 1974.

Wooster, Robert. The Military and the United States Indian Policy, 1865-1903. New Haven: Yale University Press, 1988.

Articles

Blassingame, John. "Negro Chaplains in the Civil War." Negro History Bulletin. 37 (October 1963): 23-24.

Budd, Richard M. "Ohio Army Chaplains and the Professionalization of the Military Chaplaincy in the Civil War." Ohio History. 102 (Winter-Spring 1993): 5-19.

Carle, Glenn L. "The Tragic in Black Historical Experience." Duke Divinity School Review. 38 (Spring 1973).

Helton, Charles L. "The Tragic in Black Historical Experience." Duke Divinity School Review. 38 (Spring 1973).

Hourihan, William J. "An Officer and a Gentleman: Chaplain Allen Allensworth of the Twenty-fourth Infantry." U.S. Army Chaplain Museum Association Newsletter. (July 1989).

Janda, Lance. "Shutting the Gate of Mercy: The Origins of American Total War, 1860-1880." The Journal of Military History 59 (January 1995): 7-26.

Langellier, John Philip. "Chaplain Allen Allensworth of the 24th Infantry, 1886-1906." The Smoke Signal XL(Fall 1980): 190-208.

Lowe, Chaplain (Major) Allen K. "Black Traditions in Christian Worship." Military Chaplains Review (Summer 1992).

Miles, Donna. "Buffalo Soldiers." Soldiers (July 1990): 42-44.

248

Miller, Edward A., Jr. "Garland H. White, Black Army Chaplain," <u>Civil War History</u> Vol. 43, Number 3, (September 1997): 201-218.

Newsletter from the Colonel Allensworth State Historic Park.

Park, Robert E. "The Conflict and Fusion of Cultures with Special Reference to the Negro." <u>Journal of Negro History</u>. 4 (April 1919): 111-133.

Quinby, Rollin W. "Congress and the Civil War Chaplaincy." <u>Civil War History</u>. Vol. 10, No. 3 (1964): 246-259.

_____. "The Chaplains' Predicament." <u>Civil War History</u>. Vol. VII, No. 1 (March 1962): 25-37.

Redkey, Edwin S. "Black Chaplains in the Union Army." <u>Civil War History</u> Vol. XXXIII, No. 4 (1987): 331-350.

_____. "They Are Invincible: Two Black Chaplains Get a Look at Sherman's Army. <u>Civil War Times Illustrated</u>. Vol. XXVII, No. 2 (April 1989): 33-37.

Sabine, David. "The Fifth Wheel." <u>Civil War Times Illustrated</u>. Vol XIX, No. 2 (May 1980): 14-23.

Stover, Earl F. "Chaplain Henry V. Plummer, His Ministry and his Court-Marital." <u>Nebraska History</u>. Vol. 56, No.1 (Spring 1975): 20-50.

Thompson, Julius E. "Hiram Rhodes Revels, 1827-1901: A Reappraisal." <u>The Journal of Negro History</u>. Vol. 79, No. 3 (Summer 1994): 297-303.

Wiley, Bell Irvin. "'Holy Joes' of the Sixties: A Study of Civil War Chaplains." <u>Huntington Library Quarterly</u>. 16 (May 1953): 287-304.

Williams, Sergeant Major Rudi. "Chaplain Allensworth and his all-Black colony." <u>Monmouth Messenger</u>. (3 February 1989).

Newspapers

Wiggins, Ernest L. "Group trying to preserve cemetery, history." The State. 12 May 1992. 12B.

Unpublished Sources

Armstrong, Warren Bruce. "The Organization, Function, and Contribution of the Chaplaincy in the United States Army, 1861-1865." Ph.D. diss., University of Michigan, 1964.

Brinson, Chaplain (LTC) John. "'Better Men Were Never Led:' The Battle of New Market Heights, Virginia, 29 September 1864." No date. A paper presented at the U.S. Army Chaplain Center and School, Fort Jackson, S.C.

Felton, Gayle. Class Lectures from "The Black Church in America." Duke University, 1987.

Miller, Albert George. "Theophilus Gould Steward, 1843-1924: Striving for an African-American Theology and Civil Society in the Nadir Period." Ph.D. diss., Princeton University, 1994.

Powell, Anthony L. "Black Chaplains in the United States Army, 1863 to 1945." No date. A paper presented at the United States Army Chaplain Center and School, Fort Jackson, S.C.,

"Pro Deo Et Patria, A Brief History of the United States Army Chaplain Corps." United States Army Chaplain Center and School Manual 3001 (July 1991).

Telephone interviews with General John Q. Taylor King, 5 January, 10 March 1995.

Index

252